MW01253983

SAGE was founded in 1965 by Sara Miller McCune to support the dissemination of usable knowledge by publishing innovative and high-quality research and teaching content. Today, we publish over 900 journals, including those of more than 400 learned societies, more than 800 new books per year, and a growing range of library products including archives, data, case studies, reports, and video. SAGE remains majority-owned by our founder, and after Sara's lifetime will become owned by a charitable trust that secures our continued independence.

Los Angeles | London | New Delhi | Singapore | Washington DC | Melbourne

Advance Praise

Perhaps no other journalist has utilized the RTI Act as often and as brilliantly as Shyamlal Yadav has done for a decade now. From high-level corruption to the junkets of ministers whose travel miles added up to 256 times the circumference of the earth, from insane asset declarations to money channeled to dubious NGOs, he's exposed it all, using RTI. Yet, this fine and important book is more than the sum of his own outstanding stories. It is also a concise history of the RTI, its role in a democratic society, and the powerful tool it offers the investigative journalist. Read this book. Learn about RTI—and about our society.

—P. Sainath, journalist,
Author of *Everybody Loves a Good Drought*

Shyamlal Yadav's pioneering work on RTI has made him one of India's finest investigative journalists. His book reflects his passion for truth and persistence on facts and will be an extremely useful reference and guide for any young person aspiring to join the media.

—Prabhu Chawla, renowned journalist

Shyamlal Yadav is an RTI activist of a different kind. He has married information to its rightful bride, the newspaper, and transformed it into an instrument of social change. The contents of his book show the range and depth of his inquiry. I am sure those who conceived of this law had someone like Shyamlal in their mind to take this law forward, both to expand and explore its potential and to make the powerful also accountable. RTI needs more Shyamlals.

—Satyanand Mishra,
Former Chief Information Commissioner, CIC

Shyamlal Yadav not only masters to use the Indian Right to Information law as a powerful tool for his journalistic work, even more importantly, in his role as author, Shyamlal Yadav also masters the art of inspiration and sharing. His book includes detailed practical examples as well as necessary perspectives so peers and future journalists can learn from his experiences and at the same time be encouraged to ask their own questions relevant in their own context.

—Brigitte Alfter, acclaimed FoI activist and investigative journalist of Europe; Managing Editor at Journalismfund.eu

Shyamlal Yadav is one of the main reasons that India's RTI law is so powerfully effective. He has not only shown how to collect startling documents from government but also demonstrated that these facts can be turned into powerful stories that move people to action. To those who say that we are in a "post-fact" era, I say: Look at Shyamlal Yadav. He has already earned his place as a historic figure in the global freedom of information movement, and he has only begun.

—Mark Lee Hunter, Paris-based author, scholar, and investigative journalist, Editor of UNESCO's *Global Investigative Journalism Casebook*

Journalists throughout the world who specialize in using access to information laws have learnt through experience that success needs care and determination. Shyamlal Yadav has used India's RTI law very effectively to reveal important new stories, with persistence, thorough research and ingenuity. This is his impressive account of how he did it—and how others can learn from his example.

—Martin Rosenbaum, BBC News specialist in using the FOI Act, Executive Producer in the BBC Political Programmes department

JOURNALISM through RTI

JOURNAL🖋SM through RTI

Information
Investigation
Impact

SHYAMLAL YADAV

Los Angeles | London | New Delhi
Singapore | Washington DC | Melbourne

First published in 2017 by

SAGE Publications India Pvt Ltd
B1/I-1 Mohan Cooperative Industrial Area
Mathura Road, New Delhi 110 044, India
www.sagepub.in

SAGE Publications Inc
2455 Teller Road
Thousand Oaks, California 91320, USA

SAGE Publications Ltd
1 Oliver's Yard, 55 City Road
London EC1Y 1SP, United Kingdom

SAGE Publications Asia-Pacific Pte Ltd
3 Church Street
#10-04 Samsung Hub
Singapore 049483

Published by Vivek Mehra for SAGE Publications India Pvt Ltd, typeset in 10/12 pt Palatino by Zaza Eunice, Hosur, Tamil Nadu, India and printed at Chaman Enterprises, New Delhi.

Library of Congress Cataloging-in-Publication Data

Names: Yadav, Shyamlal author.
Title: Journalism through RTI : information, investigation, impact / Shyamlal Yadav.
Description: New Delhi ; Thousand Oaks, California : SAGE Publications India Pvt Ltd, 2017. | Includes index.
Identifiers: LCCN 2017004715| ISBN 9789386062833 (print (hb)) | ISBN 9789386062857 (e pub 2.0) | ISBN 9789386062840 (e book)
Subjects: LCSH: Investigative reporting--India. | Freedom of informa-tion--India. | Press and politics--India. | Government information--India.
Classification: LCC PN5377.I58 Y33 2017 | DDC 079/.54--dc23 LC record available at https://lccn.loc.gov/2017004715

ISBN: 978-93-860-6283-3 (HB)

SAGE Team: Rajesh Dey, Guneet Kaur Gulati, Madhurima Thapa, Shobana Paul, and Kapil Gulati

*To those who have been killed fighting for information under RTI
and to those who are still fighting worldwide*

Bulk Sales

SAGE India offers special discounts
for purchase of books in bulk.
We also make available special imprints
and excerpts from our books on demand.

For orders and enquiries, write to us at

Marketing Department
SAGE Publications India Pvt Ltd
B1/I-1, Mohan Cooperative Industrial Area
Mathura Road, Post Bag 7
New Delhi 110044, India

E-mail us at **marketing@sagepub.in**

Get to know more about SAGE

Be invited to SAGE events, get on our mailing list.
Write today to **marketing@sagepub.in**

This book is also available as an e-book.

Contents

List of Figures

List of Abbreviations

ABRAJI	Association of Brazilian Investigative Journalists
ACC	Appointment Committee of Cabinet
ADB	Asian Development Bank
AG	Attorney General
AIADMK	All India Anna Dravida Munnetra Kazhagam
BJP	Bhartiya Janta Party
BJD	Biju Janta Dal
BOD	Biochemical Oxygen Demand
BPR&D	Bureau of Police Research and Development
BRDB	Border Road Development Board
BSP	Bahujan Samaj Party
C&CES	Customs and Central Excise Service
Cabsec	Cabinet Secretariat
CBDT	Central Board of Direct Taxes
CBEC	Central Board of Excise and Customs
CBI	Central Bureau of Investigation
CEO	Chief Electoral Officer
CGA	Central Ganga Authority
CIC	Central Information Commission
CMO	Chief Minister's Office
CP	Commissioner of Police
CPCB	Central Pollution Control Board
CPI(M)	Communist Party of India (Marxist)
CPWD	Central Public Works Department
CSS	Central Secretariat Services
CVC	Central Vigilance Commission
CWC	Central Water Commission
DA	Disproportionate Assets
DAF	Dr Ambedkar Foundation
DEA	Department of Economic Affairs
DEO	District Election Officer
DGFT	Director General of Foreign Trade
DGIT	Director General of Income Tax
DGP	Director General of Police

DHC	Data Harvest Conferences
DMK	Dravida Munnetra Kazhagam
DO	Dissolved Oxygen
DoE	Department of Expenditure
DFS	Department of Financial Services
DoPT	Department of Personnel and Training
DRDO	Defence Research and Development Organization
ECI	Election Commission of India
EOL	Extraordinary Leave
EOU	Economic Offences Unit
EP	European Parliament
FAA	First Appellate Authority
FCRA	Foreign Contribution Regulation Act
FIR	First Information Report
FoI	Freedom of Information
FRRO	Foreigner Regional Registration Office
GAD	General Administration Department
GAP	Ganga Action Plan
GIJC	Global Investigative Journalism Conference
GoM	Group of Members
HRD	Human Resource Development
IAS	Indian Administrative Service
ICAR	Indian Council for Agriculture Research
ICCPR	International Covenant on Civil and Political Rights
IES	Indian Economic Service
IFS	Indian Foreign Service
IFoS	Indian Forest Service
IIPA	Indian Institute of Public Administration
INSEAD	Institut Européen d'Administration des Affaires or European Institute of Business Administration
IPR	Immovable Property Return
IPS	Indian Police Service
ISS	Indian Statistical Service
JD(U)	Janta Dal (United)
JSS	Jan Shikshan Sansthan
KVK	Krishi Vigyan Kendra
LIC	Life Insurance Corporation
MEA	Ministry of External Affairs
MEPs	Members of European Parliament
MHA	Ministry of Home Affairs
MKSS	Mazdoor Kisan Shakti Sangathan

MLA	Member of Legislative Assembly
MoD	Ministry of Defence
MoEF	Ministry of Environment and Forests
MoF	Ministry of Finance
MoHRD	Ministry of Human Resource Development
MoS	Member of Service
MoUD	Ministry of Urban Development
MP	Member of Parliament
NAC	National Advisory Council
NCMP	National Common Minimum Programme
NCP	Nationalist Congress Party
NCPRI	National Campaign for People's Right to Information
NCRB	National Crime Record Bureau
NCT	National Capital Territory
NDA	National Democratic Alliance
NDAL	National Database of Arms Licenses
NDTV	New Delhi Television
NGOs	Non-governmental Organizations
NSG	National Security Guards
OGI	Open Government Information
OM	Official Memorandum
PA	Personal Assistant
PAO	Pay and Accounts Officer
PCRF	Public Cause Research Foundation
PDS	Public Distribution System
PIO	Public Information Officer
PM	Prime Minister
PMO	Prime Minister's Office
RBI	Reserve Bank of India
RTI	Right to Information
SIC	State Information Commission
SP	Samajwadi Party
SPCBs	State Pollution Control Boards
SPG	Special Protection Group
UIN	Unique Identification Number
UN	United Nations
UNESCO	United Nations Educational, Scientific and Cultural Organization
UPA	United Progressive Alliance
UPA-I	United Progressive Alliance (2004–09)
UPA-II	United Progressive Alliance (2009–14)
WOB	Wet Openbaarheid van Bestuur

Foreword

Do not speak to a single person, man, woman, or child—that was the instruction from my investigative journalism professor at the University of Southern California, Los Angeles, as she asked each of us, first-year graduate students, to pick up a slip of paper from a shoebox she had brought to class.

On mine was scrawled a street address in downtown LA.

This was 1988, I was barely months old in the city, and there was neither Google nor a cellphone, but yes, the slip of paper and a public bus led me to a crumbling townhouse and stacks of official records.

Records in the civic hall, fire department, and motor vehicles department; homeowner records; and even voters' records showed the owner was a registered Democrat—these records helped me write the story of a slumlord who owned the house; the story included his court records and a list of his many violations.

And yes, I did all this without speaking to a single person.

That was my first lesson in investigative journalism: trust in data; look at records. They speak volumes and rarely lie. They are your most trustworthy sources. Learn the art of mining them.

Shyamlal Yadav is growing to be a master of that art.

His remarkable book shows how he has used records to discover a story, to investigate it, and to reveal what would have remained hidden.

Long before social media undermined the salience of facts, long before "post-truth" became a word, Shyamlal understood the power of records—in a system where, unlike in the USA, records are notoriously concealed, trapped in files, wrapped in red tape, of course, but most importantly, kept firmly behind a wall of secrecy that is not only hard to crack but opaque as well.

Until the first hammer came along, in 2005, in the form of the Right to Information (RTI) Act.

Using this act as his veritable weapon, Shyamlal was, arguably, the first full-time journalist to start chipping away at that wall. With great effect.

The stories documented in this book show that effect.

From detailing corruption cases against top bureaucrats to members of Parliament employing members of their families as personal staff on taxpayer expense; from foreign travel of ministers to the status of funds earmarked for cleaning rivers.

Stories that go beyond the 5 Ws and 1 H—who, why, what, where, when, and how—of the classical inverted pyramid. Stories that need rigor, records, investigation, and explanation, and the subsequent backing up of interviews and field reporting. In short, good journalism.

As Shyamlal's editor at *The Indian Express* since November 2011, I have had the privilege and the pleasure to be a part of his process. I have also become one of his strongest advocates. For he and his work serve as role models in *Express* newsrooms across the country.

That's why I am delighted that he has, in this book, not only explained the reporting behind each story but also written an invaluable how-to section. This makes the book a must-have and a must-read for reporters, editors, researchers, all those who teach journalism, and, of course, citizens too, who can see for themselves what a ₹10 demand draft and a powerful law can do.

This book couldn't have come at a more relevant time.

A lot of what passes off as journalism these days is the smart quip on Twitter, the cheap shot, the put-down, the rant, or the rave. As governments and establishments get more impregnable, as leaders reach out to their constituents on social media in one-way conversations, as institutions start pulling up the drawbridge in the name of efficiency, there is a need today, more than ever, of journalism that asks questions and that strives to hold those in power to account, be it in government or business or the political system, Left or Right.

Shyamlal's work is a testament to the power of that journalism.

I hope—and I am sure—this book will inspire the next generation of reporters and editors as they fight secrecy to get to the stories that need to be done.

Raj Kamal Jha
Chief Editor
The Indian Express

Preface

It was an unusually quiet day in April 2007 at *India Today*, where I was employed, when I got an e-mail from the news coordinator S. Sahay Ranjit on behalf of the editor Prabhu Chawla. I learned later that the e-mail had been sent to every correspondent at *India Today*. Prabhu wanted us to file at least three ideas that could be investigated through the RTI Act.

Little knowing what I was getting myself into, I filed the following three ideas: first, to know the status of anticorruption cases against IAS, IPS, and IRS officers registered in the last 15 years from the CBI; second, to get details of the 10 oldest pending cases and their status from the Supreme Court; and third, to get details of foreign trips made by union ministers from the PMO. Once my e-mail reached Prabhu, Shankkar Aiyar, the then managing editor of *India Today*, called me to his room. All he said was, "You should focus on those stories that can be explored through RTI."

It was that simple, and that's how I started using RTI for my stories. I must confess I had only a faint idea of what the RTI Act was, let alone know how to use the transparency law for my work. I did remember reading about the implementation of the RTI Act but nothing more. Though I had not filed any RTI application till then, I soon realized that one can use the RTI Act without even knowing or reading it, and that is the beauty of this historic legislation.

In the coming days, I worked on ideas and conceptualized many more stories by taking the RTI route. During the course of my work, I have filed several thousand RTI applications to government offices, starting from Lutyen Hills right down to the southernmost parts of the country, from the President's Secretariat and Prime Minister's Office down to district collectors and district superintendents of police. Collecting, collating, and cross-checking replies received from every corner of the country has been an exciting journey of experience for me. Very few of the stories were possible on a single RTI, whereas for one story, to collect nationwide data on arms licenses issued to private persons, I had to file over 700 applications spanning four years. It was a gigantic task of deciphering data and information. But, it was worthy and doable, as Shrimad Bhagwad Gita (Chapter 4, Verse 17) says

karmano hyapi boddhavyam boddhavyam cha vikarmanah
akarmanaśh cha boddhavyam gahanā karmano gatih

(Must understand the nature of all three—recommended action, wrong action, and inaction. The truth about these is profound and difficult to understand.)

After all, this work has given me a new identity. The idea to write this book came from several quarters: journalists, RTI users, and government officials dealing with RTI who were aware of my work. Using RTI as a tool for my stories has been the most important and rewarding part of my professional life, and by writing this book, I wanted to share with my readers this part of my journalistic journey. The emphasis is less on theory and more on practical aspects, that is to say, text is important, but the real work lies between the words that I would like the reader to feel and understand. In a nutshell, this is a tale of RTI-based stories.

In most chapters, I have described how ideas were visualized, how information was collected through persistent efforts, how the story developed, and how the subject was followed up keeping an eye on its rightful impact. These are examples of prompting the system to reform through offbeat journalistic work. It is in no way an attempt at self-boasting; rather, it is a desire to share my journey with interested readers and, in particular, the students of journalism who want to become fellow travelers in this field.

I hope this book will be useful not only for journalists but also for RTI activists, researchers, and government officials dealing with RTI, and for any concerned citizen who wants to use RTI as a tool to reform the system.

Acknowledgments

As they say, "No duty is more urgent than that of returning thanks." I would like to express my deepest gratitude to Raj Kamal Jha, Chief Editor of *The Indian Express* for his wholehearted support. It is his guidance, patience, and faith which has helped me pursue and crack big investigations. My other pillars of support are my Editor Unni Rajen Shanker and Executive Editor Ritu Sarin, who have always been helpful with ideas and provided lots of encouragement. I admire their professional commitment and painstaking attention to detail.

My regards and respect to Aroon Purie, Editor-in-Chief of *India Today*, who in his editorial referred to me as "indefatigable." Also my sincere thanks to my previous editors particularly Prabhu Chawla, Shankkar Aiyar, and Jagdish Upasane in *India Today* who pointed me to, continuously gave me ideas, and allowed me to work on my own. I thank Raj Chengappa and Dilip Bobb, editors at *India Today*, for their help and advise whenever needed.

Also, I am thankful to Ashok Damodaran 'Damu', Ashok Kumar, Sharda Ugra in *India Today* and Rakesh Sinha, Monojit Majumdar, Ajay Shankar and Y.P. Rajesh in *The Indian Express* for anchoring my investigative stories. I must thank all the editorial staff of *India Today* and *The Indian Express* who edited my stories and made them reader-friendly.

I am thankful to all those who have encouraged me and advised wherever needed during the writing of this book: Brigitte Alfter and Staffan Dahllof (Denmark), Ides Debruyne (Belgium), Martin Rosenbaum (UK), Sheila Coronel and Jennifer LaFleur (USA), Mark Lee Hunter (France), Marcelo Moreira (Brazil), Anuska Delic (Slovenia), Umar Cheema (Pakistan), and Jitarth Rai Bhardwaj (Australia) from abroad; from India, Ram Bahadur Rai, Prabal Maitra, K.S. Sachidananda Murthy, Sushma Yadav, S.K. Singh, Sushant Singh, Yogesh Deshmukh, Anshuman Yadav, Omkar Chaudhary, Ajmer Singh, Ashutosh Shukla, M.P. Yadav, Rajesh Malhotra, Vidya Bhushan Arora, Sheokesh Mishra, Nalin

Chauhan, and Mahendra Parihar. Most of these people, including former Chief Information Commissioner Satyananda Mishra, have not only encouraged me but also given their valuable advice and inputs when needed. I am also thankful to Sudhir Pillai who helped me give shape to the chapters and made them readable. At SAGE Publications I wish to thank Shambhu Sahu and Rajesh Dey who relentlessly advised me to develop the manuscript into a book, and Guneet Kaur Gulati who managed the production of this book.

Born and brought up in a place called Bahadurpur, which is 60 km away from the district headquarters of Pratapgarh in UP, to illiterate parents, I had never thought of receiving so much exposure as I am getting today as a journalist. The fundamentals of all this are that my late father Ram Sumer Yadav was always concerned about my *sangat* (company) and my mother Pyari Yadav always preached about *achchhi aadat* (good habits). My teachers Jagdev Prasad Maurya, Devendra Pratap Singh, V.P. Singh, and Chandramohan Mishra not only gave me textbook education but also taught me how to dream and why patience is important. Maurya, my teacher at the primary level in a government school and Devendra Pratap Singh, my teacher at high school level always fought to ensure that my merit was not crushed by some of their caste-biased colleagues. I treasure their invaluable presence in my life. I always remember my teachers and try to follow their advice and respect their words along with my guide–philosopher late Jyoti Swarup whose one-liner I have adopted as my style: *Jo bhi kaam karo, deewanon ki tarah karo* (Whatever you do, do it with passion). Another line I adopted, while working as a journalist, is of Saint Kabir: *Na kahu se dosti, na kahu se bair* (Neither friendship nor enmity with anybody).

Without mentioning my better half Renu, niece Lalita, son Shikhar, and daughter Shreeti, the story would not be complete. As a matter of fact, during the last three years that I have spent in writing, mostly on leave days, my family was always around me. Without their support, it would not have been possible.

1

Advent of RTI and Role of Media

Knowledge will forever govern ignorance: And a people who mean to be their own Governors, must arm themselves with the power which knowledge gives.

—James Madison, principal author of the US Constitution, in 1822

Seeds of RTI Act in India

After an inordinate delay, Indians got their right to information (RTI) on October 12, 2005. The RTI Act is considered an extension of Article 19(1)(a) of the Indian Constitution which says: "All citizens shall have the right to freedom of speech and expression."[1] The framers of the Indian Constitution considered the freedom of the press as an essential part of the freedom of speech and expression, subject to the restrictions that are provided under Article 19(2).[2] This provision of the Constitution is the basis on which a free press functions in India.

Before efforts to bring a law for RTI in its present form gained ground, the Supreme Court had emphasized time and again that RTI is included in the freedom of speech and expression. In the well-known case of State of UP vs Raj Narain & Ors of 24 January, 1975, the Supreme Court had said,

> The people of this country have a right to know every public act, everything, that is done in a public way, by their public functionaries. They are entitled to know the particulars of every public transaction in all its bearing. The right to know, which is derived from the concept of freedom of speech, though not absolute, is a factor

---

[1] Constitution of India, Article 19(1)(a).
[2] Constitution of India, Article 19(2).

which should make one wary, when secrecy is claimed for transactions which can, at any rate, have no repercussion on public security. To cover with veil secrecy the common routine business, is not in the interest of the public.[3]

There are other cases where the Supreme Court has reiterated the same. In the matter of Indian Express Newspapers (Bombay) Pvt. Ltd vs Union of India, the Supreme Court had said, "The basic purpose of freedom of speech and expression is that all members should be able to form their beliefs and communicate them freely to others. In sum, the fundamental principle involved here is the people's right to know."[4] In the Bennett Coleman case,[5] RTI was held to be included within the right to freedom of speech and expression guaranteed in the Constitution. In the S.P. Gupta case,[6] the right of the people to know about every public act and the details of every public transaction undertaken by public functionaries was described. In the Cricket Association of Bengal case,[7] the right to impart and receive information from electronic media was included in the freedom of speech. In the People's Union for Civil Liberties case,[8] RTI was further elevated to the status of a human right, necessary for making governance transparent and accountable. It was also emphasized that governance must be participatory.

In spite of the many Supreme Court rulings that right to information included in the right to freedom of speech, it took 30 years since the first ruling of the Supreme Court for subsequent governments to finally give the citizens the RTI Act. This was 58 years after independence and 55 years after the adoption of the Constitution of India.

---

[3] State of UP vs Raj Narain & Ors (January 24, 1975).

[4] Indian Express Newspapers (Bombay) Pvt. Ltd vs Union of India (December 6, 1984).

[5] Bennett Coleman vs Union of India (October 30, 1972).

[6] S.P. Gupta vs Union of India (December 30, 1981).

[7] Secretary, Ministry of I&B, Government of India vs Cricket Association of Bengal (February 9, 1995).

[8] People's Union for Civil Liberties vs Union of India, 2004 (2) SCC 476.

Advocacy from the UN

Sweden was the first country where, introduced by Anders Chydenius,[9] RTI was implemented in 1766 as The Ordinance on Freedom of Writing and of the Press.[10] Implemented during the rule of Adolph Frederick this law of Sweden is called the world's first freedom of information (FoI) law.

But in the 20th century, the idea of 'freedom of information' was recognized by the United Nations (UN) after the end of World War II. Before that, on January 6, 1941, the US President Franklin D. Roosevelt addressed the US Congress and insisted on four freedoms: freedom of speech and expression, freedom to worship God in one's own way, freedom from want, and freedom from fear.[11] After Roosevelt's death and the end of World War II, his widow Eleanor Roosevelt took this vision and helped to enshrine it in the Universal Declaration of Human Rights.[12] She participated in the drafting of that declaration, which was adopted by the UN in 1948. The UN on December 14, 1946, stated, "Freedom of information is a fundamental human right and is the touchstone of all the freedoms to which the United Nations is consecrated."[13] As an indispensable element, FoI requires the willingness and capacity to employ its privileges without abuse. As a basic discipline, it requires the moral obligation to seek facts without prejudice and to spread knowledge without malicious intent.[14] Article 19 of the Universal Declaration of Human Rights, which was proclaimed on December 16, 1948, states: "Everyone has the right to freedom of opinion and expression; this right includes freedom to hold opinions without interference and to seek, receive and impart information and ideas through any media and regardless of frontiers."

---

[9] Anders Chydenius (1729–1803) was a Finnish priest and a member of the Swedish Riksdag of the Estates (Sweden's parliament).

[10] This is considered the world's first freedom of information law.

[11] See http://www.history.com/this-day-in-history/franklin-d-roosevelt-speaks-of-four-freedoms, accessed December 29, 2016.

[12] See http://www.un.org/press/en/2015/dsgsm924.doc.htm, accessed December 29, 2016.

[13] See https://documents-dds-ny.un.org/doc/RESOLUTION/GEN/NR0/033/10/IMG/NR003310.pdf?OpenElement, accessed December 29, 2016.

[14] Ibid.

Along with this, an academic discussion on the types of freedom and liberty was going on. In a famous essay first published in 1958, Isaiah Berlin[15] mentioned two concepts of liberty—negative and positive. The reason for using these labels is that in the first case, liberty seems to be the absence of something (i.e., of obstacles, barriers, constraints, or interference from others), whereas in the second case, it seems to require the presence of something (i.e., of control, self-mastery, self-determination, or self-realization).[16]

The International Covenant on Civil and Political Rights (ICCPR), adopted by the UN General Assembly in 1966, says:

> Everyone shall have the right to freedom of expression; this right shall include freedom to seek, receive and impart information and ideas of all kinds, regardless of frontiers, either orally, in writing or in print, in the form of art, or through any other media of his choice.[17]

Since the adoption of the 1946 Resolution, the United Nations Educational, Scientific and Cultural Organization (UNESCO) has led a global campaign to promote the freedom of expression and RTI. It was advocated again and again by UN bodies. Paragraph 10(b) of the Plan of Actions[18] states: "Governments are encouraged to provide adequate access through various communication resources, notably the Internet, to public official information. Establishing legislation on access to information and the preservation of public data, notably in the area of the new technologies, is encouraged." UNESCO's Dakar Declaration on Media and Good Governance (May 3, 2005) calls "to promote the adoption of national access to information legislation and to develop international principles on access to information."[19]

---

[15] Isaiah Berlin (1909–97) was a British philosopher, historian of ideas, political theorist, educator, and essayist. In 1958, he wrote *Two Concepts of Liberty* and in 1969 he wrote *Four Essays on Liberty*.

[16] Ian Carter, "Positive and Negative Liberty," in *The Stanford Encyclopedia of Philosophy* (Fall 2016 Edition), ed. Edward N. Zalta, http://plato.stanford.edu/archives/fall2016/entries/liberty-positive-negative, accessed December 29, 2016.

[17] See http://www.ohchr.org/en/professionalinterest/pages/ccpr.aspx, accessed December 29, 2016.

[18] World Summit on the Information Society, Geneva, December 12, 2003, http://www.itu.int/net/wsis/docs/geneva/official/poa.html, accessed December 29, 2016.

[19] Dakar Declaration, World Press Freedom Day conference, *Dakar*, Senegal, May 1–3, 2005.

But after Sweden implemented the world's first FoI Law, it took a further 200 years to reach the United States where it was implemented in 1966. Before that, Finland, a country which was part of Sweden when the first such law was passed in 1766, was the first country after World War II to enact a law in 1951 to guarantee public access to documents of a general nature. This law lays down the principle that documents of a general character prepared or received by government authorities should be accessible to all Finnish citizens without time restrictions, and lists the issues in which the government may declare that certain files are exempted from this disclosure.

The FoI Act 1966 of the United States for accessibility to public documents was followed by several other countries. There has been a revolution in the last two decades in terms of the RTI and FoI laws across the globe. Whereas in 1990, only over a dozen countries had adopted RTI or FoI laws, today there are over 100 countries with some form or the other of a law that provides the right of access to information to their citizens. Moreover, several of the remaining members of the UN are in the process to do so.

In 1967, Norway adopted a law on public administration for regulating access to certain government documents. France followed this example with a law passed in 1978, the first part of which is titled "Freedom of Access to Administrative Documents." In 1978, the Netherlands also adopted a similar law for access to government documents. Australia adopted the FoI Act in 1982. Since 1982, Canada has an "Access to Information Act" and also a "Privacy Act." Japan approved the Access to Information Held by Administrative Organs Act (RTI Act) in 1999 which was implemented in 2001. Even in China, transparency seems to be taking place; a study in 2007 said: "A strange but intriguing phenomenon is occurring in China. A country, long regarded by outsiders as the epitome of a closed, authoritarian and secretive state, has become the scene of a very rapid and extensive uptake of Freedom of Information (FoI) legislation." Shanghai (a special municipality), a further nine provinces and another special municipality (Chongqing) on the mainland of China have adopted similar legislation.[20] In 2003, the People's Republic of

---

[20] Rick Snel and Weibing Xiao, *Freedom of Information Returns to China*, https://www.law.yale.edu/system/files/documents/pdf/Intellectual_Life/

China put Open Government Information (OGI) Regulations on the legislation agenda of the State Council, which were adopted in 2007.[21] However, there are several obstacles in their proper implementation.

In South Asia, Pakistan was the first country that implemented the Freedom of Information Ordinance in 2002.[22] In April 2013, Pakistan had passed the 18th constitutional amendment which enshrined RTI as a fundamental right under Article 19A.[23] India passed the RTI Act in 2005. Maldives passed the RTI Act in January 2014. In February 2014, Bhutan also passed the RTI law. In 2015, Afghanistan also enacted the Access to Information law. Sri Lanka passed the Right of Access to Information Act on June 26, 2016, as a result of an ongoing campaign since 2004. In Sri Lanka the RTI Act has been recently implemented from February 4, 2017. Nepal adopted the RTI Act in 2007 and is the second country after Poland which has included its political parties under the purview of the RTI Act. Bangladesh implemented the RTI Act in 2009. Rapidly, RTI is being recognized as a fundamental human right by many countries.

On September 25, 2015, the UN adopted 17 sustainable development goals[24] and Goal 16 among them is on "Peace, Justice and Institutions." This goal gives targets to the member countries to substantially reduce corruption and bribery in all their forms; develop effective, accountable, and transparent institutions at all levels; ensure public access to information; and protect fundamental freedoms in accordance with national legislation and international agreements by 2030.

UNESCO decided[25] on November 17, 2015, that every year September 28 would be celebrated as the International Day for the Universal Access to Information. This day was originally

---

CL-OGI-Snell-Weibing-English.pdf, accessed December 29, 2016.

[21] See https://www.article19.org/resources.php/resource/38163/en/country-report:-the-right-to-information-in-china, accessed December 29, 2016.

[22] Media Brief, Pakistan Institute of Legislative Development and Transparency, Islamabad, September 2015.

[23] Ibid.

[24] See http://www.un.org/sustainabledevelopment/peace-justice/, accessed December 29, 2016.

[25] See http://www.freedominfo.org/2015/11/right-out-access-used-instead-for-new-unesco-day/, accessed December 29, 2016.

proposed as the "Right to Know Day" in Sofia, Bulgaria, where a number of advocates of freedom of expression from 15 countries gathered to promote the transparency and accountability of governments during a conference held from September 26 to 28, 2002. The countries participating at the event were Albania, Armenia, Bosnia and Herzegovina, Bulgaria, Georgia, Hungary, India, Latvia, Macedonia, Mexico, Republic of Moldova, Romania, Slovakia, South Africa, and the United States of America. It was also agreed at the conference on the closing day, September 28, that it should be designated as the Right to Know Day and celebrated as such each year. Now, it is decided that it will be observed as the International Day for the Universal Access to Information.

Battle for RTI in India

In India, the preamble[26] to the RTI Act defines it as follows:

> An Act to provide for setting out the practical regime of right to information for citizens to secure access to information under the control of public authorities, in order to promote transparency and accountability in the working of every public authority…. Whereas the Constitution of India has established democratic Republic; And whereas democracy requires an informed citizenry and transparency of information which are vital to its functioning and also to contain corruption and to hold Governments and their instrumentalities accountable to the governed….

Before the Central Government implemented the RTI Act, thanks to mounting pressure from mass movements in different parts of the country, states such as Assam, Goa, Madhya Pradesh, Rajasthan, Tamil Nadu, Jammu & Kashmir, Karnataka, Maharashtra, and national capital territory (NCT) Delhi had already passed such laws. The new law passed by the Central Government covers all public authorities under the Central Government, all states, and local-level public authorities (except Jammu & Kashmir which has a separate RTI Act passed by its assembly).

---

26 Preamble of the RTI Act-2005.

The RTI Act has been welcomed as a revolutionary legislation. With its implementation, the style of functioning of various governments has undergone a drastic change. In government functioning, terms such as pre-RTI and post-RTI have come up. Under the RTI Act, any citizen of India can request for information from the Central Government, state governments, and union territories or from a public authority which is established, constituted, owned, controlled, or substantially financed by funds provided directly or indirectly by the Central Government and state governments/union territory administrations. However, there are certain organizations[27] from which one can only ask for information about human rights violation and corruption. These are basically intelligence and security organizations and also the Central Bureau of Investigation (CBI), which was added later. Information[28] is defined as follows:

> Any material in any form, including the records, documents, memos, e-mails, opinions, advices, press releases, circulars, orders, log books, contracts, reports, papers, samples, models, data material hold in any electronic form and information relating to any private body which can be accessed by a public authority under any law for the time being in force.[29]

Furthermore, it defines the word 'record' as "including (a) any document, manuscript and file, (b) any microfilm, microfiche and facsimile copy of a document, (c) any reproduction of image or images embodied in such microfilm and (d) any other material produced by a computer or any other device."[30] Moreover, 'right to information' under the RTI Act, includes the right to

> (I) Inspection of work, documents, records; (II) taking notes, extracts or certified copies of documents or records; (III) taking certified samples of material; (iv) obtaining information in the form of

---

[27] Second Schedule of the RTI Act-2005: http://www.righttoinformation.gov.in/webactrti.htm, accessed December 29, 2016.

[28] Section 2 of the RTI Act-2005: http://www.righttoinformation.gov.in/webactrti.htm, accessed December 29, 2016.

[29] Section 2(f) of the RTI Act-2005: http://www.righttoinformation.gov.in/webactrti.htm, accessed December 29, 2016.

[30] Section 2(i) of RTI Act-2005: http://www.righttoinformation.gov.in/webactrti.htm, accessed December 29, 2016.

diskettes, floppies, tapes, video cassettes or in any other electronic mode or through printouts where such information is stored in a computer or in any other device.[31]

The RTI Act has certain exemptions[32] from disclosure as it says:

Notwithstanding anything contained in this Act, there shall be no obligation to give any citizen, (a) information, disclosure of which would prejudicially affect the sovereignty and integrity of India, the security, strategic, scientific or economic interests of the State, relation with foreign State or lead to incitement of an offence; (b) information which has been expressly forbidden to be published by any court of law or tribunal or the disclosure of which may constitute contempt of court; (c) information, the disclosure of which would cause a breach of privilege of Parliament or the State Legislature; (d) information including commercial confidence, trade secrets or intellectual property, the disclosure of which would harm the competitive position of a third party, unless the competent authority is satisfied that larger public interest warrants the disclosure of such information; (e) information available to a person in his fiduciary relationship, unless the competent authority is satisfied that the larger public interest warrants the disclosure of such information; (f) information received in confidence from foreign Government; (g) information, the disclosure of which would endanger the life or physical safety of any person or identify the source of information or assistance given in confidence for law enforcement or security purposes; (h) information which would impede the process of investigation or apprehension or prosecution of offenders; (i) cabinet papers including records of deliberations of the Council of Ministers, Secretaries and other officers: Provided that the decisions of Council of Ministers, the reasons thereof, and the material on the basis of which the decisions were taken shall be made public after the decision has been taken, and the matter is complete, or over, Provided further that those matters which come under the exemptions specified in this section shall not be disclosed; (j) information which relates to personal information the disclosure of which has no relationship to any public activity or interest, or which would cause unwarranted invasion of the privacy of the individual

---

[31] Section 2(j) of RTI Act-2005: http://www.righttoinformation.gov.in/webactrti. htm, accessed December 29, 2016.

[32] Section 8(1)(a) to Section 8(1)(j) of the RTI Act: http://www.righttoinformation. gov.in/webactrti.htm, accessed December 29, 2016.

unless the Central Public Information Officer or the State Public Information Officer or the appellate authority, as the case may be, is satisfied that the larger public interest justifies the disclosure of such information: Provided that the information which cannot be denied to the Parliament or a State Legislature shall not be denied to any person.

Use of the RTI Act is relatively simple. There is no standard format and one can make a request to the concerned public authority on plain paper, merely writing his/her name/address and particulars of information required. The processing fee varies among various authorities, but mostly the rules set down by the Central Government are followed, under which the processing fee is ₹10 per application with an additional charge[33] of

(a) Rupees two (₹2/-) for each page (in A-3 or smaller size paper); (b) actual cost or price of a photocopy in larger size paper; (c) actual cost or price for samples or models; (d) Rupees fifty (₹50) per diskette or floppy; and (e) price fixed for a publication or Rupees two per page of photocopy for extracts from the publication. (f) so much of postal charges involved in supply of information that exceeds fifty rupees. For inspection of records, the public authority shall charge no fee for the first hour. But a fee of rupees five (₹5) for each subsequent hour (or fraction thereof) shall be charged.

At the same time, there is a provision for a penalty of ₹250 per day to a maximum of ₹25,000 against a public authority if they fail to provide the information on time. These deterrents and the simplicity in the use of the RTI Act have given ordinary Indians courage to ask for information from government departments that could also include details of their roles and responsibilities. Success stories of common people demanding and getting the information they want have become commonplace since October 2005.

The enactment of the RTI Act was not easy. Much was said and done between 1975, when the Supreme Court first ruled that RTI was part of the right to freedom of speech, and 2005, when the RTI Act was actually implemented. In 1982, the Second Press Commission headed by Justice (Retd) K.K. Mathew

[33] See http://rti.gov.in/RTICorner/Guide_2013-issue.pdf, accessed December 29, 2016.

recommended in its report that section 5.5 of the Official Secrets
Act, 1923, be repealed and substituted by other provisions suited
to meet the needs of national security and other vital interests of
the State as well as the right of the people to know the affairs of
the State affecting them.[34] The government and its leaders continued to advocate for RTI for citizens, but no initiative was taken
to make it a law for a long time. In 1989, the then prime minister
(PM) V.P. Singh, who had won the 1989 general elections on his
promises against corruption, announced the approach of the new
government:

> An open system of governance is an essential prerequisite for the
> fullest flowering of democracy. Free flow of information from the
> Government to the people will not only create an enlightened
> and informed public opinion but also render those in authority
> accountable. In the recent past, we have witnessed many distor-
> tions in our information system. The veil of secrecy was lowered
> many a time not in the interest of national security, but to shield the
> guilty, vested interests or gross errors of judgements. Therefore,
> the National Front Government has decided to make the Right to
> Information a Fundamental Right.[35]

But his government did not last its full term and his promise
remained unfulfilled.

In 1994, the demand for RTI took the form of a mass movement.
The Mazdoor Kisan Shakti Sangathan (MKSS), an organization
headed by Aruna Roy, started a campaign in a backward region
of Rajasthan's Rajsamand district to assert people's RTI by asking
for copies of bills and vouchers and names of persons who were
paid wages, mentioned in muster rolls at the time of construction of schools, dispensaries, small dams, and community centers.
During 1994–95, several *Jan Sunwais* (public hearings) were organized by the MKSS. With its demand that people should have the
right to official information, this grassroots movement quickly
spread to other areas of Rajasthan and to some other states. In

---

[34] A.G. Noorani, First and Second Press Commission: Press Commission Report-1.
Whizcom (blog), January 23, 2011, http://whizcom.blogspot.in/2011/01/first-and-
second-press-commission.html, accessed December 29, 2016.
[35] See http://www.rrtd.nic.in/RIGHT%20TO%20INFORMATION.html, accessed
December 29, 2016.

the mid-1990s, a demand for a national law was started by the National Campaign for People's Right to Information (NCPRI). The then chairman of the Press Council of India Justice (Retd) P.B. Sawant impressed with the demand for an RTI law, organized a workshop on RTI on August 10–11, 1996, to draft a model bill on RTI. Justice Sawant stated:

> The barrier to information is the single most cause responsible for corruption in society. It facilitates clandestine deals, arbitrary decisions, manipulations and embezzlements. Transparency in dealings, with their every detail exposed to the public view, should go a long way in curtailing corruption in public life.[36]

He emphasized that in a democracy people are the masters and those utilizing public resources and exercising public power are their agents.[37]

During movements for the legislation, many prominent journalists such as Kuldip Nayar, Prabhash Joshi, and Nikhil Chakravorty were actively associated with it. A Press Council report says,

> Considering that India is literally in neck-deep corruption, scandals and scams and is operating this system for the last 50 years, the workshop was of the view that, frequent the checks and more piercing and deeper the investigation, the better is the monitoring of the system.[38]

Significantly, this bill was influenced by an earlier draft prepared during a meeting of social activists, civil servants, and lawyers at the Lal Bahadur Shashtri National Academy of Administration, Mussoorie, in October 1995.[39] The Hyderabad-based National Institute of Rural Development had also drafted a similar bill in 1997. It was in this background that the United Front government headed by PM H.D. Deve Gowda appointed a working group on January 2, 1997, under the chairmanship of consumer rights activist H.D. Shourie to deliberate on the matter. The working group

---

[36] Ibid.
[37] Ibid.
[38] Future of Print Media, Press Council of India, New Delhi, 132.
[39] See http://www.humanrightsinitiative.org/programs/ai/rti/india/articles/ The%20Movement%20for%20RTI%20in%20India.pdf, accessed December 29, 2016.

submitted its report on May 24, 1997, recommending, among other things, that the bill be named as the FoI Bill. Based on the recommendations, a conference of chief ministers was organized, but the United Front government did not complete its term so things were stuck for the time being.

Fortunately, on account of the ongoing campaign for enactment of RTI, it found a prominent voice in the election promises of political parties in the 1998 general elections. The Bhartiya Janta Party (BJP) said in its manifesto:[40]

> The BJP believes in taking concrete steps to promote transparency in the functioning of Government as a confidence-building measure. The working of a Government should not only be transparent but should be perceived to be so. We, therefore, subscribe to the principle of sharing information about the Government's work. The BJP will: 1. Enhance public access to information to the maximum extent feasible; 2. Review laws and regulations concerning confidentiality; 3. Introduce social audit of development programmes, especially in rural areas.

The Congress, on the other hand, promised[41] that "Congress will enact a Freedom of Information Act to end the culture of secrecy and to ensure openness in administration. All exercise of discretionary power by its Ministers will be made open to public scrutiny."

BJP-led National Democratic Alliance (NDA) government took oath on March 19, 1998, but the government collapsed again on April 17, 1999, leading to new elections in 1999. In its manifesto for the 1999 general elections, the Congress said:[42] "A Bill on Freedom of Information and Right to Information will be introduced soon to give citizens easy access to information at all levels." In the Agenda for a Proud, Prosperous India: Lok Sabha 1999,[43] released by the BJP-led NDA before the 1999 general

---

[40] See http://www.bjp.org/documents/manifesto/bjp-election-manifesto-1998/chapter-3, accessed December 29, 2016.
[41] See http://allindiacongress.com/admin/upload/pdf/Manifesto%201998.pdf, accessed December 29, 2016.
[42] Ibid.
[43] See http://www.bjp.org/en/documents/manifesto/nda-agenda-for-a-proud-prosperous-india-lok-sabha-1999, accessed December 29, 2016.

elections, the manifesto made no mention of it. But when the NDA came back to power in 1999, matters seemed to be moving forward. Significantly, on October 17, 1998, Ministry of Urban Development and Poverty Alleviation, under its minister Ram Jethmalani, issued an administrative order that any citizen would be entitled to inspect and take photocopies of any file in the ministry. But the government headed by Atal Bihari Vajpayee was already in process to enact a legislation in this regard, so the then Cabinet secretary Prabhat Kumar restrained Jethmalani's ministry from giving effect to its order.

When the Vajpayee government restrained Jethmalani's ministry, Prashant Bhushan's Centre for Public Interest Litigation and H.D. Shourie's *Common Cause* filed a writ petition in the Supreme Court, effectively seeking the following three reliefs:

1. That the Cabinet Secretary's restraint on Jethmalani's order be declared unconstitutional and violative of the citizens right to information; 2. That section 5 of the Official Secrets Act, which makes it an offence for a public servant to disclose any information that has come to his knowledge in his official capacity, be declared unconstitutional; 3. That the government of India be directed to frame and issue suitable administrative instructions on the lines of the Press Council's Right to Information Bill, to effectuate the citizens right to information, pending suitable legislation on the subject.[44]

Meanwhile, the Press Council of India organized a seminar on RTI on February 20, 2000, and some suggestions were sent to the government with regard to the proposed bill. Finally, the FoI Bill, 2000, was introduced in the Lok Sabha on July 25, 2000. It was thereafter referred to the Parliamentary Standing Committee on Home Affairs for examination. The Committee presented its report to both the houses of Parliament, exactly a year later, on July 25, 2001.

The Supreme Court, on its part, directed that if the legislation was not passed before the next date of hearing (January 2003), it would consider the matter on merits and pass orders. The Supreme Court further directed that even if the legislation

---

[44] See http://www.freedominfo.org/2002/12/freedom-of-information-law-approved-in-indi/, accessed December 29, 2016.

were passed, the court would examine whether the legislation was in conformity with RTI as declared by the court.[45] That was how the FoI Bill, 2002, was passed by the Lok Sabha on December 3, 2002, and by the Rajya Sabha on December 16, 2002. It then received the assent of the President of India on January 6, 2003, and it was published in *The Gazette of India* on January 7, 2003. But, since the rules were not formulated, it was not notified for implementation.

Meanwhile, the NDA government decided to hold general elections ahead of schedule in 2004. The Congress promised[46] in its election manifesto that

> Right to Information Act at the centre will be made more progressive, meaningful and useful to the public. The monitoring and implementation of the Act will be made more participatory and the penalty clauses regarding delays, illegal denials and other inadequacies relating to the supply of information to the public will be operationalised soon.

United Progressive Alliance's (UPA) National Common Minimum Programme (NCMP) had reiterated that "the Right to Information Act will be made more progressive, participatory and meaningful."[47]

After the 2004 elections, the UPA government headed by the Congress came to power and Manmohan Singh took oath as the PM. Manmohan Singh directed that "first priority should be to bring into force the Act as passed..."[48] and the Department of Personnel and Training (DoPT) began examining the draft rules framed in that regard. But, based on the recommendations of the National Advisory Council (NAC) headed by Sonia Gandhi, it was decided to repeal the earlier law passed by the Vajpayee government. Thus, the DoPT moved a proposal on December 13, 2004 to repeal the FoI Act, 2002, and the UPA government introduced the RTI Bill on December 23, 2004, in the Parliament. It was then sent to the Committee on Personnel, Public Grievances, Law and Justice to be examined. At a Cabinet meeting on December 15, 2004, it was

---

[45] Ibid.
[46] Congress manifesto for 2004 Lok Sabha elections.
[47] See http://nceuis.nic.in/NCMP.htm, accessed December 29, 2016.
[48] File No. RTI DoPT 34011–6(S)2004-ESTT-B II_Notes. Available on http://persmin.nic.in/DOPT_RTICorner_ImpFiles.asp, accessed December 29, 2016.

decided to constitute an eight-member Group of Ministers (GoM) headed by the then defence minister Pranab Mukherjee to examine the "competence or otherwise of the central government to legislate an Act to cover State governments and local bodies; to examine penalty provisions and processing fee for RTI applications."[49] Sonia Gandhi, in the meantime, wrote a letter to the PM on January 14, 2005, to examine the possibility of treating the RTI Bill, 2004, as an enactment under entry 97 (any other matter not enumerated in List II or List III including any tax not mentioned in either of those lists) of List 1 of the VIIth Schedule (Article 246) to the Constitution of India.[50] That was to follow the suggestions of the activists that "The Bill should not only apply to the Central Government and bodies owned or control by it but be extended to the states, Local Bodies or Authorities."[51] The GoM submitted its report on May 3, 2005. Finally, the RTI Bill was passed by the Lok Sabha on May 11, 2005, and by the Rajya Sabha the next day, on May 12, 2005. On receiving the assent of the President on June 15, 2005, the RTI Act, 2005, was notified in *The Gazette of India* on June 21, 2005, and became operational from October 12, 2005.

The then PM Manmohan Singh, while participating in the debate on the RTI Bill on May 11, 2005, had said:

> The passage of this Bill will see the dawn of a new era in our processes of governance, an era of performance and efficiency, an era which will ensure that benefits of growth flow to all sections of our people, an era which will eliminate the scourge of corruption, an era which will bring the common man's concern to the heart of all processes of governance, an era which will truly fulfil the hopes of the founding fathers of our Republic.[52]

In many ways, the new law started proving to be true in ways Singh had said in his address to the Lok Sabha. When enacted, the

---

[49] PMO's communication dated January 27, 2005. Available on http://persmin.nic.in/DOPT_RTICorner_ImpFiles.asp, accessed December 29, 2016.

[50] See Article 246 of Constitution of India: http://www.constitution.org/cons/india/shed07.htm, accessed December 29, 2016.

[51] From the files available on http://persmin.nic.in/DOPT_RTICorner_ImpFiles.asp, accessed December 29, 2016.

[52] See http://archivepmo.nic.in/drmanmohansingh/speech-details.php?nodeid=118, accessed February 11, 2017.

RTI Act became a tool in the hands of the ordinary citizen whose letters and applications, in most cases, had earlier did not elicit any response, let alone being taken note of by the government departments. The RTI Act gave courage to the common man who started questioning the government authorities about their pending work and also their decisions.

Approach of NDA Government Toward RTI

The NDA government boasts about its "Quest for Transparency"[53] and PM Narendra Modi seems to be one step ahead of the previous government as he has said:

> Citizens should not only have the right to get copies of documents but also ask questions and demand accountability from public authorities, because the right to ask questions is the very foundation of democracy and it will reinforce their faith in democracy.... If we limit RTI just to reply to questions, there will be no changes in governance. We have to analyse the RTI questions and ponder whether there is need to make changes in policy matters.[54]

Not only that, Modi tried to snatch credit for the RTI Act from the Congress when he said, "During Atalji's (Atal Bihari Vajpayee) time there was Freedom of Information Act, you brought Right to Information Act."[55] Notably, when Manmohan Singh had criticized the "vexatious demands for information" under the RTI Act on October 14, 2011, the then BJP president Rajnath Singh had said:

> It seems that Prime Minister is afraid of all the scams that have come to light with the help of Right to Information Act. Presently, the Congress-led UPA government is passing through a phase

---

[53] See http://www.pmindia.gov.in/en/quest-for-transparency/, accessed December 29, 2016.
[54] Narendra Modi, Prime Minister, at CIC Conference, Vigyan Bhawan, New Delhi (October 16, 2015).
[55] Narendra Modi in Rajya Sabha, replying to a discussion on Motion of Thanks to the President's Address. Modi accused Congress of copying schemes launched by NDA government headed by Vajpayee (March 3, 2015).

of depression, is under depression. The BJP would protest in the Parliament, if the government tries to dilute the act.[56]

Union Finance Minister Arun Jaitley said on October 16, 2015, at a Central Information Commission (CIC) conference,

> RTI is an exemplary law. It has transformed the society and India has passed the first stage of civilized governance. Sometimes too much openness is considered to be bad for governance. The administrators of the Act should use their discretion to prevent its misuse. The Act is of great utility to the society and will continue to grow and gain maturity.[57]

The fact that several circulars have been issued by the DoPT after the Narendra Modi government took charge indicates that the present government is as committed to the RTI Act as was the UPA. These circulars include ruling out a standard format for providing information to the applicants,[58] harmonizing the RTI (Fee and Cost) Rules and Appeal Procedure Rules[59] under the RTI Act, implementation of suo motu disclosure[60] under Section 4 of the RTI Act, uploading of RTI replies[61] on the websites of respective ministries/departments, putting frequently asked information in the public domain, and training all public authorities of the central government to maximize the use of online facilities of receiving and disposing off the RTI applications. A DoPT circular says, "The Public Authorities shall constitute Consultative Committees consisting of office bearers of key stakeholder, association on rotational basis to have a systematic and regular interaction between the officials of the Public Authorities to advice what information to be uploaded as suo motu."[62] This circular further says,

---

[56] See http://www.andhranews.net/India/2011/Rajnath-Singh-slams-PM-over-remarks-9162.htm, accessed on February 11, 2017.
[57] See http://pib.nic.in/newsite/AdvSearch.aspx, accessed December 29, 2016.
[58] See http://ccis.nic.in/WriteReadData/CircularPortal/D2/D02rti/10_1_2013-IR-06 102015.pdf, accessed December 29, 2016.
[59] See http://ccis.nic.in/WriteReadData/CircularPortal/D2/D02rti/1–5-2011-IR_10–07-2015.pdf, accessed December 29, 2016.
[60] See http://ccis.nic.in/WriteReadData/CircularPortal/D2/D02rti/RTI-29062015.pdf, accessed December 29, 2016.
[61] See http://ccis.nic.in/WriteReadData/CircularPortal/D2/D02rti/1_1_2013-IR-1-A.pdf, accessed December 29, 2016.
[62] Official Memorandum F. No. 1/34/2013-IR dated June 30, 2016, of DoPT.

In each public authority, a committee of PIOs and FAAs with rich experience of dealing with RTI applications and appeals is set up to identify the categories of information that are frequently asked by applicants. Such information must be disclosed in the public domain to make it more user friendly and should also be reviewed at regular intervals.[63]

Although there are apprehensions that governments embarrassed by the series of exposes under the RTI Act may sooner or later try to dilute the power of the RTI Act, "there will no doubt be attempts to whittle down the power of the act, to use bureaucratic legalese to deny and delay the information, to pre-empt scandals by releasing information selectively."[64]

With the change of regime at the center on May 26, 2014, when Narendra Modi took over from Manmohan Singh, several policies of the earlier government were being revised, but so far, there is no sign that the new government wants to weaken the RTI Act. But there are several officials (there are around 2,500 Central Public Information Officers in the Central Government) who have started taking RTI provisions casually after the change of regime. There are some examples: When one of the RTI applications was rejected from the Ministry of Finance, a First Appeal was filed, reminding the "Quest for Transparency" mentioned on the PMO website and saying:

> By denying the information the learned CPIO has, in my view, tried to defame hon'ble PM Narendra Modi and hon'ble FM Arun Jaitley, since they are very much in favor of transparency and in favor of RTI Act.[65]

The result was that the required information was provided after that. Similar incidents happened in other ministries including Ministry of Home Affairs as well.[66]

There are two main ways for India's RTI Act to be implemented: through the proactive disclosure of information which is of public importance, and through the creation of a system for making and responding to requests for information and appeals, if required.

---

[63] Ibid.

[64] Shankkar Aiyar, *Accidental India, A History of Nation's Passage Through Crisis and Change* (New Delhi: ALEPH, 2012), 287.

[65] Ministry of Finance's reply on appeal No. DOFSR/A/2016/60407 filed by author.

[66] Reply of MHA on appeal No. MHOME/A/2016/60066 filed by author.

An effective supply of public information at all levels of administration requires strong political will from the top level of government and a good intention toward transparency at all levels of
government. It also requires that governments deploy adequate
resources for the proper implementation of the provision of the
Act. Above all, it requires a fundamental shift from a culture of
opacity to a new culture of openness. It requires a significant commitment among political leaders, accompanied by journalists and
activists who have hunger for information of great public interest.
It requires a change of mindsets within bureaucracies. The fact is
that whether one will get the information or not depends on the
person sitting on the chair of the public authority. If he/she wants
to share the information, he/she interprets the RTI Act in favor
of disclosure and if he/she wants to hide the information, he/she
denies and lands you in a legal battle which often defeats the very
purpose of getting the information even if it is disclosed later.

On the other hand, attack on RTI from the leaders who were
part of the UPA government is being seen. Congress leader Rajeev
Shukla said:[67] "RTI act is grossly misused and people are taking
wrong benefits. People have printed visiting cards like 'RTI Activist'
is some designation. People are blackmailing, making money...."
Praful Patel, who was the civil aviation minister in UPA-I (2004–09)
when the RTI Act was passed, said that "Objectivity (from decision
making process) is lost... Now everybody is concerned that this
law was passed in hurry. Anybody from a beetle seller to tea seller
can ask any information after paying ₹10. He can get information
about who made country's missile...."[68] And Naresh Agrawal, a
Member of Parliament (MP) from the Samajwadi Party (SP), which
supported the UPA government when it enacted the RTI Act, said
that the RTI Act was passed "under pressure of USA";[69] the statement was opposed by Congress MP Jairam Ramesh.[70] This all
shows that no matter how much the ruling classes are disturbed
from the transparency law, still there is no sign from the Central
Government that it wants to dilute the law.

In general, in the minds of the people of India, it is not relevant
who implemented the RTI Act. Although Manmohan Singh, who

---

[67] In Rajya Sabha question hour on April 28, 2016.
[68] Ibid.
[69] Ibid.
[70] Ibid.

spoke against "vexatious" use of the law, has said nothing on RTI since his party's defeat in the 2014 Lok Sabha elections, leaders such as Sonia Gandhi and Rahul Gandhi have only praised this act even after the departure of their government at the center in the 2014 elections. Sonia Gandhi has always termed it as the first significant achievement of the UPA government. She said in May 2015 in the Lok Sabha: "It is through this very legislation that millions were empowered to ask questions from their government about how schemes and public works are being implemented and how public authorities are functioning."[71] Rahul Gandhi said: "If you look at what we did with regard to corruption. RTI is the single biggest tool against corruption."[72] It is a fact that parties and their leaders are using the law when they are in the opposition.

It is also a fact that despite all the lofty statements made by Manmohan Singh, it was pressure from activists and the media that forced the UPA government from making major amendments in the Act in order to dilute it.

In Vijai Sharma's words, "There is no change (towards RTI in the new government) because the RTI Act, the system itself, is channelized and has been given a certain direction. RTI is widely accepted as a lifeline."[73] His predecessor Satyananda Mishra, who headed the CIC bench that delivered the order declaring political parties as public authorities under the RTI Act, says: "I don't think RTI can be abolished by any government. It would require extra ordinary courage almost verging on an autocratic attitude to be able to really recall the RTI Act."[74]

---

[71] Sonia Gandhi, Congress President, in Lok Sabha on May 6, 2015, http://www. inc.in/In-focus/420/Congress-President-Smt-Sonia-Gandhis-speech-in-Lok-Sabha, accessed December 29, 2016.

[72] In an interaction with students at Mount Carmel College, Bengaluru, on November 25, 2015.

[73] Vijay Sharma, "You can't use RTI to light up every corner," *The Indian Express* (December 22, 2015), http://indianexpress.com/article/india/india-news-india/you-cant-use-rti-to-light-up-every-corner-chief-information-commissioner-vijai-sharma/, accessed December 29, 2016.

[74] Ritu Sarin, "'There is a problem in demanding far too much freedom for our institutions. How do you establish their accountability?'" *The Indian Express* (November 11, 2012), http://archive.indianexpress.com/news/-there-is-a-problem-in-demanding-far-too-much-freedom-for-our-institutions.-how-do-you-establish-their-accountability--/1029862/, accessed December 29, 2016.

RTI and the Media

Much before the RTI Act was passed, the Press Council of India and some leading media personalities were actively associated with the activists demanding the legislation. The significance of RTI for the media was reflected in the Press Council's report, which was released as early as March 2001. The report said:

> At present, one of the stumbling blocks in the path of investigative, analytical and popular journalism is the difficulty in getting access to the official information. The bureaucracy, the police, the army, judiciary and even the legislature guard information regarding even the most mundane subjects with astonishing zeal. Few journalists are able to break this iron curtain of the official non-cooperation. The Right to Information will encourage journalists and society at large to be more questioning about the state of affairs and will be a powerful tool to check the unmitigated goings-on in the public realm and will also promote accountability. No longer will scribes have to depend on conjecture, rumour, leaks and sources other than knowledgeable sources. The legislation when enacted will pose an antidote to vested interests which try to conceal or misinterpret information or which try to manipulate media directly or indirectly to plant misinformation. Through this legislation, transparency in public, professional, social and personal sphere can be achieved.[75]

On February 17, 2009, speaking at a seminar on "Future of Print Media," Justice (Retd) G.N. Ray, the then chairman of the Press Council of India, had said:

> The legislation on access to information from all authorities from local to the national level and from all institutions whether in the private or public sector whose activities have a bearing on public welfare should be insisted on. Ultimately, it is the media which can deliver the benefits of such information to the people and also pursue it. The media also then does not have to depend upon speculation or unreliable secondary information to inform and educate the people.[76]

---

[75] Future of Print Media (New Delhi: Press Council of India), 135, 136.
[76] Inaugural address by Justice (Retd) G.N. Ray, Chairman, Press Council of India at a seminar on "Future of Print Media" on February 17, 2009, at Surendranath College for Women, Kolkata.

For journalists, FoI or RTI was always considered necessary equipment. UNESCO constituted a commission in 1979 in the chairmanship of Sean Mac Bride of Ireland in which the late Indian journalist BG Verghese was also a member. The commission submitted its report in 1980 which said:

> It is of course true that the right to seek and impart information, and the right to express opinions, should be enjoyed by everyone. But journalists need to exercise these rights as a basic condition of doing their job effectively, and they are particularly vulnerable to constraints by authority. They are often placed, whether they wish it or not, among those who find themselves in the front line of defence of freedom.[77]

The Mac Bride commission further said:

> Active pursuit and disclosure of facts which are of public interest is one of the criteria to judge a journalist's professional capacities. The role of the investigative journalist is to question and probe the action of all those in authority and to expose them wherever there is abuse of power, incompetence, corruption or other deviations.[78]

Mac Bride commission recommended that:

> Communication needs in a democratic society should be met by the extension of specific rights such as the right to be informed, the right to inform, the right to privacy, the right to participate in public communication—all elements of a new concept, the right to communicate. In developing what might be called a new era of social rights, we suggest all the implications of the right to communicate be further explored.[79]

Now, in many countries where the RTI or FOI law has been implemented, it is considered a tool of investigative reporting. A leading RTI advocate says: "The right to information is also a key tool in combating corruption and wrongdoing in government. Investigative journalists and watchdog NGOs can use the right to

---

[77] Many Voices, One World, Sean MacBride Commission Report (UNESCO, 1980), 233.
[78] Ibid., 234.
[79] Ibid., 265.

access information to expose wrongdoing and help root it out."[80] The Director-General (DG) of UNESCO says: "Social justice, empowerment, and development are all hampered if individuals do not enjoy access to information which relates, for example, to basic services and social programs they are entitled to, or to educational opportunities that have the power to transform lives."[81] In her lines, media can see a message to use RTI and help the citizenry in their empowerment. UNESCO organized a conference on Media and Good Governance in 2005 which called "to promote the adoption of national access to information legislation and to develop international principles on access to information."[82]

In India, during the initial years of RTI, the applications of common people were seen to be focused on their personal problems such as ration cards, passports, school admissions, departmental proceedings, electricity bill, and several other such issues related to daily life. Gradually, even ordinary citizens started to use the new law to explore issues of public concern. From the far-off North East to the far corners of the southern states, from the remotest areas of Jammu & Kashmir to Odisha, Bihar, UP, and Maharashtra, everywhere a large number of RTI activists emerged. There are certain common citizens who claim to have filed hundreds and thousands of RTI applications in government offices. There are not many such activists from the journalistic fraternity.

But, inspired by the success stories coming from RTI users from the remotest corners of the country, editors' belief further strengthened that RTI could be converted into an effective mean for investigative reporting. Delhi-based journalists in media organizations such as *India Today*, *The Indian Express*, and language newspapers based outside Delhi such as *Prabhat Khabar*, a Hindi daily from Ranchi, and *Amar Ujala*, another prominent Hindi daily of north India, also started taking recourse to the RTI Act to explore investigative stories. *The Indian Express*, which is known for investigative reporting, has been using the RTI Act since its inception in 2005. This newspaper's correspondents are regularly being trained to use this new means of investigative reporting, and they are regularly using the law to explore stories and getting published.

---

[80] Toby Mendel, The Right to Information in Latin America, UNESCO, 2009.
[81] Irina Bokova, Director-General of UNESCO, Brisbane, Australia, May 2, 2010.
[82] Dakar Declaration, Dakar, Senegal, May 3, 2005.

When RTI was implemented in India, common citizens such as Subhash Agrawal[83] served media men in accessing RTI-based stories. For years, he has been regularly accessing RTI-based stories and supplying them to journalists; the stories get published prominently. In matters such as the asset declaration system for the judges of the Supreme Court and High Courts, he has fought tremendous legal battles before CIC, Delhi High Court, and Supreme Court.[84] What he has done is an excellent job as a concerned citizen, but Indian media could have produced dozens of persons from within who could use RTI to investigate stories and make changes in the system.

But, with some exceptions, most of the RTI-based media reporting in newspapers, TV channels, and other media outlets has been just reporting of RTI happenings, decisions of CIC and state information commissions (SICs), and information accessed by ordinary citizens, nongovernmental organizations (NGOs), and RTI activists. While it is true that sometimes activists unearth major public interest issues, many of them may be driven by their own agendas. Therefore, while utilizing the information accessed by NGOs and activists, the need for media is to visualize and explore the information of public interest and follow up on the stories on their own. Some of the efforts of media men have been really impact-making.

Some stories that were investigated through RTI have created a huge impact. In December 2015, when the Supreme Court directed[85] that the Reserve Bank of India (RBI) is bound to give information regarding banks, Utkarsh Anand of *The Indian Express* filed an application to the RBI without wait. He received information which said that 29 state-owned banks wrote off a total of ₹1,140 billion of bad debts between financial years 2013 and 2015, much more than they had done in the preceding nine years. The RBI disclosed that while bad debts stood at ₹155.51 billion for the financial year ending March 2012, they had shot up by over three times to ₹525.42 billion by the end of March 2015. This story had

---

[83] Well-known RTI activist based in Delhi.

[84] See https://en.wikipedia.org/wiki/Subhash_Chandra_Agrawal, accessed December 29, 2016.

[85] See http://supremecourtofindia.nic.in/FileServer/2015–12-16_1450252953.pdf, accessed December 29, 2016.

the desired impact as the Supreme Court took suo motu cognizance and asked the RBI to provide it with the list of defaulters.[86]

Very recent are the revelations in the Ishrat Jahan case. This
case has been among India's biggest political controversies in the
last few years. The truth, for around a decade, was hidden in a
series of documents. Times Now, a news channel, accessed the file
related to Ishrat Jahan by using the RTI Act from the Ministry of
Home Affairs (MHA). The file, containing 70 pages of government
notings, signatures, legal documents, and annexures, had never
been made public before.[87]

Lok Sabha members declare their assets since 2004, and they
are supposed to update it annually. Ritu Sarin of *The Indian
Express* came to know in response to an RTI application in 2008
that barely 10 Lok Sabha members of the 14th Lok Sabha had
updated the list of their assets they filed when they got elected in
2004. Congress Vice President and MP Rahul Gandhi was one of
them. In a declaration filed on July 24, 2006, he submitted that he
had bought two medium-sized shops in the plush Metropolitan
Mall in Saket in south Delhi for a price of ₹13.4 million.[88]

The Manmohan Singh government came to power in June
2004. After nearly four years, an interesting effort was made by
Ravish Tiwari of *The Indian Express*. Using RTI, he inspected the
documents related to all Cabinet meetings that had taken place
during the Manmohan Singh government tenure till then.[89] The
story says that the PM had convened 217 Cabinet meetings till
June 2008—about one meeting per week—to deliberate over 1,800
proposals. But senior Cabinet ministers such as Textiles Minister
Shankersinh Vaghela, Commerce Minister Kamal Nath, and
Railways Minister Lalu Prasad Yadav attended less than half of all
Cabinet meetings. Vaghela, who attended just about 35 percent of
the meetings, tops the list of absentees, followed by Kamal Nath

---

[86] See http://indianexpress.com/article/india/india-news-india/bad-debts-rbi-
supreme-court-bank-defaulters/, accessed December 29, 2016.

[87] See http://timesofindia.indiatimes.com/india/Ishrat-Jahan-encounter-case-
Chidambaram-had-also-signed-first-affidavit/articleshow/51886383.cms, accessed
February 11, 2017.

[88] See http://archive.indianexpress.com/news/rahul-updates-his-assets-list-two-
shops-for-rs-1.34crore-in-south-delhi-mall/378051/0, accessed December 29, 2016.

[89] See http://archive.indianexpress.com/news/the-case-of-the-missing-cabi-
net/355477/, accessed December 29, 2016.

and Lalu. Only 13 ministers attended more than 70 percent of the meetings. Many ministers were also absent from meetings where a proposal moved by their ministry was on the agenda. Topping the list in this category was HRD Minister Arjun Singh, who was absent on 22 occasions when a matter moved by his ministry was to be discussed, followed by Lalu (21 meetings), Finance Minister P. Chidambaram (19), and External Affairs Minister Pranab Mukherjee (19). Ten of Mukherjee's 19 absences, however, were recorded after he took over the External Affairs portfolio, which requires frequent overseas travel, in 2006.

One such story was that of Saikat Dutta which was carried in *Outlook*.[90] In 2007, the Center had put a ban on the export of non-basmati and 25 percent broken rice to strengthen food security in India. This was done for deflecting high inflation and ensuring that there were enough food grains within the country at all times to distribute to those below the poverty line under the Public Distribution System (PDS). Soon thereafter, since India is a major rice exporter, the prices of rice in the international markets sky-rocketed. Almost three months after the ban was imposed in 2007, the government soon decided that since the ban had caused a shortage in foreign markets, if requests came for rice from poorer nations, the grains would be released on humanitarian grounds. Twenty-two countries, mostly African, were hence exempted from the ban. This was when the private companies connived with the government officials to make the most of the demand.[91] Dutta filed RTI applications to the Ministry of Consumer Affairs, Food and Public Distribution, Ministry of Commerce and Industry, Ministry of External Affairs (MEA), and Director General of Foreign Trade (DGFT) to inspect all documents related to the issue of this notification. The documents revealed that all procedures had been violated. The case was referred to the CBI.

But the fact is that in comparison to the media in many other countries, the Indian media has not done enough to explore the potential of the RTI Act. In Europe, for instance, journalists resort to Wobbling[92] [Wet Openbaarheid van Bestuur (WOB)

---

90 See http://www.outlookindia.com/magazine/story/whose-name-on-a-grain-of-rice/250566/, accessed January 2, 2017.

91 See http://www.rtiawards.org/saikatdutta.html, accessed December 29, 2016.

92 See http://www.wobbing.eu/ and http://journalismfund.eu/, accessed December 29, 2016.

in Dutch]—a common journalistic slang which means getting documents through FoI. There are certain groups of journalists in Europe who use the FoI Act exclusively for their stories. They gather regularly to share their experiences and get training in new techniques. Tony Blair, in whose tenure as PM the FoI legislation was implemented in the UK, was quite embarrassed because of a series of exposes by media using the new law; he had this to say about it in his memoirs:

> Freedom of Information. Three harmless words. I look at those words as I write them, and feel like shaking my head till it drops off my shoulders. You idiot. You naive, foolish, irresponsible nincompoop. There is really no description of stupidity, no matter how vivid, that is adequate. I quake at the imbecility of it.[93]

Blair went on to say that the

> FoI Act is not used, for the most part, by 'the people'. It's used by journalists. For political leaders, it's like saying to someone who is hitting you over the head with a stick, 'Hey, try this instead', and handing them a mallet.... It's used as a weapon.[94]

He further stated, "The power it (the FoI Act) handed to the tender mercy of the media was gigantic. We did it with care, but without foresight."[95]

This was the same Tony Blair who had said at the Campaign for FoI awards ceremony in 1996:

> It is not some isolated constitutional reform that we are proposing with a Freedom of Information Act. It is a change that is absolutely fundamental to how we see politics developing in this country over the next few years...information is power and any government's attitude about sharing information with the people actually says a great deal about how it views power itself and how it views the relationship between itself and the people who elected it.... People often say to me today: everyone says this before they

---

[93] A Journey, memoirs of Tony Blair, published on September 1, 2010, Random House. p. 516.
[94] Ibid., 517.
[95] Ibid., 127.

get into power, then, after they get into power you start to read the words of the government on the screen and they don't seem so silly after all.[96]

FoI had featured in the Labour Party's 1997 manifesto—the sixth successive time that the party had promised it to the electorate since the early 1970s.[97] Tony Blair became the PM of the UK in 1997 and was on the post till 2007. His government brought FoI in the UK which was implemented on January 1, 2005.

For the first time, journalists representing all European member states teamed up to file complaints with the European Court of Justice against the European Parliament (EP). They were refused access to information related to how the 751 Members of the European Parliament (MEPs) spend their allowances. As an example of a coordinated effort of European journalists, this team of 29 led by Slovenia-based Anuska Delic has now filed complaints with the Court of Justice on November 13, 2015.[98]

Besides the UK and other European countries where FoI is being utilized by the media proactively, globally, wherever there is an RTI or FoI law, it has impacted on media reporting. For instance, in Australia, the FoI Act was implemented in 1982 at the federal level and, over the years, separate legislations were passed at the state level. For instance, in Queensland (Australia), the RTI Act was implemented in 2009 and a study of media reporting during pre- and post-RTI law conducted by their Office of Information Commissioner says: "Accessing government information, open discussion of problems including investigating or resolving problems, and issues of government transparency have received more media attention since the RTI reforms were introduced. There is a discernible shift in the way FoI and RTI are used to source stories."[99]

---

[96] Tony Blair, leader of the Labour Party, March 25, 1996 https://www.cfoi.org.uk/?s=Tony+Blair, accessed December 29, 2016.

[97] See https://www.opendemocracy.net/ourkingdom/maurice-frankel/roots-of-blairs-hostility-to-freedom-of-information, accessed December 29, 2016.

[98] See http://gijn.org/2015/11/20/european-parliament-taken-to-court-by-journalists-from-all-eu-countries/, accessed December 29, 2016.

[99] See https://www.oic.qld.gov.au/__data/assets/pdf_file/0009/7794/research-report1-changes-media-reporting-after-rti-laws-qld.pdf, accessed December 29, 2016.

In the United States,[100]

> Journalists and scholars have used FoI Act, Federal Advisory Committee Act and the Sunshine Act to investigate a variety of news stories and historic events. Their discoveries, based on documents they received or discussions they witnessed, have often brought about crucial change to many aspects of public life.

To use the US's FoI Act, one need not be a citizen of that country.

In Brazil, where RTI was implemented only in 2012, the Association of Brazilian Investigative Journalists (ABRAJI) coordinates a 25-NGO coalition named Forum for the Right to Access Public Information. Just over a year after the implementation of the law, ABRAJI conducted a study of three newspapers (namely, *Folha de S. Paulo, O Estado de S. Paulo,* and *O Globo*) and found that: "The Access to Information Law is incorporated into the routine of newsrooms. The fact that more than six dozen reporters from three newspapers have used the law demonstrates that obtaining public information is already a constant tool in journalistic investigations."[101] Marcelo Moreira, the president of ABRAJI, says: "The approval of Access Act was one of the most important achievements for the Brazilian journalism in recent years and allowed the most reporters and editors seek information to which access was difficult before."[102]

Even in Pakistan, a group of journalists has excessively used the law and created embarrassment for the ruling classes. Journalists have done breaking stories about the secret funds of the Pakistan government to influence journalists, and also about the huge expenses on foreign travels by the PM among others.[103]

In India, with very few exceptions, hardly any government official has tried to hide information because of the fear of its use by the media. Moreover, no senior political leaders have been known to express the fear of the use of RTI by the media. There

---

[100] See http://www.rcfp.org/federal-open-government-guide/introduction, accessed December 29, 2016.
[101] Details of the study shared with author by Marina Iemini Atoji, Executive Manager, ABRAJI.
[102] Marcelo Moreira, the president of ABRAJI, in conversation with author.
[103] Author's interaction with Umar Cheema, an Islamabad-based investigative journalist.

are of course complaints and criticism of excessive use by people who 'misuse' the law as well. Most of the applications that are being called as misuse of law are sometimes nonserious, vague, and unspecific. Public authorities find it difficult to provide information to such queries, and their concerns may be genuine, because many such applications can be quite disconcerting and a wastage of time. An example of such frivolous misuse of the Act is one where officials dealing with a sensitive department of the Government of India got an application where the applicant asked, "How many statues of Mahatma Gandhi are installed in the country.... How many statues of Jawaharlal Nehru.... (He had asked similar information regarding around 60 personalities).... One of the queries was whether his (applicant's) statue could also be installed in this country somewhere?"[104] Then, there are queries more than 20 pages long which contain questions rather than requests for particular information. Such things remain in implementation of every law, and every law is often abused and misused. But these are mere exceptions, whether it is the RTI Act, 2005, or any other law like the Dowry Prohibition Act, 1961. The problem is somehow related to the awareness and education level of ordinary Indians, and things will certainly change gradually.

RTI was implemented without providing any extra remuneration to government employees. It has been observed that most public authorities are not afraid to disclose information, but the fact is that due to the extra hours of work, lack of compensation, and shortage of staff, they criticize RTI out of their own frustration. Their voice was echoed by Manmohan Singh when he spoke on the sixth anniversary of its implementation:

> A situation in which a public authority is flooded with requests for information having no bearing on public interest is something not desirable. We must, therefore, pool all our wisdom, our knowledge, and our experiences to come to a conclusion on how to deal with vexatious demands for information without, at the same time, hindering the flow of information to those whose demands genuinely serve public interest.[105]

---

[104] An officer showed this application to the author.
[105] PM's address to 6th annual convention of information commissioners at New Delhi on October 14, 2011.

Again, a year later, Manmohan Singh said at a CIC conference:

> There are concerns about frivolous and vexatious use of the Act
> in demanding information the disclosure of which cannot possi-
> bly serve any public purpose. Sometimes information covering a
> long time-span or a large number of cases is sought in an omni-
> bus manner with the objective of discovering an inconsistency or
> mistake which can be criticized. Such queries besides serving little
> productive social purpose are also a drain on the resources of the
> public authorities, diverting precious man-hours that could be put
> to better use.[106]

But the fact is that a large number of RTI users are from the government itself. Vijai Sharma says, "There is a trend of disgruntled
employees filing applications driven by grudge or vendetta. This
is not what the RTI system was meant for. But the law doesn't
disallow them from filing RTI applications."[107] Before him, the
second Chief Information Commissioner A.N. Tewari had a different other experience when he said:

> The Commission had observed a trend of the civil servants using
> the RTI Act to save themselves from disciplinary and vigilance
> inquiries. If we make an analysis, almost 15 percent cases we are
> hearing can fall in this category. The trend is rampant in PSUs and
> even in ministries like Home and DoPT. Civil servants are using
> the Act to deflect and stall proceedings against them and we have
> to find a way out of this pattern.[108]

The media can change this situation by proactively using this historic legislation to provide bona fide information to the public.

The Supreme Court's observation, made in their order dated
August 9, 2011, also says: "The nation does not want a scenario
where 75% of the staff of public authorities spends 75% of their
time in collecting and furnishing information to applicants

---

[106] PM's address to 7th annual convention of information commissioners at New
Delhi on October 12, 2012.
[107] See http://indianexpress.com/article/india/india-news-india/you-cant-use-rti-
to-light-up-every-corner-chief-information-commissioner-vijai-sharma/, accessed
December 29, 2016.
[108] See http://indianexpress.com/article/news-archive/web/rti-used-as-a-tool-not-
to-give-information, accessed December 29, 2016.

instead of discharging their regular duties."[109] In several cases, the Supreme Court has been seen standing behind the information seekers. For example, on December 16, 2015, the Supreme Court had said:

> It had long since come to our attention that the Public Information Officers (PIO) under the guise of one of the exceptions given under Section 8 of RTI Act, have evaded the general public from getting their hands on the rightful information that they are entitled to.[110]

There have been success stories for the media and common RTI users who have exposed the ill-doings of the government at the center and state governments. Several scams have been exposed using the RTI Act post 2005, including the Adarsh Housing scam, which resulted in the exit of the Chief Minister of Maharashtra Ashok Chavan. RTI was also used extensively in exposing scams such as 2G, coal block allocations, and Commonwealth Games scandals which resulted in huge embarrassment to the governments and disgraced many leaders. This law has given little power to the powerless people whether they are ordinary citizens, leaders of opposition parties, victimized bureaucrats and government employees, and many other sections of the society who can question the powerful with RTI in their hand. This law has brought embarrassment to the ruling classes and to them who are running the high offices of the country, and that is the reason they are resisting it.

What Media Can Do

Having access to and understanding the functioning of the government machinery, starting from the Central Government based in Delhi to the grassroots level, makes it easy for journalists to identify issues of public interest and expose the wrongdoings of government authorities, and prompt them to reform.

---

[109] Justices R.V. Raveendran and A.K. Patnaik on August 9, 2011.
[110] Justice M.Y. Eqbal and Justice C. Nagappan in Reserve Bank of India vs Jayantilal N. Mistry and others.

The RTI Act has given the media an opportunity to unearth the mismanagement of public money and expose the misdeeds of public servants, but in general, it has so far not been successful in doing that as effectively as it should have. The use of the RTI Act for investigative journalism needs a lot of patience, persistent effort, and the acceptance that many of these efforts may often go waste. Considering the tremendous growth of print, electronic, and social media in recent times, the increasing number of dedicated journalists coming into the profession can change the entire approach to and style of reporting. But several journalists have preferred approaching activists to file an RTI for them. A greater number of journalists need to accept the RTI Act as a crucial tool of journalistic investigation.

While the RTI Act needs to be taught to every Indian, its knowledge and techniques of use are the need of the hour for journalists to utilize it as an impact-making and reform-oriented law. This will certainly make journalists' job more relevant, more impact-making, and more reform-oriented. Journalists' use of RTI on focused issues will also avoid criticism because it may not have 'vexatious' and 'frivolous' queries. Journalists need to consider it as a crucial law vis-a-vis Article 19-1(A) of the Constitution and try to utilize it on their own rather than depending on activists for information. And, at all times, they need to take every precaution to protect it from any possible dilution by the governments.

2

Foreign Travels of Ministers: 256 Rounds of the Globe

Travels abroad are expensive, both in terms of the time and the money spent on them, and also cause disruption in work, and hence must be kept to the barest minimum. No doubt, certain visits are necessary and unavoidable; important international conferences and meetings of international organisations in which the country's representation is necessary fall in this category. Except for these, other travel abroad by Ministers should be undertaken only when these are inescapable.[1]

—Cabinet Secretariat to all departments of Government of India, on
August 21, 1996

Table 2.1:
Highlights of RTI filed to get information on foreign travel of union ministers

Information	Foreign travel of union ministers
Authority	Prime Minister's Office, Cabinet Secretariat and all union ministries
Problems	PMO provided dates of visit and city/country visited. For expenses, I had to approach every ministry; despite that, several ministries did not give expenses—at least three did not respond.
Applications and appeals	59 for first story (excluding those filed for the follow-up).
Time taken	Over four months
Story	The Flying Cabinet: 71 union ministers made foreign travels equal to 256 round of the globe in three and a half years. (*India Today*, February 18, 2008).
Impact	PM Manmohan Singh wrote to union ministers to curtail the foreign travel expenses.

(Continued)

---

[1] DO No 21/1/7/95-Cab dated August 21, 1996: http://cabsec.nic.in/showpdf.php? type=circulars_f21aug1996&special, accessed December 30, 2016.

(Continued)

Follow up by me	Many other aspects of ministers' foreign trips were investigated, such as who uses their mileage points, with whom they travel, and where they go on personal trips.
Follow up by others	Widely followed up by other media.

Source: Author.

In July 1991, with the announcement of its new economic policy of liberalization, privatization, and globalization, India began to open up to the outside world, encouraging economic reforms and foreign investment. Today, in an increasingly inclusive world, India has emerged as one of the most vibrant economies, a key player in geopolitics, and, as we are proud to assert, the world's largest democracy. With over 1.2 billion people, India's recent growth and development has been one of the most significant achievements of our times and India's growing voice on the international stage is in keeping with its enormous size and potential.

In this scenario, it becomes more necessary than ever before to make one's presence felt in the global arena, and in doing so, for government officials to travel abroad. The UPA government under Manmohan Singh would seem to have taken this a wee bit too seriously, for ministers and bureaucrats have been guzzling up frequent-flyer miles with unprecedented rapidity. The benefits of foreign travel have never before been so widely utilized. Economic progress in our country is hampered at every step by corruption, widely accepted as endemic and engulfing every aspect of politics and society.

Once I was assigned the job of using transparency law for investigative reporting, I started thinking of several ideas to explore through RTI. By visiting websites of concerned departments, discussing with the sources in the government departments, and going through the reports and other available documents about the functioning of various departments, several ideas of public interest were coming to mind. Foreign travel made by union ministers became the first big investigation using the transparency law. After going through the circulars and instructions with regard to foreign travel of union ministers and government officials available either on the websites of Department of Expenditure (DoE) and Cabsec, or in some books compiling such circulars, an RTI application was filed with the PMO, requesting for details of foreign jaunts of union ministers. It was my first story broken through the RTI Act to reconnoiter information from the government for journalistic use. The application was drafted without so much as going through the transparency law. Rather brazenly, and in very basic terms, the PMO was asked about the foreign trips made by union ministers: "Please provide the following information under the RTI Act: Name of minister, country/cities visited, dates of travel, purpose of visit, total expenses incurred."[2]

That was the humble beginning of what became my chosen journalistic pursuit. It has taken me through a protracted, time-consuming, and often frustrating journey, which after all makes for an interesting reading.

My first RTI query elicited an early reply, as in a letter the PMO advised to pay ₹66 as photocopying charges at ₹2 per page as the requisite information was in 33 pages. I was delighted nonetheless to get a reply from the PMO, convinced that it would not have been possible had the RTI not been in place. The fee was paid and the information was received (but only a part of it as I was soon to learn).

In the meantime, realizing that the PMO's response also did not have full details of travel expenses incurred by ministers, a different approach was applied: knock at each union ministry's door to extract details of foreign travels by their concerned ministers. Finally, except for the Ministry of Panchayati Raj,[3] all others yielded. The information was checked and cross-checked doubly to be sure that everything was right. Then two replies—one provided by the PMO and the other by the ministries concerned— were carefully compared.

After that, an excel sheet detailing all aspects of foreign trips made by every minister in the Manmohan Singh-led UPA-I was meticulously prepared. Details of Natwar Singh and Ghulam Nabi Azad were left out since the former had resigned following revelations of the Volcker Committee Report and the latter to take over as Chief Minister of Jammu & Kashmir. The PM's visits abroad

---

[2] RTI application dated September 27, 2007 filed by the author.
[3] Shyamlal Yadav, "Frequent Fliers," *India Today* (February 8, 2008), http://m.indiatoday.in/technology/story/Frequent+fliers/1/4364.html, accessed December 30, 2016.

were also excluded. And finally the calculation came out: in 1,287 days of the UPA government, till November 30, 2007, 71 of the 78 UPA ministers (seven had not ventured out of the country) had made 786 foreign trips spending about 3,798 days' travel time.[4]

Three months had passed since the investigations began, and now Shankkar Aiyar, the then managing editor of *India Today*, came up with something very interesting. He asked to calculate the total distance travelled by each minister during that time. Taking the help of a website and from documents spread over 700 pages, it took over 15 days to calculate the total kilometers travelled by the 71 ministers and punch in the data in the excel sheet.

A shocking figure arrived which was over 10.2 million km. Then this figure was divided by the circumference of the earth (40,008 km) and the result was 256. This number became the punch line of the story: 71 UPA ministers had made foreign trips equaling 256 rounds of the earth in less than three and half years. It was after that when the main story, along with a one-page info-chart on each minister, was written.

That was the chronicle of first major investigation using RTI, but the story had to wait for publication because it was felt that the story needed to make comparisons with foreign jaunts of ministers of previous governments. A comparative assessment of similar trips made during the NDA regime would no doubt have made a better impact, but the almost four years that had passed meant that to unearth those details would have been a time-consuming and laborious process. Therefore, the idea was dropped and the UPA story was finalized. The story was published as a cover story running into 14 pages.

Some extracts from the story:[5]

> This is one high-flying government. In this globalised world, it is now in the nature of official business to travel to different parts of the earth making new friends, lesser enemies and influencing people.... As a rising economic power, it is perhaps more necessary than ever before to make your presence felt at global high

---

[4] Ibid.
[5] Ibid.

tables and international conference podiums.... But even by that yardstick, the UPA Government would seem to be in an overdrive or rather turbo-charged, its ministerial representatives raking up frequent-flier miles at a frenetic pace.... Whether it's a case of Democracy on the Move or the New World Order, the perks of foreign travel have never been so widely utilised."

Besides the prominence and importance given to the story, what motivated me more was the 'Letter from the Editor' written by Aroon Purie. His editorial said:[6]

When the Right to Information (RTI) Act was passed in 2005 it was welcomed as a landmark legislation that would lead to transparent governance. For journalists, the Act promised to be the key to unlock doors which usually stayed shut due to the government's obduracy. We decided to launch a series of investigations that would use the RTI Act to get information on how the Government deploys its funds.

This issue features the first of those investigations....

Our cover story this week is an exhaustive detailing of this expenditure of taxpayers' money. It was researched by our indefatigable Principal Correspondent Shyamlal Yadav from *India Today* Hindi, who has now become the in-house expert on the RTI Act. It took him 59 applications over four months and much persistence to get the information we wanted. At the end of this game of intra-governmental badminton, we discovered: that the UPA Government has an extraordinary appetite for overseas travel and that it requires an Olympian stamina to make the full use of the RTI Act.

.... Whatever be the reason, it seems that if you joined the UPA Cabinet, you could see the world—at someone else's expense, of course.

The 'Frequent Fliers' story gave a great new identity which I did not have earlier, though I had already won a few awards, including the prestigious Statesman Rural Reporting Award (First Prize) for stories on rural India, but after this first RTI-based story was published in *India Today*, I got congratulatory calls from

---

[6] Aroon Purie, "Letter from the Editor," *India Today* (February 18, 2008).

unexpected quarters—some politicians, including Congress leaders, and several senior journalists.

Impact and After Effects

With travel details of 71 ministers, backed by extensive data, there were apprehensions that many angry rejoinders and demands for corrections were bound to follow. Fortunately, we did not get many. A call was received from Minister of State Chandrashekhar Sahu[7] complaining that figures of his expenses were wrong. But when he was given sufficient proof citing the original documents, he was convinced.[8]

There were facts, there were documents, and there were certified copies of information supplied under the RTI Act. It was realized how powerful and effective a mechanism the RTI Act is for investigative journalists, as every piece of information comes from the government itself, officially. That is the beauty of the RTI Act for a journalist.

The impact was clear. On June 4, 2008, PM Manmohan Singh wrote a letter[9] to his ministers:

> It cannot be denied that there is substantial scope to reduce expenditure on travel and administration. As we ask the people to bear some of the financial burden of our oil imports, it is not only necessary from resources conservation point of view but also as a moral duty to cut out all wasteful expenditure in our own establishments.... I am, therefore, writing to ask you to severely curtail expenditure on air travel, particularly foreign travel, except in cases where it is deemed to be absolutely necessary. This economy may be made applicable immediately for your own self and also for all senior functionaries in your ministry.... While instructions will be issued to the Cabinet Secretary to introduce more rigorous scrutiny of foreign travel proposals, the prudence can be exercised at your own level with regard to both foreign and local travel for

---

[7] Sahu was Minister of State, Ministry of Labour and Employment and later Ministry of Rural Development during UPA-I government under Manmohan Singh.

[8] Author's own records.

[9] Letter was accessed by the author under the RTI Act from the PMO.

you and your offices. I seek your full co-operation in this matter of importance and urgency."

This letter of the PM was more than sufficient endorsement of the issues raised in the story.

For the follow-up stories, RTI applications were being sent regularly to keep chasing the PMO, Cabsec, and various ministries. Later, the Pay and Accounts Office (PAO) of Cabinet Affairs informed[10] that while the foreign travel expenditure of union ministers (Cabinet Ministers and Ministers of State) was ₹1.2279 billion during 2007–08, it had come down to a mere ₹203.7 million in 2008–09. Although, admittedly, in 2006–07, the expense on foreign travel of union ministers was ₹149.8 million, the year 2007–08 had seen a huge surge in spending. It was clear that the story had its desired impact, prompting the government to take austerity measures which saved over ₹1 billion of the public exchequers in the next financial year.

Air India and Frequent-flyer Mileage Points

To keep an eye on ministers' foreign trips, an RTI application was filed with Air India to find out the frequent-flyer mileage points that ministers under the UPA-I had earned out of their foreign visits and who had travelled using those points. Curiosity was to know how the ministers utilize the mileage points they earn from official trips.

This was based on a hunch that ministers must be receiving mileage points and utilizing them for personal travel and for those of their relatives and friends. Within a week of filing the application, a reply[11] was received from the deputy general manager at IGI Airport, Bharat Chaturvedi, who said,[12] "We are forwarding your application to our headquarters and shall revert." After waiting for over a month a reminder was sent to Chaturvedi. He replied[13] the same day: "This is an extensive/voluminous exercise

---

[10] Vide letter dated October 16, 2009, to author on RTI.
[11] Letter dated January 30, 2008, received from Air India on RTI.
[12] Letter dated February 5, 2006, to author on RTI.
[13] E-mail received from Chaturvedi on March 6, 2008.

in nature and being worked out. Same shall be completed within next week or so. In view of the above, we shall revert to you at earliest, possibly before March 20, 2008." On March 20, the given date, Chaturvedi responded,[14] "As per the information we received from headquarters the information on your question is being compiled and we shall revert on receipt reply from them."

But then a reply[15] was received from the central public information officer (CPIO) of Air India:

> The information requested by you includes commercial confidence, the disclosure of which would harm the competitive interest of the passengers as also the airline which is exempted from disclosure under section 8(1)(d) of the RTI Act. Further, the information which is available with us is in fiduciary relationship and we do not feel that larger public interest warrants the disclosure of this information.

When I called the concerned officer informally to understand the reason behind the unexpected response, he clarified that he had all the information compiled, but before dispatching it, had consulted the concerned joint secretary who had advised him not to dispatch it, but to issue a denial.[16] So, crucial information of public interest was kept from being disclosed and remained in its secret domain.

The very same day, a first appeal was filed before Jitender Bhargava, Executive Director, Corporate Communications, Air India. He responded[17] justifying the CPIO's response:

> While I do agree that the information sought by you is in public interest, there is another aspect to it that of Air India's commercial interests. If Air India makes public the information with respect to use of frequent flier mileage earned by ministers of the Union Cabinet, the airline runs the risk of losing business as some of these ministers, as well as other government officials, who generally travel on Air India, could think of shifting to private carriers.

In response, a second appeal was filed on April 21, 2008, to the CIC. This appeal was heard on July 17, 2008, and was my first

---

[14] E-mail dated March 20, 2008, to the author.

[15] Response of Air India dated March 31, 2008, to author on RTI.

[16] Author's own records.

[17] Bhargava's response dated April 8, 2008, to author on First Appeal under RTI.

appearance before an information commissioner. When I appeared before Commissioner M.M. Ansari, the Air India representative had already left. I clearly remember what Ansari had asked me that day: "What will you do with the information?"[18] I said that being a journalist I needed it for news story. During hearing of the matter, Ansari said that the information I sought was personal information and has commercial confidence.[19] Reminding him that ministers were public figures and information about them was of public interest, I left his chamber.

A couple of days later the order was uploaded on the CIC website, which upheld the decisions of the CPIO and the First Appellate Authority (FAA). The CIC order[20] said:

> Almost all the airlines have been offering incentives to the passengers irrespective of their official status. The Government and public servants have been availing of such incentives provided by the respondent and other airlines with which it has been competing. The disclosure of selective information in respect of the identified Ministers could be misused for humiliation and harassment of any passenger. Almost every commercial entity offers certain incentives to promote its business and the respondent is no exception. In view of this, the denial of information on the ground of commercial confidence u/s 8(1)(d) of the Act is justified.

What was becoming increasingly apparent was a clear case of double standards being played out. There were no provisions to stop ministers from using the mileage points they earned from official trips for their personal use. The DoE issued a circular[21] for government officials banning use of frequent-flyer mileage points earned during official trips for personal travel.

> All mileage points earned by government employees on tickets purchased for official travel shall be utilised by the concerned department for other official travel by their officers. It is the responsibility

---

[18] Author's own records.
[19] Ibid.
[20] See http://www.rti.india.gov.in/cic_decisions/MA-17072008–03.pdf, accessed December 30, 2016.
[21] F. No.7(1)/E.Coord./2008 dated July 17, 2008: http://www.rti.india.gov.in/cic_decisions/MA-17072008–03.pdf, accessed December 30, 2016.

of the officer concerned to ensure that free mileage points are used only for official travel and not for personal trips.

When the DoE was asked whether the circular was applicable for union ministers too, it replied:[22] "Orders are applicable to Central Government Employees only." So, ministers keep enjoying mileage points earned from their official trips on their personal trips as usual.

Later, the Ministry of Consumer Affairs, Food and Public Distribution responded that the minister's wife accompanied[23] as free companion during his three foreign visits between September 13, 2009, and February 2012. The Ministry of Minority Affairs also informed[24] that the minister's spouse visited the USA in May 2010 as his free companion. It may be the practice in other ministries as well, but other ministries did not respond to the queries asked by the author or did not provide such information.

The Montek Singh Ahluwalia Story: One Trip Every Nine Days

The frequent-flyer story and the data collected thereof brought up many more ideas to be followed up. From the information, a large number of names were of people who availed the rank of union cabinet minister or minister of state, but their names were not included in the frequent-fliers story, only of the members of the union council of ministers. From the list provided by the PMO, it was noticed that Deputy Chairman of the Planning Commission Montek Singh Ahluwalia was among the most frequent foreign travelers. So, to get more related details, another RTI application was filed on February 11, 2008, seeking details of foreign trips made by Ahluwalia since taking charge.

The CPIO concerned did not respond on time so a first appeal was filed with the FAA. On April 11, 2008, many details were received[25] about the foreign trips made by Ahluwalia and other

---

[22] Response dated February 2, 2009, from DoE to author on RTI.
[23] Response of the Ministry dated June 27, 2012, to author on RTI.
[24] Response of Ministry dated July 17, 2012, on RTI to author.
[25] In response to an RTI filed by the author.

members of the Planning Commission since his taking over in June 2004. But the information was insufficient so further applications were filed. Information was received in many parts but finally it was interesting. On January 21, 2011, the Planning Commission provided the updates of Ahluwalia's foreign trips on another RTI application. But the information had many inconsistencies, so again an application was filed on March 28, 2011, seeking details of all foreign trips of Ahluwalia since June 2004. Thus, all details[26] of his trips along with dates of visit, countries/cities visited, names of companions, and total expenses incurred arrived. These were those trips which he had made in his official capacity.

Based on calculations of his trips, it was discovered that since taking office in June 2004, and up to January 2011, Ahluwalia had made 42 official foreign trips and spent 274 working days abroad.[27] This brought forth the startling fact that he had spent every ninth day abroad in his seven-year tenure and this without even including travel time! It was found that 23 of his 42 trips had been to the United States while the other destinations included the UK, Muscat, Dubai, Ethiopia, Australia, South Korea, Canada, Morocco, Bahrain, Singapore, Japan, and China.

The exact expenditure incurred on official travel of ministers is difficult to calculate considering the multiplicity of authorities involved, but going by the Planning Commission's own submission (three replies had contradictory figures so the lowest amounts were taken), he had spent ₹23.4 million on those trips. It was not clear whether the figures included expenses incurred by Indian embassies abroad on frills like hiring limousines. What was clear was that his globe-trotting had certainly affected the functioning of the Planning Commission as the approach paper for the 12th Five Year Plan, which was supposed to be ready by the end of 2010, was not submitted until May 2011.

It was difficult to get Ahluwalia's version before the story went in for publication. Despite repeated reminders, through e-mails and phone calls, all that was received from his staff was the standard line that the request was pending with Ahluwalia and that

---

[26] On April 26, 2011, on an RTI filed by author.
[27] Shyamlal Yadav, "One in every nine days..." *India Today* (May 23, 2011).

only he would respond. Finally, since he did not respond despite all efforts, the story was run. It appeared as a one-page story.[28]

The story did not make the kind of initial impact which was expected. But that was belied by what noted journalist and Magsaysay awardee P. Sainath later wrote in *The Hindu*:[29]

> That Dr Ahluwalia practices austerity himself is evident from two RTI queries. Both fine examples of RTI-based journalism, but failing to get the attention they deserved. Both exploring the anatomy of his austerity. One was a story in *India Today* (covering Dr Ahluwalia's foreign trips between June 2004 and January 2011) by Shyamlal Yadav. This journalist (now with *The Indian Express*), has done outstanding RTI-based stories in the past as well.

Personal Foreign Trips: The Dubious Dubai Connection

Going through the vast foreign travel data, another idea came: to get details of personal foreign trips made by union ministers and bureaucrats. RTI applications were being put regularly and data were being updated. From their responses, another interesting trend was noticed: the frequent trips made by union ministers to Dubai.

Dubai, the most populous city in the United Arab Emirates, is known for its friendly tax regime, low property rates, and lucrative investment opportunities. So investors flock to Dubai from across the globe. And, the facts were clearly indicated that one out of five personal trips made by union ministers was to Dubai.

Of the 128[30] personal foreign trips by 39 ministers in the 20 months of United Progressive Alliance (UPA-II), 27 had UAE, particularly Dubai, as their destination. Of the 39 union ministers who had travelled abroad in their personal capacity, since June 15, 2009, 15 had visited the UAE at least once, if not more. The names of ministers included then Minister of Textiles Dayanidhi Maran, Human Resource Development (HRD) Minister Kapil Sibal, Law Minister M. Veerappa Moily, Minister of State for External Affairs

---

[28] Ibid.

[29] P. Sainath, "Austerity of the Affluent," *The Hindu*, New Delhi (May 21, 2012).

[30] Based on various RTI applications to MEA and PMO filed by the author during 2009–12.

E. Ahamed, Urban Development Minister Kamal Nath, Heavy Industries Minister Praful Patel, Agriculture Minister Sharad Pawar, Coal Minister Sriprakash Jaiswal, New and Renewable Energy Sources Minister Farooq Abdullah, Minister of State for Information and Broadcasting S. Jagathrakshakan, Minister of State for Consumer Affairs K.V. Thomas, Minister of State for Railways K.H. Muniyappa, Minister of State for Tribal Affairs Mahadev S. Khandela, Minister of State for Petroleum and Natural Gas R.P.N. Singh, and MoS for Tourism Sultan Ahmed.

While some took families, the clearance given by the MEA did not reflect any names of companions for other ministers. This story was published in *India Today*.[31] It is matter of further investigation that why majority of Indian politicians visit Dubai again and again on personal trips.

Summing Up

Even after ministers' foreign travel stories had been published in *India Today*, efforts were continued on further aspects of the story, especially those to do with expenditure incurred by ministers. It was an onerous task because of the involvement of multiple agencies in India and abroad. In response to the first RTI query on the subject, the PMO had provided details of foreign trips of ministers, but refused to disclose the expenses incurred. It said:[32] "The culled out expenses does not include expenditure involved in each trip which this office does not maintain and may be obtained from individual ministries." When the individual ministries were approached, most of them took positions that they were not concerned with the ministers' expenses and advised to approach the PAO, Cabinet Affairs, saying:[33] "The public authority maintaining details of approximate expenditure on Minister's foreign trips is PAO, Cabinet Affairs."

But the PAO, Cabinet Affairs, repeatedly responded[34] in much the same manner: "As per existing Receipts and Payments Rules

---

[31] Shyamlal Yadav, "Hi, Dubai," *India Today* (May 16, 2011).
[32] PMO's letter dated November 2, 2007, to author on RTI.
[33] Over a dozen ministries answered this way during 2008–09 on RTI applications filed by the author.
[34] Response of the Cabinet Affairs, MHA on author's RTI.

the details of each and every payment to the individual concerned are made through the Drawing and Disbursing Officer (DDO). Hence, the entire initial records are being maintained by the DDO of that Ministry."

Things appeared to be at a dead end.

Then, on March 29, 2011, on an appeal, Chief Information Commissioner Satyananda Mishra sent a directive[35] to the Cabsec:

> We think that it would be in the interest of transparency if some key information about the domestic and international travel by Union Ministers could be maintained centrally in the Cabinet Secretariat itself especially since the PAO under it is responsible for all accounting details for payment of the salary and reimbursement of their travel expenditure. We direct the CPIO to bring this to the notice of the competent authority in the Cabinet Secretariat for appropriate action.

Later, the DoPT issued an official memorandum (OM)[36] to all ministries and departments of Government of India:

> Public authorities are receiving RTI applications frequently asking for details of the official tours undertaken by ministers and other officials of the Ministries/Departments concerned. In compliance with the provisions of Section 4 of the RTI Act, 2005, it is advised that public authorities may proactively disclose the details of foreign and domestic official tours undertaken by minister(s) and officials of the rank of Joint Secretary to the Government of India and above and Heads of Departments, since January 1, 2012. The disclosure may be updated once every quarter from July 1, 2012. Information to be disclosed proactively may contain nature of the official tour, places visited, the period, number of people included in the official delegation and total cost of such travel undertaken.

This advisory, the OM states, would not apply to security intelligence organizations and chief vigilance officers (CVOs) of public authorities.

---

[35] See http://www.rti.india.gov.in/cic_decisions/CIC_WB_A_2010_000015-SM_M_54250.pdf, accessed December 30, 2016.

[36] Official Memorandum F. No.1/8/2012-IR of DoPT dated September 11, 2012.

Quoting the CIC order of March 29, 2011, when the PAO, Cabinet Affairs was asked[37] about the details of expenses made on foreign travel of every minister, the office responded[38] that, "It has been decided that RTI application seeking information regarding expenditure incurred by Ministries may be handled in Ministry of Home Affairs." All it provided was the consolidated amount spent on the foreign travel of Union cabinet ministers as ₹6.61 billion and on union ministers of state as ₹49.9 million during 2011–12; ₹2,169 million and ₹48.60 million during 2012–13; and ₹194.5 million and ₹11.39 million during 2013–14 (till July 31, 2013) respectively.[39]

When the DoPT was asked on February 1, 2013, that how many departments had followed the OM dated September 11, 2012, and how many were defaulters, the DoPT responded:[40] "No deadline was given to Ministries/Departments to implement the said OM. As to how many departments have implemented the order, no such data is maintained."

Interestingly, while the Cabinet Affairs passed the buck to MHA for minister-wise information, the MHA, in turn, did the same when it said[41] that

> The MHA is concerned with the making of only budgetary provisions for tours of ministers (both cabinet and state) as a whole for a financial year. As per procedure, sanction is to be issued by the concerned Ministry and bills in respect of such expenses are raised and submitted in Pay and Accounts Office, Cabinet Affairs for payment.

Changing Trends

After Narendra Modi's taking oath as the PM, the new government advised its ministers to curtail their travels abroad, and this advice, initially at least, seemed to have had an impact. When the information on foreign trips made during the first six months of the

---

[37] By the author under RTI.
[38] Response dated July 15, 2013, to author on RTI.
[39] Response dated July 23, 2013, and September 10, 2013, to author on RTI.
[40] Response dated February 8, 2013, on author's RTI application.
[41] In a response dated November 13, 2013, to author under RTI.

Modi government with that of the previous year under UPA-II for the same duration was compared, one interesting change noticed was that fewer ministers, as compared to an increasing number of senior officials on government duty, were being cleared for trips abroad. The MEA had cleared 23 ministers for 74 foreign trips between May 26 (the day the BJP-led government took charge) and November 25. During the same period in 2013, 64 UPA ministers were cleared for 221 foreign trips.[42] Admittedly, one reason could be that the Modi government had only 44 ministers until November 9. Cabinet expansion later raised that number to 65. But, undoubtedly, more senior bureaucrats are heading abroad on official visits under the Modi government—136 secretaries and officers of their rank were cleared for 285 trips. During the same period under the UPA-II, just 58 officials were given the green signal by the MEA for 67 trips abroad. Clearly, the number of trips by secretaries and the officers of their rank have risen by more than four times when compared with the last government.

However, PM Narendra Modi has been travelling abroad more than his two predecessors—Atal Bihari Vajpayee and Manmohan Singh. According to the data[43] released on the website of PMO, Narendra Modi has spent almost every ninth day abroad (till December 31, 2016), Singh had spent his every 11th day, and Vajpayee had spent his every 17th day abroad.[44] The PMO website has put the details of all foreign trips made by three PMs since 1998. While Vajpayee had made 19 foreign trips and spent 133 days abroad in his 2,255 days in office, Manmohan Singh spent 317 days on his 73 foreign trips in total in his 3,289 days in office. But Modi has made 27 trips and spent 114 days in his just 946 days in office (till December 31, 2016). While Modi is traveling more than his two predecessors, his ministers' foreign trips have shown decreasing trend in his government's first one year in office.[45] But

---

[42] Shyamlal Yadav, "The Coin flips..." *The Indian Express*, New Delhi (December 21, 2014).

[43] Details of three PMs are now posted on PMO website www.pmindia.gov.in

[44] Author's calculation based on data (till December 31, 2015) available on PMO website.

[45] Shyamlal Yadav, "Foreign trips for NDA Ministers less than half of UPA's, reveals RTI reply," *The Indian Express*, New Delhi, July 18, 2015, http://indianexpress.com/article/india/india-others/foreign-trips-for-nda-ministers-less-than-half-of-upas/, accessed December 30, 2016.

whether this decreasing trend will continue in coming years, let us wait and watch.

Foreign travel of ministers became a talking point in media because of the RTI-based stories and their follow-up stories. If the RTI Act was not there, it would have been very difficult, if not impossible, to bring out these facts and figures from government records. The government and departments have issued circular after circular to curtail the foreign travel expenses of ministers in the last few years and new PM started discouraging ministers from foreign trips. This can be seen one of the big success stories using the transparency law.

But, despite the CIC order of 2011 and the 2012 OM of DoPT, most ministries and departments have not put the foreign travel details of ministers and government functionaries on their websites. One of the departments which is regularly putting foreign travel details in the public domain and updating them regularly is the PMO. Some of the departments did put it up initially, but it was never updated. So, while ministers make merry abroad, the authorities continue to hide details and prevent government functioning from becoming transparent and open.

3

Foreign Travels of Bureaucrats: 74 Up–Down Trips to the Moon

There is an increasing tendency on the part of government officials to travel by air in order to gain mileage points which are then used by them for private travel. All mileage points earned by government employees on tickets purchased for official travel should be utilised by the concerned department for official travel itself. Any usage of these mileage points for private travel by an official should be duly acted upon.[1]

—Sixth Pay Commission headed by Justice (Retd) B.N. Srikrishna

Table 3.1:
Highlights of RTI filed to get information on foreign travel by bureaucrats

Information	Foreign travel by bureaucrats of the Central Government
Authority	All union ministries and departments
Problems	Most of the departments provided all required details such as country/city/dates/purpose/expenses/companions
Applications and appeals	80 for first story (excluding those filed for the follow-up)
Time taken	Over six months
Story	Babus' Flights of Fancy: 1,576 officials of 46 central ministries have traveled 56,562,426 km, which is equivalent to 74 trips to the moon and back. They collectively stayed abroad for 24,458 days (over 67 years) (*India Today*, September 15, 2008)
Impact	Ministry of Finance issued circular to stop the use of mileage points on their personal trips if they are availed against official trips
Follow up by me	Many other aspects of ministers' foreign trips were investigated, like who uses their mileage points, and in-depth details from particular departments
Follow up by others	Widely followed up by other media

Source: Author.

---

[1] Government of India, Para 4.2.31, Report of the Sixth Central Pay Commission, 237, http://finmin.nic.in/6cpc/6cpcreport.pdf, accessed January 4, 2017.

If used effectively, the RTI Act can be a powerful and often lethal tool for investigative journalism. What is important is to get the exciting ideas and have the ability to pursue one's stories with relentless energy, dogged perseverance, and due diligence. Lethargic government machinery can be forced to change and improve its functioning, and government functionaries can be made to change and reform their mind-sets, provided the media keeps following up issues with persistent efforts. Many government servants who are concerned with the rotting of the system, come forth with information and sometimes they themselves give ideas, especially when they realize the seeker of information is doing so in the public interest.

But having said that, and despite the RTI Act, getting crucial information from the government is a tough, time-consuming, and often tedious task.

Foreign travel story had not ended with ministers. Many of my sources in political circles and junior level officers in different ministries felt that what was exposed so far was only the tip of the iceberg and the foreign travel records of senior bureaucrats must also be dug out.

There are several circulars and guidelines applicable on foreign travels of government officials—starting from limiting foreign trips of any particular official in a year to deputing junior rank officials and sending only technical experts and officers directly connected with the concerned trips abroad, but seniors always prefer to go, and technical expertise and direct connection with work are hardly considered. The fact is that the officers who are better placed and those who are well connected with their senior bureaucrats and political bosses are very often deputed abroad utilizing flexibility of all applicable rules, instructions, and circulars.

Taking the advice of sources and in much the same fashion as the ministers' story was explored, fresh RTI applications were filed with all the Union Government departments except a few sensitive ones such as the Department of Space and Department of Atomic Energy, and indeed the MEA, as foreign travel is part of their job. These departments were asked for details of foreign trips made by officials of the rank of director and above during almost same period as in the case of ministers. There were, at that time, around 1,200 directors, around 300 joint secretaries, around 150 additional secretaries, and 120 secretaries and officers of their

rank in the Union Government.[2] The desired information took
a period of over six months to materialize and was extensive,
spread over 1,297 pages.[3]

The tedious and often frustrating exercise saw the filing of
over 80 RTI applications, clarifications, appeals, and reminders.
Some ministries replied only after their CPIOs were personally
approached who, on their part, often required much persuasion
to divulge information. In some cases, responses were possible
only after first appeals were filed before their appellate. Despite
all efforts, the ministries of Railways, Earth Sciences, and the
DoPT were adamant in their refusal to divulge information.

As done earlier, data were compiled in an excel file which,
when completed, had details of around 10,000 foreign trips by
1,576 officers.[4] Extended trips for fellowships and scholarships
were excluded from this list. Cross-checking the gamut of information was a mammoth task, but it was done over and over to
avoid inaccuracies that would invite the inevitable rejoinder. It
was not only about compiling data from several scattered papers,
but calculating the distance of every trip and keying it in excel.

There were a number of senior bureaucrats in the list who
would hit back if there was even a single error. After checking and
rechecking every minute detail, finally all the travel information
was available in excel file, in ascending and descending order,
incorporating the total number of trips undertaken and the km
travelled. The distances were calculated with the help of Geobytes.[5]

The bottom line of the story was this: 1,576 officials of the
rank of director and above had traveled more than 56.5 million
km and stayed 24,458 days (more than 67 years) abroad, during
a period of 40 months (from January 1, 2005 to April 30, 2008),
spending over ₹563,803,300. The distance the babus had traveled was around 74 up and down trips to the moon,[6] though full
details of expenses incurred were not made available. Topping
the list of frequent-flyers was the Ministry of Commerce whose
101 officials had traveled more than 11.20 million km, spending

[2] Informal research by the author.

[3] Shyamlal Yadav, "Babus' Flights of Fancy," *India Today* (September 15, 2008).

[4] Ibid.

[5] www.geobytes.com

[6] Shyamlal Yadav, "Babus' Flights of Fancy," *India Today* (September 15, 2008).

5,751 days abroad and incurring a cost of ₹89.9 million. Six other ministries—Water Resources, Finance, Home Affairs, Information & Broadcasting, Agriculture, and Science & Technology—also earned the distinction of being high on the frequent-flyers list. Each of these ministries had logged 1,000 days or more of travel abroad.

Frequent-flyer Mileage Points

The story "Babus' Flights of Fancy" was published in *India Today*. It prompted the government to implement a particular recommendation of the Justice (Retd) B.N. Srikrishna headed Sixth Pay Commission which said that if any government official earned frequent-flyer mileage points against his/her official air travel, those points should be used for other officials' travel or other official trips of the same officer rather than for his/her private trips. The commission said[7]: "There is an increasing tendency on the part of government officials to travel by air in order to gain mileage points which are then used by them for private travel." The commission further recommended: "All mileage points earned by government employees on tickets purchased for official travel should be utilised by the concerned department for official travel itself. Any usage of these mileage points for private travel by an official should be duly acted upon."[8]

Nearly two weeks after publication of the story, a circular[9] was issued by the DoE which said:

> All mileage points earned by government employees on tickets purchased for official travel shall be utilised by the concerned department for other official travel by their officers. It is the responsibility of the officer concerned to ensure that free mileage points are used only for official travel and not for personal trips. Any other incentives and similar packages like free companion etc. should be so negotiated by ministries/departments so that the benefit comes to the department.

---

[7] Government of India, Para 4.2.31, Report of the Sixth Central Pay Commission.
[8] Ibid.
[9] http://finmin.nic.in/6cpc/TA%20Allowance.pdf dated September 23, 2008; http://finmin.nic.in/6cpc/TA%20Allowance.pdf

These 'austerity measures' were applicable to government employees only and not to the ministers.[10] After that, the government issued some more austerity measures on October 1, 2008.[11] as well.

The Sixth Pay Commission recommendations and the DoE circular led to a smoke screen of austerity measures being introduced by the government to restrict the babu traffic to overseas destinations. As has become a convention with the Union Government, it begins enforcing austerity measures during June–November and by the beginning of summer starts announcing relaxations. Sometimes, such instructions are issued every year, sometimes every alternate year. In this case too, while none of the government departments took the mileage points restrictions seriously, the free companion scheme was soon opened to officials. Just eight months after the austerity circular was issued, the DoPT issued a clarification[12] on June 3, 2009, saying:

> A review of these instructions (of October 1 and September 23, 2008) was done in consultation with the Ministry of Finance and it has been decided to modify the instructions contained in the said OM to the extent that the government servants shall be allowed to avail the facility of free companion tickets offered by airlines for international travel.

There is still no apparent mechanism in place in many departments to ensure beneficial usage of mileage points as suggested in the DoE circular. Most officials, therefore, continue to make the best use of the mileage points for their and their relatives' personal trips; the more cautious ones do not use them at all, and they get wasted. If government departments had followed the Sixth Pay Commission recommendations, and enforced the circular, hundreds of free trips could have been gained from it for other government officials' official trips. Interestingly, the circular had warned that it would be the responsibility of the officer concerned to ensure that free mileage points were used only for official travel

---

[10] Response dated February 2, 2009, of DoE on author's RTI.

[11] http://finmin.nic.in/the_ministry/dept_expenditure/notification/emre/ExpMangement_TADA2008.pdf, accessed March 22, 2017.

[12] See http://ccis.nic.in/WriteReadData/CircularPortal/D2/D02est/11013_7_2008-Estt.(A)0001.pdf, accessed December 30, 2016.

and not for personal trips. The government, including the PMO under Manmohan Singh did not show the will or the courage to implement changes; no one, therefore, enforced the restrictions, no action was taken, and a huge number of mileage points were either misused or wasted, therefore, no benefit was reached to government exchequer as thought by the Sixth Pay Commission.

Games Bureaucrats Play

However, persistent efforts were going on to track the issue, the replies received on RTI applications were quite telling. It was clear that once bureaucrats made up their minds on what was good for them and in their best interests, nobody could enforce anything to the contrary. Ideally, the government should have approached the airlines to persuade them to change the mechanism of availing mileage points but all that was done was just formality, it shows. Several departments including PMO approached the airlines, including the national carrier Air India, to open corporate accounts in the name of departments and to ensure that mileage points earned by a particular official must be clubbed with the points of other officials or their departments. But these airlines were able to convince the departments on their existing mechanism. All that the replies from departments under RTI did was to confirm the sorry state of affairs prevalent within the government—how senior officers didn't care a hoot for a government circular, and how the government couldn't enforce its decision on the airlines. Or, what was more likely, departments must have been in cahoots with the airlines to let the old practice continue. Figure 3.1 elaborates the situation.

An Ignorant PMO

Here, it would be prudent to take a hard and reflective look at the helplessness of the highest office in the country—the PMO. On July 2, 2009, through an RTI query, the PMO was asked that what mechanism it had evolved to utilize the mileage points earned

Figure 3.1:

Officials fly frequently, their points keep government guessing

Officials fly frequently, their points keep govt guessing

Austerity drive meant to club frequent flier points in departments, it remains a non-starter 3 years later

SHYAMLAL YADAV
NEW DELHI, MAY 31

IN October 2008, the Department of Expenditure announced a "austerity measure" over the use of frequent flier mileage points earned by government employees from official air travel in India and abroad. Three years on, not only does the measure appear a non-starter but any possible misuse of such points for personal travel, too, continues unchecked.

The Department of Expenditure under the Finance Ministry had issued a circular stating: "All mileage points earned by government employees on tickets purchased for official travel shall be utilised by the concerned department for other official travel by their officers. It added that it would be the responsibility of the officer concerned to ensure that free mileage points are used only for official travel and not for personal trips.

Some departments, including the Prime Minister's Office, had suggested a scheme where frequent flier points earned during official travel could be clubbed into a corporate account for subsequent use.

Replies received from departments through the Right To Information (RTI) route, however, reveal that most ministries and departments have not maintained any record of mileage points earned by their officials or of points transferred to the department. Those that have tried to abide by the circular are still trying to figure out how the points should be transferred for travel of other officials.

While many departments provided the number of points acquired by officers from air travels, they have admitted they do not have any information whether the officers deposited these points with departments' accounts — considering there are no such accounts in the first place.

Shortly after the 2008 circular was issued, the PMO had written to seven airlines, including Air India, to find a way of implementing the Ministry of Finance's instructions. An RTI reply shows that the PMO

THERE IS no information if officers have deposited their points into departments' accounts — there are no such accounts

requested airlines to "Open a corporate account of PMO for domestic and foreign travels which could be quoted by officers of this office while booking tickets".

However, airlines categorically said such measures were difficult to enforce. Air India, for instance, informed the PMO that "We are not in a position to club mileage points of different members or open corporate mileage accounts."

The most detailed response has been received from divisions of the Ministry of Defence. A calculation shows that the headquarters of the integrated defence staff and the finance division amassed 4,19,290 frequent flier points between 2008 and January 2010 from travel of 26 senior officers.

However, the MoD admitted, "On liaison with Air India it has emerged that mileage points can only be awarded to the individual undertaking the journey. There is no government account in which these mileage points can be credited."

A bureaucrat of joint secretary rank posted with the PMO recently compiled all his mileage points earned over a period of three-and-a-half years and is in the process of dispatching it to the DoE for them to devise a method to credit or utilise them.

On behalf of the DoE, the spokesperson of the Finance Ministry, DS Malik, said the circular was issued "in the nature of policy guidelines/instructions and their implementation rests with the respective departments/ministries".

Source: The Indian Express (June 1, 2012).

by government officials on their official travels in order to the circular of DoE dated October 1, 2008. It replied:[13] "This office had requested Air India and six other private airlines to open a corporate account for Prime Minister's Office so as to implement the said circular in totality. No reply has been received from any of the airlines except Air India." In effect, private airlines Jet Airways, Kingfisher Airlines, American Airlines, British Airways, SpiceJet Airlines and IndiGo Airlines did not care to respond to PMO's request. On their part, Air India responded[14] to the PMO that: "In terms of the current programme structure and rules, we are not in a position to club mileage points of different members, or open corporate mileage accounts." While the PMO tamely conceded helplessness in ensuring compliance of the circular, the curt and predictably dismissive response[15] of the MEA was equally appalling: "Ministry is no longer availing of this facility of free mileage points. Air India has not agreed to club mileage points of different members, or open corporate mileage accounts. Therefore, ministry is no longer availing of this facility of free mileage points." The response of the Ministry of Defence (MoD),[16] to another RTI query, was echoing the same sentiments: "On liaison with Air India, it has emerged that Mileage Points can only be awarded to the individual undertaking the journey. There is no government account to which these mileage points can be credited."

Some Honorable Men

It wasn't for lack of trying or a lack of will. In the absence of clear modalities, there was a complete deficiency of clarity on the issue. Concerned officers like the then Joint Secretary in the Department of Economic Affairs (DEA) K.P. Krishnan, kept pointing out the lacunae in implementation. He wrote[17] to the DoE mentioning his

---

[13] PMO's letter dated August 1, 2009, to author on RTI.
[14] Air India letter dated February 20, 2009.
[15] Dated August 21, 2009, to author.
[16] MoD letter dated February 24, 2010, to author.
[17] On April 9, 2009, letter accessed from DoE under RTI by author.

six trips: "This is to seek your advice on the account to which these miles need to be credited and the procedure therefore." The DoE responded[18] with its ambiguous best:

> Department of Economic Affairs (where Krishnan was posted) is advised to take up the matter with the airlines, to ascertain in what manner the benefits can be passed on to the administrative department. Alternatively, mileage points earned by officers can be used for their own official travel in future.

The rot in the system was to blame. The Cabsec wrote[19] to the DoE saying, "In the absence of clear cut instructions regarding procedure to be followed for putting the above instructions in position, the secretariat is facing problem in implementing the DoE's instructions in the matter. DoE is therefore, requested to provide necessary advise in the matter." The Cabsec wrote[20] again to the DoE, "It may please be clarified whether Department of Expenditure have laid down any modalities for utilisation of mileage points earned by government employees on tickets purchased for their official travel by the concerned ministry/department for other official travel by officers/employees of that ministry/department." The response[21] was the same.

An interesting correspondence between the Rajya Sabha Secretariat and the DoE with regard to implementation of the said austerity circular is notable. The Rajya Sabha Secretariat wrote:[22]

> To clarify the mode of operation by which mileage points earned by government employees against their individual frequent flyer registration number, on tickets purchased for official travel, are to be utilised by the organization concerned. A clarification is particularly necessary as presently it appears that Frequent Flyer Number is allotted by airlines only to individuals and not to the organization.

---

[18] On April 22, 2009, letter accessed from DoE under RTI by author.
[19] On December 1, 2008, to DoE, letter accessed from DoE under RTI by author.
[20] On July 23, 2009, to DoE, letter accessed from DoE under RTI by author.
[21] Dated July 28, 2009, from DoE to Cabinet Secretariat accessed by author under RTI Act.
[22] Through letter dated December 10, 2008, letter accessed from Rajya Sabha under RTI by author.

The DoE responded:[23] "It is clarified that it is the duty of the department to collect the Mileage Points earned by the government employees on tickets purchased for official travel and utilise it for the other officials' travel of their department."

Unconvinced with the DoE's reply, the Rajya Sabha Secretariat again wrote[24] to the DoE:

> The Frequent Flyer Scheme, as it exists at present, operates on the basis of individual accounts of beneficiaries. It does not provide for opening of an account (Frequent-flyer number) in the name of an organization. The scheme also does not contain any provision for transfer of Mileage Points from one account to other. As such, it is not clear as to how the Mileage Points earned by individual officers in their accounts for official journeys can be utilised by the department for other official travels.

To this letter, the DoE reverted[25] to the Rajya Sabha Secretariat with the advice: "Frequent-flyer Accounts may be opened in the name of Under Secretary/Deputy Secretary. The points will accrue to this common account and can be utilised centrally by the concerned ministry/department."

But this reply too did not satisfy the Rajya Sabha Secretariat, which again reverted[26] to the DoE.

> The scheme does not permit crediting of mileage points earned on journeys undertaken by a person in an account existing in the name of any other person. As such, even if a Frequent-flyer Account is opened in the name of Under Secretary/Deputy Secretary, only mileage points in respect of journeys taken by the very Under Secretary/Deputy Secretary in whose name the account has been opened, would be credited in that account in respect of journey undertaken by other officers of this secretariat. In short, the scheme is individual based and does not permit crediting of points of a group of persons in one account. In view of it, it does not appear feasible to implement the new guidelines on Mileage Points earned

---

[23] Letter December 17, 2008, of DoE to Rajya Sabha accessed by author under RTI Act.

[24] On January 27, 2009, letter accessed from DoE under RTI by author.

[25] On February 18, 2009, letter accessed from DoE under RTI by author.

[26] On April 6, 2009, letter accessed from DoE under RTI by author.

on official journeys in the manner stipulated in the same OM of Ministry of Finance, Department of Expenditure.

This time around, the DoE passed the buck as it replied:[27] "Rajya Sabha secretariat is advised to take up the matter with airlines, to ascertain as to in what manner the benefits can be passed into the administrative department. Alternatively mileage points earned by officers can be used for their own official travel in future."

Free Companion Travel and Other Matters

The DoPT withdrew its directive banning the free companion scheme for international travel of bureaucrats within a year of the much publicized austerity measures initiated to affect economy in the matter of expenditure on air travel by Government of India officials while on official tour. When a number of officials wanted to know if the said scheme would also apply to domestic travel, the Department of Expenditure clarified to the DoPT:[28] "Free companion/spouse ticket offers in the case of domestic travel, which are made on payment of full fare can't be availed of."

RTI applications were being filed asking the various departments about the implementation of the circular banning personal use of frequent-flyer mileage points. From some departments, replies were in most interesting ways[29]: When they were asked, "Whether your department is implementing the said circular?" They replied "Yes." When they were asked, "Whether your department faced any problems in implementation of the said circular?" They said "No." When they were asked "Whether any of the foreign travelling officers have deposited any frequent flyer mileage points in your department's account?" They replied "No." And, finally when they were asked, "What mechanism has your department evolved to utilise the Mileage Points on official

---

[27] On April 17, 2009, letter accessed from DoE under RTI by author.
[28] Vide letter dated July 22, 2010, letter accessed from DoE under RTI by author.
[29] Based on responses from various ministries such as Mines, Earth Sciences, HRD during 2009–10.

trips?" most of the departments replied, "We have circulated a copy of the said circular to the concerned officials."

When the queries were put to the Ministry of Communications, it responded[30] :

> Instructions have been circulated to all officers in this case eligible for travel by air in this office. No Mileage Points earned by any officer have so far been intimated... It is the responsibility of the officer concerned to ensure that free Mileage Points are used only for official travel.

The DoPT was also asked whether action had been taken against any Indian Administrative Service (IAS) officer for violation of the austerity circular. The DoPT responded[31] that it "has not received any proposal for initiation of disciplinary action against any such IAS officer since the issuance of aforesaid circular."

The underlying message of all these replies was clear that all these austerity measures were issued just as a formality without going much into practical details. Interestingly, many departments later provided the lists of officials along with the frequent-flyer mileage points earned by each out of their international trips. While some officers said that they earned the points but did not utilize them, most officers did mention that they had earned points, but did not provide details of how those points were utilized. It was clear that many officials continued to utilize the mileage points, but departments were hardly interested in checking it. Few officers may not be utilizing their mileage points due to fear of departmental action and their points might be getting wasted, therefore, government exchequer got nothing out of these instructions.

It seems that when it comes to foreign travel, there seems to be a happy nexus between babus (bureaucrats) and *mantris* (ministers). But if the RTI Act was not there, it was not possible to track the problem at every stage and bring the problem into notice.

Foreign trip proposals of joint secretaries and officers of their rank are cleared by concerned ministers, while trips of secretaries and officers of their rank are cleared by Committee of Secretaries

---

[30] Vide letters on January 27, 2010, and May 14, 2010, to author.
[31] On September 2, 2011, to author under RTI.

headed by Cabinet Secretary. On the other hand, ministers' foreign trips are cleared by the PMO whether it is personal trip or official. For official trips, political clearance from the MEA is mandatory and it also needs Foreign Contribution Regulation Act (FCRA) clearance from the MHA if foreign hospitality is involved during personal trips as well.

The new NDA government, which took charge on May 26, 2014, initiated some additional steps to curtail the trips of secretaries. Cabinet Secretary Ajit Seth wrote[32] a letter to all Union Government departments saying that "The Prime Minister has, in the context of a proposal for deputation abroad, observed that 'foreign as well as domestic tours of secretaries should be planned only if the Joint Secretary/Additional Secretary-level officers are not likely to address needs." He further wrote[33] that the PM's observation "may kindly be kept in mind for strict compliance, while considering any proposal involving domestic and foreign tours."

In an attempt to simplify procedures, the new government headed by Narendra Modi revised[34] the format submitted with foreign travel proposals of officials. The old format—last revised on December 11, 2007—had 24 questions; the new one was finalized with only 19. The DoE under the Ministry of Finance issued the new format on July 2, 2014, and Para 15 (iv) of the said circular says: "Justification be given as to why this (videoconferencing) facility cannot be utilised." Para 15 (i) says: "Why cannot the purpose be served by deputing officers at the functional level viz. Director/Dy. Secretary, instead of deputing officers of higher level(s)." The problem is that while senior officers visit abroad to study a subject, many of them are transferred when they come back, making their foreign trip useless. It is due to emphasis on sending abroad 'functional level' officers that the New Delhi Municipal Council (NDMC) sent some ground level employees[35]

---

[32] Letter dated September 26, 2014, by Ajit Seth. Available on http://cabsec.nic.in/showpdf.php?type=circulars_f26sep2014&special, accessed December 30, 2016.
[33] Ibid.
[34] See http://indianexpress.com/article/india/india-others/foreign-trips-under-scanner-why-fly-when-you-can-talk/, accessed December 30, 2016.
[35] Shyamlal Yadav, "Delhi sweepers to fly to Japan, S. Korea for hygiene lessons," *The Indian Express*, New Delhi (November 14, 2015). Available on http://indianexpress.com/article/india/india-news-india/delhi-sweepers-to-fly-to-japan-south-korea-for-hygiene-lessons/, accessed December 30, 2016.

consisting sweepers and *beldar*s (diggers) to visit Tokyo and South Korea in November 2015.

Although there are instructions regarding submission of detailed report after coming back from official foreign trips, this is just-for-formality, if at all it is followed. RTI came as a weapon using which it became easy to enter government offices and trace the stories in official records. Huge information of foreign travel of bureaucrats was accessed, analyzed, and published which made some impact. If the RTI Act was not there, this would not have been possible. It is another issue which proves that RTI has a potential of reforming the functioning of government set-up and force them to change.

4

I Hereby Declare: Assets' Declarations in Public Domain

*One is this, namely, that we should require by law and by Constitution—
if this provision is to be effective—not only that the Ministers should
make a declaration of their assets and their liabilities at the time when
they assume office, but we must also have two supplementary provisions.
One is that every Minister on quitting office shall also make a declaration of his assets on the day on which he resigns, so that everybody who
is interested in assessing whether the administration was corrupt or not
during the tenure of his office should be able to see what increase there is in
the assets of the Minister and whether that increase can be accounted for
by the savings which he can make out of his salary…. The other provision
would be that if we find that a Minister's increases in his assets on the day
on which he resigns are not explainable by the normal increases due to his
savings, then there must be a third provision to charge the Minister for
explaining how he managed to increase his assets to an abnormal degree
during that period. In my judgment, if you want to make this clause effective, then there must be three provisions as I stated. One is a declaration
at the outset; second is a declaration at the end of the quitting of this office;
thirdly, responsibility for explaining as to how the assets have come to be
so abnormal and fourthly, declaring that to be an offence, followed up by
a penalty or by a fine.*[1]

—Dr B.R. Ambedkar in his reply in the Constituent Assembly on
December 31, 1948, on the proposal made by members K.T. Shah
and H.V. Kamath that ministers should be obligated to declare their
interests, rights, and properties before they assumed office.

From Table 4.1, it would appear that with the achievement of
independence, corruption in public life had already raised its
ugly head. Elimination of corruption is not merely a moral and
ethical need but an economic inevitability for a nation aspiring to
catch up with the rest of the developed world.

---

[1] See http://164.100.47.192/Loksabha/Debates/Result_Nw_15.aspx?dbsl=609,
accessed February 11, 2017.

Table 4.1:
Highlights of RTI filed to know the assets of ministers

Information	Assets of union ministers
Authority	Prime Minister's Office and Cabinet Secretariat
Problems	Both offices forwarded application to each other. Copies of their letters were sent to each other by the author. This mess was itself a story.
Applications and appeals	Five, for first story (excluding those filed for the follow-up and other related stories).
Time taken	Over two months.
Story	The Open Secret: Despite the prime minister's claim of transparency, efforts to get information under the RTI Act are often stonewalled. (*India Today,* June 30, 2008)
Impact	After new government came to power in 2009, all ministers declared their assets on given time.
Follow up by me	Several more applications were filed related to assets of union ministers, ministers of state governments, bureaucrats, MP, MLAs and stories were brought. All of them paved way for proper mechanism of filing assets.
Follow up by others	Widely followed up by other media.

Source: Author.

Government's effort to keep track of the assets and liabilities of its ministers can effectively be said to date back to the year 1964.[2] The Union Cabinet adopted a code of conduct for ministers at the Center and in the states, with provisions for annual updates in case of any change. It was decided that all union ministers before assuming office should make a declaration of their assets to the PM. The same would apply to ministers in the states, who would make such declarations to their chief minister.

The code of conduct states:[3]

In addition to the observance of the provisions of the Constitution, the Representation of the People Act, 1951, and any other law for the time being in force, a person immediately after entering office as a Minister, and in any case within two months from the date

---

[2] Letter of Home Minister Y.B. Chavan, dated June 10, 1969, accessed by Venkatesh Naik of CHRI through PMO letter dated November 10, 2009, using RTI.
[3] Accessed by author under RTI in 2008, now it is available on MHA website.

of assumption of office, shall: a) Disclose to the Prime Minister, or the Chief Minister, as the case may be, details of the assets and liabilities, and business interests, of himself and of members of his family. The details to be disclosed shall consist of particulars of all immovable property and the total approximate values of (i) shares and debentures, (ii) cash and (iii) jewelry; b) Sever all connections, short of diverting himself of the ownership, with the conduct and management of any business in which he was interested before his appointment as Minister; and c) With regard to a business concern which supplies goods or services to the Government concerned or to undertakings of that Government (excepting in the usual course of trade or business and at standard or market rates) or whose business primarily depends on licenses, permits, quotas, leases, etc., received or to be received from Government concerned divest himself of all his interests in the said business and also of management thereof.

The government modified it from time to time.

Along with the code of conduct, the government also addressed the question of employment of dependents of ministers. A confidential letter by then Minister of Home Affairs Y.B. Chavan to all union ministers stated:[4]

You would recollect that in 1964, we adopted a Code of Conduct for Ministers of the Central Government, and also asked State Governments to adopt it in respect of the Ministers of the State Governments.

While the Code of Conduct provides guidance on several aspects, it does not include any guidelines concerning employment of sons and daughters or dependents of Ministers under foreign governments in embassies in India or abroad, or under other foreign organizations (including commercial concerns). It has been felt that there is need for adopting some conventions in this regard. Recently, a question was also asked in the Parliament regarding such employment.

Following careful consideration of the problem, the Prime Minister has come to the conclusion that wives and dependents of Ministers should not accept employment under a foreign government in India or abroad, or in a foreign organization (including commercial

---

[4] Letter of Home Minister Y.B. Chavan, dated June 10, 1969, accessed by Venkatesh Naik of CHRI through PMO letter dated November, 10, 2009 using RTI.

concerns) without her (PM's) prior approval.... I am addressing the Chief Ministers of the State also be consider adopting a similar policy in respect of Minister in the State Governments.

Copies of the letter were forwarded to every state government for their action, but since it was not mandatory, it hardly received the attention it deserved.

On taking the oath of office, every minister is handed a copy of the code of conduct which says, among other things, that ministers should disclose to the PMO details of their assets, liabilities, and business interests along with those of their family members.

Manmohan Singh, during his stewardship of the UPA government, made valiant efforts to keep up the tradition in the best interests of transparency. Toward the middle of 2007, there were reports that the PM was unhappy about his ministers repeatedly ignoring reminders from the Cabsec to file details of their assets and liabilities. In the end, however, the PM's brave efforts proved to be just words and nothing else.

* * *

To understand the status of its implementation, I filed separate RTI applications to the PMO and Cabsec on November 6, 2007. They were asked to provide particulars of those ministers who had filed details of their assets and liabilities, and those who were defaulters. They were also asked for copies of reminders, if any, which may have been sent to the defaulters. Both offices responded quickly, but their replies were scandalous, to say the least. The PMO is headquartered at South Block and the Cabsec is inside the Rashtrapati Bhavan premises; the distance between the two is a mere 300 m. But 43 years after the resolution was adopted, responses on RTI applications show that these two high offices had no knowledge of which department was responsible for maintaining and processing the required information.

The PMO had forwarded the RTI application to the Cabsec with these words:[5] "An application dated November 6, 2007, received from Shri Shyamlal Yadav on the above noted subject is transferred under section 6(3) of the RTI Act for appropriate action."

[5] Letter dated November 19, 2007, of PMO was also endorsed to the author.

A copy of this letter was also marked to the applicant. A week later, in a clear case of passing the buck, the Cabsec responded[6] to the application: "It is stated that the information asked for pertains to the Prime Minister's Office and the Cabinet Secretariat is not directly concerned with the subject matter." In retaliation, it was decided to send back both the replies, but with a difference. The Cabsec's response was sent to the PMO and the response of PMO was sent to the Cabsec. In an apparent attempt at washing its hands off the matter, the Cabsec now responded:[7] "The matter is under consideration of the competent authority and the information/reply will be sent to you in due course."

But despite three subsequent reminders,[8] there was no response, either from the CPIO or FAA of the Cabsec. In the third reminder, on March 13, 2008, they were asked what was the stipulated time frame to reply to such queries, and demanded to know when they would be replying to the requests. Under the RTI Act, they are supposed to respond to all queries within 30 days. Disheartened with the approach of the Cabsec officials, a complaint was moved before the CIC on March 17, 2008. The reason cited for the complaint was that neither the CPIO, nor the First Appellate responded providing the information.

Toward the end of May 2008, at a function to commemorate the UPA government's completion of four years in office, PM Manmohan Singh had spoken with great pride about his government's achievements, making a special reference of its contribution to open governance:[9] "The UPA Government has set a new standard for accountability and transparency in governance," he had emphasized.

Manmohan Singh said this at a time when I was struggling for information and sending reminders, and failing to get responses from the PMO and Cabinet Secretariat. Then it was thought that denial of information would also make a good story. It was published in *India Today*.[10]

---

[6] Cabsec's letter dated November 26, 2007, was also endorsed to the author.

[7] Cabsec's letter to author dated December 24, 2007.

[8] Sent by the author to Cabsec on February 11, 2008, March 7, 2008, and March 13, 2008.

[9] PM's Address at the Fourth Anniversary of UPA government, presentation of Report to the People, 2008.

[10] Shyamlal Yadav, "Open Secret," *India Today* (June 19, 2008). Available on http://indiatoday.intoday.in/story/Open+secret/1/10097.html, accessed December 30, 2016.

CIC's Knee-jerk Reaction and Misplaced Judgment

Apparently, the story did not have the desired effect. But efforts to get more information were continued. The complaint, which was filed on March 17, 2008, was pending before then Chief Information Commissioner Wajahat Habibullah, and his order[11] stated:

> Because the first appellate authority has not addressed the questions of appellant, which are of direct concern to his public authority and because the complainant has pleaded no ground for making a direct complaint to us u/s 18(1)(e), the Commission has decided to remand this complaint to the First Appellate Authority Ms Vini Mahajan JS, Prime Minister's Office, New Delhi to dispose of the complaint of Shri Yadav within ten working days from the date of receipt of this decision.

He further said in the order[12] that in doing so, she will make reference to CIC decision in appeal Nos. CIC/WB/A/2009/00038 & WB/C/08/868 SC Agrawal vs PMO[13] announced on March 16, 2009 that:

> It is clear that the information sought, as is recognised by the Lok Sabha rules quoted above, is held in confidence, thus warranting of reference to third party u/s 11(1) before proceeding with any disclosure. However, because under the Lok Sabha Rules cited above such information is not disclosable except with the permission of the Speaker, the matter will be referred to Shri Somnath Chatterjee, Speaker of the Lok Sabha, for disclosure of such information as relates to those members of the Council of Ministers who are members of the Lok Sabha. If there is any equivalent rule with regard to the Rajya Sabha, this may also be exercised, although, we were not told of existence of any such rules during the hearing. If no such rules in fact exist, the matter will be referred to the third parties concerned as per the process mandated u/s 11 subsection (1) of the RTI Act 2005.

---

[11] See http://ciconline.nic.in/rti/docs/cic_decisions/WB-28072009-03.pdf, accessed April 1, 2017.

[12] Ibid.

[13] Agrawal had filed an Application to Cabsec on April 28, 2008, which was forwarded to PMO but when he did not get information, he filed a complaint and Second Appeal to CIC.

.

Clearly, what the CIC had done was put the ball in the Lok Sabha/Rajya Sabha's court, unnecessarily. CIC erred in its judgment in more ways than one. Provisions for declaration of assets and liabilities by ministers and MPs are governed by different procedures. Lok Sabha MPs file it before the Speaker under the Members of Lok Sabha (Declaration of Assets and Liabilities) Rules, 2004 and Rajya Sabha MPs file it before the chairperson of that House under the Members of Rajya Sabha (Declaration of Assets and Liabilities) Rules, 2004. What the union ministers file before the PMO is entirely different and comes under the Code of Conduct for Ministers adopted by the Union Cabinet in 1964. Therefore, in disclosing the declarations made before the PMO, there was no need to forward the query to the Lok Sabha Speaker or Rajya Sabha Chairperson.

However, Speaker of the Lok Sabha Somnath Chatterjee and Chairperson of Rajya Sabha Hamid Ansari did give their consent and the details of assets were disclosed.

But a little before the 'irrelevant' decision of the CIC had been followed upon, the PMO, apparently apprised of the content of application, forwarded the following information:[14] "The Cabinet Secretariat circulates the Code of Conduct for Ministers among the members of the Council of Ministers and periodical reminders are being sent by the Cabinet Secretariat to Minister for observing the Code of Conduct." Accordingly, the PMO had provided the list of ministers under UPA-I, with the date of their declarations and their updates which made it clear that 16 ministers had filed their declarations only in 2008, that is, four years after they took oath as ministers, and eight other ministers had never filed their declarations. That is what was asked for in the application. In fact, the copies of the declarations made by ministers were not asked for, but it seems that all of these authorities responded considering that request was for copies only. Cabsec also now responded[15] that "No specific reminder has been sent to Ministers who have not submitted the statement of their assets and liabilities. However, general reminders are being sent from time to time."

---

[14] PMO's response dated January 9, 2009, on the RTI filed by the author on November 6, 2007.
[15] Cabsec's response dated February 13, 2009, to author on application dated November 6, 2007.

After getting the status of UPA-I ministers, it was thought that it would only be fair to also probe the status of declaration of assets by previous governments. Therefore, another RTI application was filed with the PMO seeking details of ministers in the NDA government (1998–2004) under Atal Bihari Vajpayee. The PMO clarified:[16] "There is no information on record in this office for the period as requested by the applicant." It shows that there had been no clarity or concern on this issue earlier.

When an application was filed about the declarations made by ministers of UPA-II, the response was sufficient to show the impact of the earlier exercise.[17] It was informed that all the ministers had filed their declarations of assets and liabilities within the stipulated time. But, on another application, the PMO clarified[18] that the code of conduct is not applicable in the case of persons availing rank of cabinet ministers and ministers of state outside the Union Council of Ministers, "The Code of Conduct issued by Ministry of Home Affairs is not applicable to persons who are not members of the Union Council of Ministers."

These case studies clearly show how the ruling class does not take seriously the provisions it itself frames. And even the little that was managed to procure would not have been possible without the RTI Act. Assets declarations of functionaries of the government are one thing which was not possible if the RTI Act was not in place.

Subhash Agrawal's Crusade

Subhash Chandra Agrawal, the intrepid crusader for the RTI Act based in Delhi, had done much work on RTI and has made a huge impact through his revelations using the RTI Act. One of his success stories is ascertaining the assets and liabilities of judges of the Supreme Court and High Courts. He had demanded answers from the Supreme Court, reminding it of the resolution[19] passed at a meeting held in 1997 chaired by the Chief Justice of India,

---

[16] PMO's response dated June 23, 2011, to author on RTI.
[17] PMO in response dated November 10, 2009, to Venkatesh Naik of CHRI on RTI.
[18] PMO's response dated January 8, 2013, to author on RTI.
[19] Resolution adopted in full court meeting on May 7, 1997. Available on https:// indiankanoon.org/doc/155236387/ accessed February 14, 2017.

which said: "Every judge should make a declaration of all assets in the form of real estate or investment held in their names, in the name of their spouses or any other person dependent on them, to the Chief Justice."

Agrawal's efforts under RTI finally saw Supreme Court judges posting details of their assets and liabilities on the Supreme Court website in November 2009. This was followed by the judges of several High Courts also filing details of their assets and liabilities.

Lok Sabha and Rajya Sabha

The Members of Lok Sabha (Declaration of Assets and Liabilities) Rules, 2004 states:[20]

> Every elected candidate for the House of the People shall, within ninety days from the date on which he makes and subscribes an oath or affirmation for taking his seat, furnish as in Form I the following information as required to be furnished by him to the Speaker in pursuance of sub-section (1) of section 75 A, namely: (i) the movable and immovable property of which he, his spouse and his dependent children are jointly or severally owners or beneficiaries; (ii) his liabilities to any public financial institution; and (iii) his liabilities to the Central Government or to the State Governments.

Similarly, the Members of Rajya Sabha (Declaration of Assets and Liabilities) Rules, 2004 states:[21]

> Every member of the Council (Rajya Sabha) shall, within ninety days from the date on which he makes and subscribes an oath or affirmation for taking his/her seat, furnish as in Form-I the following information as required to be furnished by him to the Chairman in pursuance of sub-section (1) of section 75A, namely: (i) the movable and immovable property of which he/she, his/her spouse and his/her dependent children are jointly or severally owners or beneficiaries; (ii) his/her liabilities to any public financial institution; and (iii) his/her liabilities to the Central Government or to the State Governments.

---

[20] See http://164.100.47.132/bull2/2009/27.11.09.pdf, accessed December 30, 2016.
[21] See http://rajyasabha.nic.in/rsnew/members/declaration_assets_rules_2006.pdf, accessed December 30, 2016.

These provisions, not applicable in the case of nominated members, were implemented in August 2004.

As per the information provided by the Lok Sabha Secretariat, there were only 11 defaulters till the date of response. Declarations made by most MPs were copies of the declaration they had made during filing of their nomination papers for election. The information provided by the Rajya Sabha Secretariat stated that there were 13 defaulters till the date of response which was January 30, 2009.

There are many instances in which the Lok Sabha and Rajya Sabha secretariats provided the copies of declarations made by certain members under the RTI Act, but these are not being posted in public domain. While PMO has put the declarations of all union ministers and the ministers of state it is yet to be implemented in the Parliament, though these are being provided under the RTI Act. Lok Sabha Secretariat has said:

> Rule 4(4) of The Members of Lok Sabha (Declaration of Assets and Liabilities) Rules, 2004 states that the information relating to declarations of Assets and Liabilities of the Members of Lok Sabha shall be treated as confidential and it shall be made available to any person except with the written permission of the Speaker.[22]

On the other hand, the declaration of business interests of members is implemented in Rajya Sabha where all the upper house members are supposed to declare their business interests, the Lok Sabha is yet to take any call on it. It is under the consideration of Committee of Ethics of Lok Sabha.

Games Played Out in the States

While the resolution passed by the Union Cabinet in 1964 was forwarded to the state governments as well, next curiosity was to know that what was taking place in the states. Moreover, a curiosity was that whether state assemblies have taken any inspiration from both houses of Parliament to frame same rules for their members. Therefore, in a massive exercise, applications were filed

---

[22] Response of Lok Sabha Secretariat dated February 26, 2016, to author on RTI.

in June 2008 to every chief minister's office (CMO) and to every assembly secretariat. In some cases, the replies took over eight months to reach. What was clear from the information that only three states' ministers had submitted details of assets and liabilities to their chief ministers. It is ironical that in a country having 28 states (now 29 with the creation of Telangana), only two had the system in place to declare details of their ministers and member of legislative assemblies (MLAs) and to place that in public domain.

Gujarat's then chief minister, Narendra Modi, had asked his ministers to file details of their assets and liabilities at a cabinet meeting on January 30, 2008, and every minister had done so.[23] In Kerala, pursuant to Section 22 of the Kerala Lok Ayukta Act, 1999, the ministers in Kerala and Chief Minister V.S. Achuthanandan's government had also submitted statements of their assets and liabilities.[24] Rajasthan Cabsec said, "Chief Minister asked from the ministers their details of assets and they have submitted."[25]

In Haryana, Himachal Pradesh, and Uttarakhand, the CMOs had issued repeated reminders to their ministers, in some cases exceeding 10, but with no action taken by majority of the ministers. In Haryana, despite repeated reminders from then Chief Minister Bhupinder Singh Hooda, five ministers had not responded.[26] Some of those defaulter ministers, including the Deputy Chief Minister Chandra Mohan, who left the government later, and Power Minister Randeep Singh Surjewala, had been reminded up to nine times but in vain.

In Himachal Pradesh, BJP's Prem Kumar Dhumal, who was the chief minister at that time, had directed his cabinet of nine ministers to file details of assets on January 28, 2008, but "The details from four Ministers have been received."[27] In Uttarakhand, then Chief Minister B.C. Khanduri's directive was issued on September 13, 2007, with, "None of the ministers have submitted details of their assets and liabilities."[28] Despite the fact that the Uttar Pradesh Ministers and MLAs (Declaration of Assets and Liabilities) Act, 1975 is applicable in UP as well as in Uttarakhand.

---

[23] Response dated July 15, 2008, to author from Gujarat government.
[24] CMO office's letter dated July 18, 2008, to author.
[25] Letter dated February 18, 2011, to author.
[26] Response of Cabinet Branch, Haryana Government dated August 8, 2008, and January 27, 2011, to author.
[27] Response of GAD, Himachal Pradesh dated August 4, 2008, to author.
[28] Response 463/XXI/2008 dated August 1, 2008, from Government of Uttarakhand to author.

In Maharashtra, much like what the PMO and Cabsec had done at the Center, the letter-forwarding game was reenacted. The CMO forwarded[29] the application to the General Administration Department (GAD) asking it to reply directly. The latter promptly sent it back to the CMO saying[30] that according to the Representation of People's Act, ministers are supposed to file details of their assets and liabilities to the chief minister directly. "If the ministers have filed such details, the CMO certainly have this information," it said. The CMO did not revert back after that.

In Bihar, Chief Minister Nitish Kumar's Cabsec replied, "The requisite information is not concerned with the cabinet secretariat. Therefore, it is not possible for this department to provide such information."[31] From Jharkhand's Cabsec, the response[32] was, "No information is available in this regard."

Uttar Pradesh Chief Minister Mayawati's office apparently sent out necessary instructions[33] to the principal secretary, Home and Confidential Department, but despite three reminders, they said, no reply was received. Following this, the CMO remained mum, and so a First Appeal was filed, but that was also not replied to. After a year, on June 8, 2009, there was a news item in some newspapers that the Mayawati Cabinet held a meeting where a decision[34] was taken that matters related to the Code of Conduct of Ministers would be exempted from the RTI Act.

Punjab's then Chief Minister, Akali Dal stalwart, Prakash Singh Badal's office was very matter-of-fact. It said: "The Chief Minister has not issued any directions to the ministers to file the details of their assets and liabilities and no such information has been made available by the ministers to the government."[35]

The CMO under Sheila Dikshit in Delhi was even more taciturn. "No such information is available in this office,"[36] it informed on

---

[29] Vide letter dated July 30, 2008, to author.
[30] Response dated August 27, 2008, from GAD, Government of Maharashtra to author.
[31] Letter dated July 17, 2008, from CM Office to author on RTI.
[32] Dated October 15, 2008, to author on RTI.
[33] Vide letters dated June 30, 2008, and March 30, 2009, copies endorsed to author on RTI.
[34] Press statement issued on June 7, 2009, by then Cabinet Secretary of UP Shashank Shekhar.
[35] Response dated September 6, 2008, from Punjab Government's Cabinet Affairs branch to author on RTI.
[36] Response dated May 22, 2008, from CM Office, Delhi to author on RTI.

RTI application. The office of then Puducherry Chief Minister V. Vaithilingam was provokingly dismissive: "The Hon'ble Chief Minister is under no legal obligation to require the ministers to furnish particulars of properties owned by them. Hence, furnishing information in this regard does not arise."[37]

Things were no different in the Northeast. Sikkim Chief Minister Pawan Kumar Chamling's office advised[38] to look at the Election Commission of India (ECI) website for the details. In Assam, then Chief Minister Tarun Gogoi sent a letter to all his ministers (this was after receiving my RTI application, dates reflect)[39] saying, "In pursuance of the directions of Shri M. Veerappa Moily, CWC member and in charge of Assam, and also decision taken in the meeting of the APCC Co-ordination Committee, the Members of Council of Ministers are to submit their statement of Assets at the earliest." Whatever the outcome was, it was not known. In Tripura, Chief Minister Manik Sarkar's secretariat said that the Tripura Assembly had sought information as per the format under the Tripura State Legislature (Declaration of Assets and Liabilities) Act, 2006 and as such, the chief minister had not felt it necessary to ask individual members of the council of ministers to furnish details of their assets and liabilities, separately. Much similar was the case with Arunachal Pradesh[40] headed by Dorjee Khandu.

In Mizoram, under Pu Zoramthanga, the CMO said: "Besides the declaration made at the election, the Hon'ble Chief Minister did not ask the ministers to file the details of their assets and liabilities."[41] The justification for a nonresponse from Nagaland was revealing and worthy of note as the office of Chief Minister Neiphiu Rio said: "In the State of Nagaland, which is predominantly tribal in population, the people do not pay income tax, hence filing of annual returns/tax are not required. Therefore, the details sought by you are not available."[42]

Other states simply chose to be silent and did not respond.

---

[37] Response of CMO dated July 17, 2008, to author on RTI.
[38] Response dated August 4, 2008, of Home Department, Sikkim to author on RTI.
[39] RTI was filed on June 18, 2008, and CM wrote to his ministers on July 1, 2008 to author.
[40] Letter dated June 15, 2008, to author on RTI.
[41] Letter dated July 3, 2008, to author on RTI.
[42] Letter dated August 4, 2008, from CM Office, Kohima to author on RTI.

Meanwhile, in the Chhattisgarh Assembly, Congress MLA Dharmjeet Singh asked a question,[43] "Whether Ministers and Parliamentary Secretaries including the Chief Minister have declared details of their properties for the year 2009–10 to Chief Minister? If yes, provide the details of their properties along with their names." To which Chief Minister Raman Singh replied:[44] "No. Therefore question does not arise." But this was a starred question and, therefore, later, the same day, Raman Singh declared in the assembly that his cabinet colleagues and party MLAs will submit a declaration of their assets on the floor of the assembly by April every year.[45]

In Uttar Pradesh, Chief Minister Akhilesh Yadav took oath of office on March 15, 2012. I spoke to him on the phone to get his version for a story the same day. Reminding him of the directive of his predecessor Mayawati's government that issues related to the code of conduct of ministers will be beyond the purview of the RTI Act, he was asked, "Will you revoke the said directive in the interest of greater transparency?" He replied, "I will ask my ministers to declare their property details. I will declare my property details first." While the decision of Mayawati cabinet to exempt Code of Conduct of Ministers from RTI is still in force, Akhilesh declared his details and those were put on the government website, but none of his ministers' assets were available online even after completing his term in government. When BJP government was formed on March 19, 2017, Chief Minister Yogi Adityanath asked his ministers to declare their assets and liabilities. But thanks to the decision of Mayawati cabinet no one can get the information about these declarations under the RTI Act.

State Assemblies

On the other hand, on applications, the responses were not satisfactory from state assemblies either. Replies from their secretariats

---

[43] Available at http://www.topnews.in/law/chhattisgarh-chief-minister-legislators-declare-assets-211211, accessed on March 9, 2010.

[44] Ibid.

[45] Available at http://www.topnews.in/law/chhattisgarh-chief-minister-legislators-declare-assets-211211, accessed on March 28, 2017.

showed that speakers of state assemblies had made little effort to call for such details from the MLAs. Only Karnataka, Kerala, Uttarakhand, Odisha, and Tripura had such system. Not surprisingly, therefore, only these states had given convincing replies to the RTI applications.

According to Section 22 of the Karnataka Lokayukta Act, 1984, which came into effect on January 15, 1986, an MLA is supposed to file such details before June 30 each year. Explaining the procedure, the response of the Karnataka Assembly Secretariat concluded that "Most of the members are filing their details as per the provision. And there is no defaulter." The Kerala Assembly secretariat said:

> As per the Kerala Lok Ayukta Act 1999 and the Kerala Lok Ayukta (Furnishing Property Statement) Rules 1999, it is mandatory for the members of the Kerala Legislative Assembly to file their details of assets and liabilities... This act took effect on March 4, 1999.[46]

The Kerala Raj Bhavan said that only three MLAs were defaulters.[47] Tripura Assembly said that it, "Has sought information"[48] from MLAs under Tripura State Legislature (Declaration of Assets and Liabilities) Act, 2006.

In Uttarakhand too, such rules exist since 1975 (when Uttarakhand was part of UP, those rules are applicable in Uttarakhand as well)[49] but their reply indicated that out of the 70 MLAs, only nine had filed the details of assets and liabilities. Delhi assembly said,[50] "MLAs are not supposed to declare their assets and liabilities before the Speaker's office." A similar response[51] was from Madhya Pradesh assembly. Meghalaya assembly said that it "has not framed any rule of law."[52] And Mizoram assembly said that "Filing of details of assets and liabilities of MLA has not been done in the Mizoram Legislative Assembly." Bihar, Manipur, and Goa assemblies said that they have no such provisions.

---

[46] Letter dated June 27, 2008, to author.
[47] Raj Bhawan's response dated July 5, 2008 to author.
[48] Response dated June 27, 2008, to author.
[49] Uttarakhand Assembly response dated July 22, 2008, to author.
[50] Response dated April 29, 2008, to author.
[51] Response dated August 13, 2008, from Madhya Pradesh assembly to author.
[52] Response dated July 2, 2008, to author.

Gujarat assembly said, "There is no law/statute under which MLAs are required to produce information about their holdings of assets and liabilities."[53] Himachal Pradesh assembly said, "There are no rules/regulations available in this Secretariat governing filing of such details."[54] However, Himachal Pradesh assembly, Arunachal Pradesh assembly, Rajasthan assembly, and Jharkhand assembly as well advised to consult ECI for the declarations filed during the nomination for elections.

In Odisha, there are no statutory provisions but the assembly had passed a code of conduct on April 6, 2005 for its 147 MLAs that they should declare their assets and liabilities to Speaker within 30 days of taking oath, but only one MLA had followed it.[55] And West Bengal assembly said,[56] "It is not mandatory for the members of the West Bengal Legislative assembly to file the details of their assets and liabilities as member of this legislature."

It was clear from the many replies that in a majority of states, provisions to get declared assets and liabilities of MLAs do not exist. It was also clear from the replies of state assemblies and the CMOs that a top-down lack of transparency continues to plague the democratic system in the country. When this is the condition at the Parliament and assemblies, one can imagine the level of transparency at the village, block, and district panchayats and urban local bodies. Worse, there were an insignificant few who questioned the dismal state of affairs. But probing the status of state governments and assemblies was almost impossible without the RTI law.

Bureaucrats: Modern Day Chanakyas

After plodding through the labyrinth of information on assets and liabilities of union ministers, MPs, ministers of state governments and MLAs of state assemblies, next thing came to mind was to know the status of bureaucrats' assets.

---

[53] Response dated July 17, 2008, from Gujarat assembly to author.
[54] Response dated August 11, 2008, from Himachal Pradesh assembly to author.
[55] Response of Odisha assembly dated August 7, 2008, to author.
[56] Letter dated August 29, 2008, from WB Assembly Secretariat to author.

These are the people who virtually run the system. There is a system for declaration of assets and liabilities for them as well. All India Service (Conduct) Rules, 1968 states:[57]

> Every person shall...on his first appointment to the Service, submit a return of his assets and liabilities in such form as may be prescribed by the Government giving the full particulars regarding; (a) the immovable property owned by him, or inherited or acquired by him or held by him on lease or mortgage, either in his own name or in the name of any member of his family or in the name of any other person; (b) shares, debentures, postal Cumulative Time Deposits and cash including bank deposits inherited by him or similarly owned, acquired or held by him; (c) other movable property inherited by him or similarly owned, acquired or held by him and; (d) debts and other liabilities incurred by him directly or indirectly.

The rule further states:[58] "Every member of the Service shall intimate the Government in respect of each transaction, whose value exceeds ₹15,000 within a month of the completion of such transaction." This amount of ₹15,000 has been revised[59] now to two month's basic salary of the particular officer.

The officers are also supposed to update their declarations annually. Rule 16(2) states:[60]

> Every member of the Service shall submit an annual return in such form as may be prescribed by the Government in this regard, giving full particulars regarding the immovable property inherited by him or owned or acquired by him or held by him on lease or mortgage, either in his own name or in the name of any member of his family or in the name of any other person.

So, in effect, all government officials are expected to annually file details of their assets and liabilities. As per the said rule, they are

---

[57] Rule 16 of the All India Service (Conduct) Rules, 1968. Available on http://persmin.gov.in/DOPT/Acts_Rules/AIS_Rules/Revised_AIS_Rules_Vol_I_Updated_Upto_31Oct2011/Revised_AIS_Rule_Vol_I_Rule_10.pdf, accessed December 30, 2016.
[58] Ibid.
[59] Government of India, through amendments dated May 5, 2011. Available on http://ipr.ias.nic.in/Docs/AIS_ConductRules2011.pdf, accessed December 30, 2016.
[60] Rule 16 of the All India Service (Conduct) Rules, 1968: http://persmin.gov.in/DOPT/Acts_Rules/AIS_Rules/Revised_AIS_Rules_Vol_I_Updated_Upto_31Oct2011/Revised_AIS_Rule_Vol_I_Rule_10.pdf, accessed December 30, 2016.

also supposed to do so at the time of joining service. But most of the officers hardly own any movable or immovable property at the time of joining. Rule 16(2) is their savior in this regard as under this rule they are not supposed to declare any movable property, only to update the transactions of immovable properties. But with the Lokayukta Act, the things are changing now.

The Indian Government has over 75,000 Group-A officers and around over 189,000 of that of Group-B besides other government employees.[61] There are around 4,800 IAS officers and 3,500 Indian Police Service (IPS) officers among the Group-A.[62] Since it was not possible to analyze the assets of every official, a selective list was prepared and copies of assets and liabilities of all secretary rank officers serving under Government of India was asked for. In order to check the progression and growth of their properties and assets, copies of their first (one which they submitted at the time of joining the service) and latest declaration of assets and liabilities were asked. The whole gamut of initially filing the RTI application, First Appeal, and finally the Second Appeal, gave lot of gratification and satisfaction as it paved the way to unearth the disclosure of returns filed by these officials.

As a first step, on January 22, 2009, an application was filed before the DoPT to know the number of secretary rank officers in the Government of India. Copies of their first and latest declarations of assets and liabilities were also asked. The CPIO of the DoPT while declining to submit copies of declarations said:[63] "The requisite information being personal in nature is exempted under section 8 (1) (j) of RTI Act."

Aggrieved with the said response, a First Appeal was filed on March 17, 2009, quoting CIC order[64] delivered by A.N. Tewari, which said: "All public authorities are urged that in order to open the property returns of all public servants to public scrutiny, the public authorities may contemplate a new and open system of filing and retention of such returns."

---

[61] Data received on various RTI applications from DoPT by the author.
[62] Ibid.
[63] Response of DoPT dated February 26, 2009, to author.
[64] See http://www.rti.india.gov.in/cic_decisions/Decision_10072006_14.pdf, accessed February 14, 2017.

First Appeal filed before DoPT said:[65]

Request is related to secretaries who are very senior officers of the government and people keep watch on their actions like the ministers and other elected leaders. You must be aware that the MPs and MLAs are bound to file the details of their assets and liabilities during election itself which is always in the public domain and could be accessed from the Election Commission of India website. This step was taken to bring probity and transparency in public life. Obviously, like ministers and elected representatives, the secretaries are also public servants.

But the first appellate decided[66] that: "I find nothing irregular in the reply of the CPIO. The appeal petition is accordingly disallowed." Thus, the Second Appeal was filed before the CIC.

The DoPT, CPIO, and First Appellate's responses denying copies of assets and liabilities of bureaucrats were despite the fact that some information commissions had already directed the disclosure of assets of officers in some states. In Punjab, the SIC P.K. Grover had directed[67] the Punjab Civil Secretariat to disclose the returns of some officers saying that

There seems to be no reason why they should not be freely disclosed. This should also be considered as a step to contain corruption in government offices since such disclosures may reveal instances where property has been acquired, which is disproportionate to known sources of income.

Earlier, UP Information Commissioner Gyanendra Sharma had directed[68] the UP Government on October 10, 2008, to "Disclose the details of immovable assets of all IAS officers." A copy of this order was also attached with Second Appeal.

A similar order[69] was passed by the Madhya Pradesh Chief Information Commissioner P.P. Tewari to disclose the property

---

[65] From the first appeal filed by the author.

[66] Order dated April 1, 2009, by DoPT on author's first appeal.

[67] Decision dated December 14, 2009, AC-711 of 2009 in HC Arora vs Punjab Civil Secretariat.

[68] On complaint no. S9–651©/08 dated October 10, 2008, in Brijesh Mishra vs Appointment Department, UP.

[69] On February 15, 2010, on appeal A-1646/SCI/15–20/Bhopal/2009 and A-1608/SCI/18–10/Bhopal/2009.

returns of certain officials on an appeal filed by deputy leader in the state assembly, Chaudhary Rakesh Singh. In fact, Singh had filed an application to the GAD asking for details of properties filed by certain senior IAS and IPS officers posted at the state government secretariat. But some officers—whose views were taken as if they were third parties—and the PIOs objected to the disclosure saying that this is personal information and exempted under section 8(1)(j) of the RTI Act. Of the officials whose views were taken as third party, some had also responded to the SIC that there was no harm in such disclosure. Chaudhary Rakesh Singh pleaded his case and asked, "When the privacy of Lok Sabha and Assembly candidates is not invaded by disclosing their property details how can the declaration of properties of public servants be invasion of their privacy?" Tewari directed the GAD and the Home Department of the MP Government to provide the requisite details within 15 days.

Madhya Pradesh Chief Minister Shivraj Singh Chouhan went an extra mile when he declared[70] his assets and liabilities. Later, the state government directed its officials to put the details of their immovable property on the websites of their respective departments by April 30, 2010. By that time, Bihar government, headed by Nitish Kumar, had also directed its officials to declare their assets and liabilities to be put in public domain.

Second Appeal was heard by then Chief Information Commissioner Wajahat Habibulla, a former IAS officer, who, in his order[71] said:

It is clear that the property statements are statements regarding private individuals serving in government and become part of government records. However, although by no means can they then be treated as information held in confidence, they certainly constitute personal information, disclosure of which can amount to invasion of privacy under section 8 (1) (j), unless the public interest in disclosure is demonstrated. For this reason, it is appropriate to make such disclosure after reference to the third party under section 11 (1) within the time limit prescribed under section 11 (1). The third

---

[70] See http://www.thaindian.com/newsportal/politics/shivraj-singh-chouhan-discloses-assets-in-state-assembly_100325023.html, accessed February 12, 2017.
[71] Central Information Commission, dated August 25, 2010. Available on http://www.rti.india.gov.in/cic_decisions/CIC_WB_A_2009_000669_M_40680.pdf, accessed December 30, 2016.

party, under section 11 (2) is expected to make any representation that he/she wishes within 10 days from the date of receipt of such notice by him/her. As discussed above, therefore, the order of Shri Anil Kumar (First Appellate) of 1.4.2009 is set-aside. The appeal is allowed. CPIO Shri Deepak Israni will now issue notice to third parties within five working days of receipt of this decision notice and proceed to disclose the information sought by appellant Shri Shyamlal Yadav, if no viable objection based on exemption under section 8 (1) is received within 10 days of the date of issue of such notice by CPIO.

This order was little protective of the officers, as it was clear that the details of the assets and liabilities of an officer can only be disclosed after taking their views.

After the CIC order, DoPT's Under Secretary Deepak Israni wrote to all secretary rank officers: "You are requested to make submission in writing or orally whether the requisite information may be disclosed, as requested by the applicant, within ten days from the receipt of the notice failing which the case will be decided ex-parte."[72]

On the one hand, the DoPT fought legal battle with me at CIC but in the meanwhile it realized the need for disclosure and supported it. While most of the officers fell in line, 19 secretary rank officers objected to the disclosure of their assets. For example, TCA Anant, Secretary, Ministry of Statistics and Programme Implementation wrote to DoPT:[73] "Property returns containing details of property, its value etc., as furnished by me is purely personal information and therefore, the same disclosure may not be disclosed." Other IAS officers who opposed[74] the disclosure were then Secretary Urban Development Navin Kumar, Secretary Public Enterprise Bhaskar Chatterjee, and Secretary Micro Small and Medium Enterprises Uday Kumar Verma. Furthermore, MHA told[75] that Commerce Secretary Rahul Khullar and Ashok Kumar (IAS cadre AGMUT [Arunachal Pradesh, Goa, Mizoram and Union Territories] 1974) were also against disclosure. The disclosure of assets and liabilities of secretary rank officers

---

[72] Letter dated September 24, 2010, DoPT endorsed copy to author.
[73] On October 13, 2010, letter no. 12016/1/2010-APAR, DoPT endorsed copy to author.
[74] List provided by DoPT vide letter October 29, 2010 to author.
[75] MHA response dated November 24, 2010, to author.

belonging to the Indian Foreign Service (IFS) was opposed by the MEA itself as the ministry said: "Information sought in your RTI application cannot be disclosed under Section 8(1) (j) and 11(1) of the RTI Act."[76] Also, Omita Paul, then advisor to Minister of Finance Pranab Mukherjee and later Secretary to President Pranab Mukherjee objected to the disclosure. A letter[77] of the DEA informed that: "Smt Omita Paul, advisor to Finance Minister, who is of the rank of Secretary in this department, under section 11(2) of the RTI Act, has desired not to share information with you."

But, in effect, besides engaging in legal battle at CIC and later providing the requisite copy of declarations, the DoPT took an initiative to put the details of all of the officers of All India Services and Central Civil Services in public domain. In this regard, the then DoPT Secretary Shantanu Consul wrote[78] to Home Secretary G.K. Pillai, IAS Association President Sudha Pillai, and Secretary Environment and Forest Vijay Sharma:

> The DoPT is considering a proposal that the asset declarations made by All India Service Officers under rule 16(2) of the All India Service (Conduct) Rules, 1951 should be placed on website of Ministries of respective Cadre Controlling Authorities. The objective is to set a standard which may not be presently prescribed by law but is likely to advance the cause of transparent and accountable bureaucracy. In such matters, AIS (All India Services i.e., IAS, IPS and Indian Forest Service) should take a lead and walk an extra mile than what is necessitated by the law. I would request you to kindly furnish your considered views on the above proposal. The views of the Officers Association may also please be ascertained and communicated.

The communication also took into consideration the views of the IPS association and the Indian Forest Service (IFoS) association. IAS, IPS, and IFoS associations gave their consent. Speaking on behalf of the IFoS officers, the Ministry of Environment and Forests (MoEF) conveyed to the DoPT its concurrence[79] to the proposal for posting declarations made by the members on the website.

---

[76] MEA's response dated November 4, 2010, to author.

[77] Dated March 3, 2011, DoPT endorsed copy to author.

[78] DO Letter No. 11017/03/2010-AIS(III) of Shantanu Concul dated February 24, 2010, accessed by author using RTI.

[79] Letter of MoEF dated July 19, 2010, copy accessed by author using RTI.

Home Secretary G.K. Pillai conveyed[80] to the DoPT that: "This ministry has no problem for placing the Annual Property Return of IPS officers on the website of the MHA." Before doing that, the MHA took the advice of the IPS association which gave its consent to the MHA after taking advice of its state chapters. The Tamil Nadu chapter of the IPS association, for instance, wrote:[81] "There is nothing wrong in displaying the property details of IPS officers in the official website of MHA as its being done in the case of High Court and Supreme Court judges."

Later, the same instructions[82] were sent to all Group-A central services, who started posting their annual property returns (APRs) one after the other. Some services were still hesitant. Reminders[83] were issued by DoPT on May 23, 2011, June 8, 2011, August 2, 2011, August 25, 2011, and October 20, 2011. In spite of this, many continued to hold back. Later, the DoPT asked for clarification from all the services:[84]

The PMO have directed this department to seek clarification from the respective Cadre Controlling Authorities on the following: 1. Reasons for delay in placing the APRs of the officers on the website of the cadre controlling authority, or for not placing details on the website, 2. What are the actions proposed to be taken by the cadre controlling authorities in order to secure compliance by officers?"

It is astonishing that even the OM issued by the DoPT on September 27, 2011,[85] made no impact on certain obdurate service officers: "Vigilance clearance shall be denied to an officer if he fails to submit this annual immovable property return of the previous year by January 31 of the following year, as required under Government of India decisions."

A complete lack of accountability among some services as a whole, and many officers individually, seems to be the preferred

---

[80] Letter of G.K. Pillai dated July 26, 2010, copy accessed by author using RTI.
[81] IPS Officers' Association, Tamil Nadu chapter, letter dated August 10, 2010, copy provided to author by IPS Association informally.
[82] Vide letter dated April 11, 2011, to all ministries/departments of Government of India.
[83] Accessed by the author on February 29, 2012 using RTI act from DoPT.
[84] DoPT Secretary Alka Sirohi's letters dated December 5, 2011, accessed by author using the RTI Act.
[85] Accessed by the author using RTI.

choice of behavior, especially since there was no strict monitoring and no fear of reprisals.

But things have been changing rapidly in the style of government functioning after the implementation of the RTI act and growing demand of transparency and accountability in public life. Now, the Lokpal and Lokayuktas Act, 2013 states:[86]

(1) Every public servant shall make a declaration of his assets and liabilities in the manner as provided by or under this Act.

(2) A public servant shall, within a period of thirty days from the date on which he makes and subscribes an oath or affirmation to enter upon his office, furnish to the competent authority the information relating to—(a) the assets of which he, his spouse and his dependent children are, jointly or severally, owners or beneficiaries; (b) his liabilities and that of his spouse and his dependent children.

(3) A public servant holding his office as such, at the time of the commencement of this Act, shall furnish information relating to such assets and liabilities, as referred to in subsection (2), to the competent authority within thirty days of the coming into force of this Act.

(4) Every public servant shall file with the competent authority, on or before the 31st July of every year, an annual return of such assets and liabilities, as referred to in sub-section (2), as on the 31st March of that year.

(5) The information under sub-section (2) or sub-section (3) and annual return under sub-section (4) shall be furnished to the competent authority in such form and in such manner as may be prescribed.

(6) The competent authority in respect of each Ministry or Department shall ensure that all such statements are published on the website of such Ministry or Department by 31st August of that year.

Accordingly, the DoPT issued a notification[87] on July 14, 2014, directing all government officials to declare details of cash in hand; deposit in bank accounts (fixed deposit receipts [FDRs], term deposits, and all other types of deposits including saving accounts); deposits with financial Institutions, non-banking

---

[86] See http://ccis.nic.in/WriteReadData/CircularPortal/D2/D02ser/Notification_Lokpal_14July_2014_Eng.pdf, accessed December 30, 2016.
[87] Ibid.

financial companies and cooperative societies, and the amount in each such deposit; investment in Bonds, debentures/shares and units in companies/mutual funds and others; investment in the National Savings Scheme (NSS); postal savings; insurance policies and investment in any financial instruments in post office or insurance companies; deposits in provident fund/new pension scheme; personal loans/advance given to any person or entity including firm, company, trust and so on; and other receivables from debtors and the amount (exceeding (a) two months basic pay, where applicable, (b) Rupees 0.1 million in other cases); motor vehicles/aircrafts/yachts/ships (details of make, registration number and so on, year of purchase, and amount); and jewelry, bullion and valuable thing(s) with details of weight. The format for declaration of immovable properties has also been revised. While earlier format had only eight columns, the format issued under the Lokpal and Lokayuktas Act, 2013 has 12 columns and needs more detailed information. A DoPT circular issued to chief secretaries of all states dated December 29, 2014, said that, "The Prime Minister has further directed that all preparatory steps be put in place for this purpose by January 31, 2015." This last date of filing details has been extended again and again. And, the DoPT has clarified[88] on July 3, 2015, that "The public servants who have filed declarations, information and annual returns of property under the provisions of the rules applicable to such public servants, shall file the revised declarations, information or as the case may be."

In the meantime, the department-related Parliamentary Standing Committee on Personnel, Public Grievances, Law and Justice headed by E.M.S. Natchiappan had said in its report dated December 7, 2015, that:[89] "Immovable assets acquired by the public servant whether in his/her name or in the name of any family member or any other person to be declared. Movable assets of only public servant to be declared." Last dates of such declarations are being extended again and again considering the reluctance from public servants. A major twist to the issue came up with a

---

[88] See http://ccis.nic.in/WriteReadData/CircularPortal/D2/D02ser/407_12_2014-AVD-IV-B-03072015.pdf, accessed December 30, 2016.
[89] See (p. 10): http://164.100.47.5/newcommittee/reports/EnglishCommittees/Committee%20on%20Personnel,%20PublicGrievances,%20Law%20and%20Justice/77.pdf, accessed February 14, 2017.

notification[90] dated June 20, 2016, issued by the DoPT including the office bearers of societies (NGOs) under these provisions saying that their directors, managers, secretaries, or other officers needed to file such declarations under Lokpal and Lokayuktas Act, 2013 to the departments from where the concerned NGO has received highest amount of funds and need to file such declarations till they fully utilize such funds. It was clarified that the NGOs included in this category are those which received funds in excess of ₹1 million from a foreign source or in excess of ₹10 million from state governments or the central government. In a clarification dated July 20, 2016, MHA said "Any person who is or has been a director, manager, secretary or other officer of every other society or association of persons or trust (whether registered under any law for the time being in force or not), in receipt of any of any donation from any foreign source under the Foreign Contribution (Regulation) Act, 2010 (42 of 2010) in excess of ₹10 lakh rupees in a year"[91] is required to furnish such details. On July 25, a group of MPs including Sharad Pawar (Nationalist Congress Party [NCP]), Digvijaya Singh (Congress), Anu Aga (Nominated, Rajya Sabha), Naresh Gujral (Shiromani Akali Dal [SAD]), Rajeev Chandrasekhar (independent, Rajya Sabha), Neeraj Shekhar (SP), T.K. Rangarajan (Communist Party of India (Marxist) [CPM]) and D. Raja (Communist Party of India [CPI]) met PM Mr Modi.[92] On July 29, 2016 the Lokpal and Lokayuktas (Amendment) Act, 2016 was passed which said that: "On and from the date of commencement of this Act, every public servant shall make a declaration of his assets and liabilities in such form and manner as may be prescribed." Thus, on December 1, 2016 the DoPT issued a circular and clarified: "Under the Public Servants (Furnishing of Information and Annual Return of Assets and Liabilities and the Limits for Exemption of Assets in Filing Returns) Rules, 2014 there is no requirement for filing of declarations of assets and liabilities by public servants now. The Government is in the process

---

[90] See http://ccis.nic.in/WriteReadData/CircularPortal/D2/D02ser/Lokpal-24062016.pdf, accessed December 31, 2016.

[91] See https://fcraonline.nic.in/Home/PDF_Doc/Notice_Form_Lokpal_20072016.pdf, accessed December 31, 2016.

[92] See http://indianexpress.com/article/explained/lokpal-bill-narendra-modi-loksabha-pm-narendra-modi-govt-lokpal-and-lokayuktas-act-ngo-2941254/, accessed December 31, 2016.

of finalising a fresh set of rules."[93] It is clear that every section is reluctant toward transparency about their assets and liabilities. It is despite the fact that the most detailed format of disclosure is already in practice for electoral candidates of the Parliament and state assemblies.

Electoral Candidates and Others

The debate on putting declarations of assets and liabilities of public servants in public domain, in fact, caught momentum after the well-received Supreme Court order of May 2, 2002, giving directions to the ECI that:[94]

> A person shall not be qualified to file his nomination for contesting any election for a seat in the House of the People, the Council of States Legislature Assembly or Legislative Council of a State unless he or she files—(a) a declaration of all his assets (movable/ immovable) possessed by him/her, his/her spouse and dependent relations, duly supported by an affidavit, and (b) a declaration as to whether any charge in respect of any offence referred to in section 8B has been framed against him by any Criminal Court.

And after that, it has now become mandatory to file such details with nomination forms.

It would appear that almost every section of persons in public life is today expected to declare their assets and liabilities, but the format for doing so may vary from section to section and in many cases from individual to individual. For electoral candidates, it is mandatory to declare their assets and liabilities because, without it, their nomination would not be accepted.

But in reality, the declarations of assets and liabilities never reflect the real worth of the persons and, therefore, its very purpose is defeated as it is not being implemented in the spirit that it should be. It is just one step toward bringing transparency and probity to public life.

---

[93] http://dopt.gov.in/sites/default/files/407_16_2016-AVD-IV-LP-01122016A.pdf

[94] See http://judis.nic.in/supremecourt/imgst.aspx?filename=18463, accessed December 31, 2016.

There are many government organizations such as banks and insurance companies where officials are more prone to corruption, but their declarations are never made public. The purpose of these declarations would be served only if they are made available in the public domain and people are able to analyse them.

There was provision for almost every section of the public servants, it is clear, but the truth was brought under the RTI Act that these provisions were not being taken seriously. Earlier, they were not being even declared in many cases to put in secret files; now several declarations are available in public domain. In conclusion, if the RTI Act had not been there, fight for disclosure of assets and liabilities of ministers, MPs, MLAs, judges, and bureaucrats would have been very difficult. Had these issues not been raised and followed up by the RTI applicants repeatedly and persistently, things may not have changed to the extent it has. This was another example of RTI exercise through which numbers of news stories were brought, and these prompted little change in the government system.

5

India's Steel Frame: Corruption Cases Against IAS/IPS/IRS

Corruption is an enemy of the nation and tracking down corrupt public servants and punishing such persons is a necessary mandate of the PC (Prevention of Corruption) Act, 1988.[1]

—Supreme Court, May 6, 2014, in the matter of
Dr Subramanian Swamy vs CBI

When implemented, the RTI Act was considered as a tool to expose corruption. But within six years of its implementation, the same government which implemented it exempted CBI, the agency involved in investigation of corruption cases, from the RTI Act. But till the CBI was under RTI, several efforts were there to track the cases of corruption it had booked. I also did a massive exercise to track such cases.

Table 5.1:
Highlights of the RTI filed on anti-corruption cases against bureaucrats

Information	Anticorruption cases against bureaucrats
Authority	Central Bureau of Investigation, Central Vigilance Commission, Department of Personal and Training, Ministry of Home Affairs, Ministry of Finance
Problems	Some of units of CBI did not provide complete information, CBDT under Ministry of Finance did not provide any required detail
Applications and appeals	100 (excluding those filed for the follow-up and other related stories)
Time taken	Over one year

(Continued)

---

[1] See http://judis.nic.in/supremecourt/imgst.aspx?filename=41503, accessed December 31, 2016.

(Continued)

Story	A Lot to Hide: Status of long pending cases against civil servants prove that the cozy relationship that bureaucrats share makes the wheels of justice grind real slow. (*India Today*, April 7, 2008)
Follow up by me	Several more applications were filed to get related information from CBI, CVC, DoPT, MHA, Ministry of Finance and follow-up stories were done.

Source: Author.

On an RTI application, the fact came out that since 1992 the CBI had registered corruption cases against 163[2] officers from three prominent services—Indian Administrative Service (IAS), Indian Police Service (IPS), and Indian Revenue Service (IRS). The IRS list includes Customs and Central Excise Service (C&CES) officers. Yet, most of them were continuing to be in service and getting most other service benefits.

This exercise under the RTI Act was undoubtedly one of the most challenging tasks: getting details of over 275 corruption cases registered against IAS, IPS, and IRS officers spanning over 15 years. But in the end, after over a year, and well over 100 applications, reminders and appeals, all the required information came out.

RTI helped to get the major part of the information needed for the story. An application was filed to the Director (Prosecution), CBI Headquarters, on April 7, 2007, asking for details of disproportionate assets (DA) cases registered under the Prevention of Corruption Act, 1987, pertaining to the three prime civil services. The director (prosecution) forwarded the application to each of the 67 CBI units to respond directly.

In the meantime, the DoPT—the cadre-controlling authority for the IAS—was asked to provide information on the action taken against IAS officers against whom corruption cases were filed. Similar requests were sent to the MHA regarding IPS officers and to the Ministry of Finance, Central Board of Direct Taxes (CBDT) and Central Board of Excise and Customs (CBEC), for details on IRS and C&CES officers. It was also followed up with letters to

---

[2] Information received from all units of CBI during 2007–08 by the author. http://indiatoday.intoday.in/story/A+lot+to+hide/1/6290.html, accessed December 31, 2016.

the CVC, which is the recommending authority for departmental action in all corruption cases.

Gradually, replies started trickling in from every unit, with names of the accused officers, their service, batch, cadre, and date of registration of first information report (FIR) with their present status. After meticulously going through the vast information received, a detailed list of indicted officers was compiled. But the process was long winded and complicated, entailing many subsequent applications, appeals and requests, and facing many refusals.

Some units from the agency played truant. Praveen Salunke, Superintendent of Police at the Anti Corruption Branch (ACB), Mumbai, denied information saying: "The details of assets recovered cannot be provided as this information relates to personal information the disclosure of which has no relationship to any public activity or interest and there are no larger public interest justifying the disclosure of this information." Similarly, Superintendent of Police of Dhanbad ACB informed that "Information cannot be given to the applicant as it may affect the outcome of the prosecution/trial of the cases."[3] S.J.M. Gillani, Superintendent of Police of Special Crime Branch (SCB), Delhi said: "Information pertaining to cases under investigation is exempted from disclosure."[4] Keshav Mishra, Superintendent of Police of Economic Offences Unit (EOU)-2, said: "The information requested by you cannot be provided since the same would impede the process of investigation and in the apprehension/prosecution of offenders."[5] Neerja Gotru, Superintendent of Police of EOU-1 also sent a similar response.[6]

In view of the denials, First Appeals were filed. But on the first appeal only Superintendent of Police/CBI/ACB/Chandigarh provided the requisite information, not others. On appeal against the denial form Gotru and Mishra, FAA Harbhajan Ram justified their denials by saying that they have "correctly applied the provisions"[7] in rejecting the request. The next option under the

---

[3] Response dated December 31, 2007, to author on RTI.
[4] Letter dated June 8, 2007, to author on RTI.
[5] Letter dated May 29, 2007, author on RTI.
[6] Dated May 28, 2007, to author on RTI.
[7] Both orders dated November 8, 2007, on author's first appeals.

circumstance was to file a Second Appeal before the CIC, but considering the delay in disposal of appeals by the CIC, it was not the right option.

Therefore, a letter was written to the director, CBI before approaching to CIC. The letter was sent with all attachments on December 14, 2007, requesting then Director Vijay Shankar to "look into the matter and intervene." He was told that different CBI units have interpreted RTI provisions differently to provide or deny the information.

This plan worked as I got an acknowledgement from his office the very next day assuring that they will respond very soon. In due course, I received a call from Joint Director (Co-ordination) N.R. Wasan[8] who told that he had asked all officials concerned to provide the information and in the event of the information not reaching within a week I should contact him again. As promised, every unit responded with a great deal of information and so a better part of the list was complete. But the story was not complete. Some important details such as dates of arrest of the accused, dates of bail, and action taken thereafter were still missing. So, again an application was drafted to all CBI units concerned.

The list of IAS, IPS, and IRS officers was segregated. Then, the list of IAS officers was sent to the DoPT, the list of IPS officers to the MHA, and the list of IRS and C&CES officers to the CBDT as well as the CBEC under the Department of Revenue in the Ministry of Finance. All these departments were asked to provide details of departmental action taken against those accused officials till that time and also their posting details since registration of cases. Then, the lists were also forwarded to the CVC asking for details of action recommended and action taken against them.

After months of persuasion and many reminders and personal visits to the offices concerned, information was received from the DoPT, MHA, CVC, and CBEC, but not from the CBDT. The Department of Revenue had forwarded the list of IRS officials to both CBEC and CBDT since the IRS and C&CES were bifurcated. CBDT replied:[9]

---

[8] Is now retired as DG, Bureau of Police Research and Development (BPR&D), MHA, New Delhi.

[9] On February 4, 2008, on author's RTI.

The objective of getting such detail is to write an article for publication by the media regarding these officers accused of corruption. Providing such details for publication in media would not be appropriate as in several such cases investigation might still be continuing and premature disclosure of the details of the case may jeopardize or impede the process of investigation.

When a first appeal was filed, CBDT's vigilance directorate said:[10] "The purpose does not appear to be public interest. No public interest is going to be served by any premature disclosure of information pertaining to any ongoing investigation or enquiry. Therefore, it is informed that the requisite information cannot be provided."

When the director general of income tax (DGIT) was approached through another appeal, that their brother organization CBEC had provided all requisite details about C&CES officers and, therefore, there was no logic in hiding the information about CBDT officials, the CBDT questioned the purpose of publishing an article in the media about the accused officials and again denied the information.

The CBDT is one of the most obdurate organizations, with regard to RTI implementation. Similar information was received from every other concerned department, but the CBDT repeatedly kept fogging me off, insisting that the information was exempted and, what is more, questioning the purpose of filing RTI application despite that asking the purpose of seeking information is not permissible under the RTI Act.

On another application requesting for a list of suspended IRS officers, CBDT's Additional Director (Vigilance) L.K.S. Dahia replied on September 15, 2009: "As the investigations/inquiry are in progress the details sought by you are claimed exempt." It was ridiculous because the names of suspended officers are regularly disclosed in the Civil List of IRS officers, which is always in public domain. RTI application was filed because updated list till that date was needed. On the application dated February 9, 2009, for "[d]etails of IRS officers who are under suspension as on date," it was claimed to be exempted. They merely provided the number of officers (18) who were under suspension. Again, on December 1, 2011, another application was filed seeking the "[l]ist of IRS

---

[10] Response dated February 11, 2008, of Directorate of Vigilance, CBDT, New Delhi to author on RTI.

officers who are under suspicion now along with their name/
batch/designation-rank/date of suspension." The response[11] was,
"Information cannot be provided to the applicant as information
pertains to third parties and the disclosure of the same has no
relationship to any public activity or interest and would cause
unwarranted invasion of the privacy of individuals." Even, when
it was asked to provide the list of IRS officers who have been
terminated/dismissed from service, the response[12] was, "Name of
the officers cannot be disclosed to the applicant as this is information is third party information" (Figure 5.1).

Figure 5.1:
Reply to one of the RTI applications filed by the author to DGIT (Vigilance)

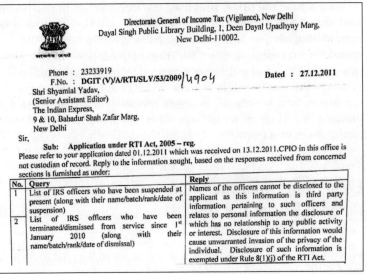

Source: Author.

There was another rather disconcerting rejoinder from the
DoPT. This is what they had to say:[13]

Right to Information is available to all Citizens, whereas the present
request has been received in this Department as from the Principal

---

[11] CBDT (DG, Vigilance) letter dated January 23, 2012, to author.
[12] Response dated December 27, 2011, by CBDT (DG Vigilance) to author.
[13] Response of DoPT dated March 19, 2008, to author.

Correspondent of *India Today*. Further, you have also stated in your request that you (*India Today*) are working on a story on the officials accused in various corruption cases and you need the information for that purpose. Thus, it is clear that the present request for information is from Shyamlal Yadav, Principal Correspondent, *India Today*, and not from Shyamlal Yadav, a Citizen. In view of the above it is regretted that the present request for information is not covered with the provisions of the said Act.

But what was ironical, and totally unexpected, was when I got a call from an officer working in the DoPT requesting me to visit his office. When I did so the next day, I was provided all the requisite information off the record.

Meanwhile, the MHA provided the information in one go but said that,[14] "Departmental action, if any, will be taken only on culmination of cases before the Courts, and on the basis of the outcome of the investigation by CBI." Rest of the details were received from the CVC,[15] but only after repeated telephonic reminders.

In the end, as a result of over 100 RTI applications, appeals, reminders, and telephonic requests spread over a year, there was plenty of information which was short listed, analyzed, and finalized in form of a story.[16]

Exemptions from the RTI Act: Defense Forces and the CBI

When the legislation was being framed, no need was felt to include the CBI in the second schedule (the list of organizations which are exempted from RTI except regarding matters related to Human Rights violation and Corruption) of the RTI Act because it is mainly involved in investigating anticorruption cases. Even the second administrative reforms commission (ARC) headed by M. Veerappa Moily had not recommended exemption to the CBI. The CBI was given exemption only in June 2011, and interestingly the CBI

---

[14] Response of MHA dated March 12, 2008, to author.
[15] Vide letter dated March 19, 2008, to author.
[16] See http://indiatoday.intoday.in/story/A+lot+to+hide/1/6290.html, accessed December 31, 2016.

demanded to exempt its only units involved in intelligence collection but the government granted the exemption to CBI as a whole.

Unlike in the case of the CBI, the second ARC headed by M. Veerappa Moily recommended the defense forces to be included in the second schedule of the RTI Act. In its letter[17] written with "approval of Defence Minister," the Ministry of Defence demanded exemption for the defense forces from RTI. The letter said:[18]

> The nature and duties carried out by the Defence Forces encompasses both internal and external security and sensitive intelligence material. The Coast Guard is tasked with protection of the Exclusive Economic Zone and has to ensure compliance of various local laws relating to environment, customs etc. As such, it handles sensitive information, the disclosure of which will be prejudicial to its operational efficiency. Thus the Defence Forces i.e., Indian Army, Indian Navy and Indian Air Force, Coast Guard and the Border Road Development Board (BRDB) also fulfil the requirements of Section 16 of the Freedom of Information Act-2002 and deserve to be included in the schedule thereto.

The letter also demanded exclusion for the Defence Research and Development Organization (DRDO) from the RTI Act. While DRDO was granted exemption from RTI, regarding other organizations, then Secretary of DoPT A.N. Tewari wrote[19] back to Defence Secretary Shekhar Dutt:

> The Army, Navy, Air Force and Coast Guard need not to be exempted from disclosure by inclusion in the Second Schedule in view of the fact that Section 8(1) (a) of the RTI Act, 2005 already provides adequate protection for information which could affect the sovereignty and integrity of India, security, strategic, scientific or economic interests of the State, relations with foreign States or lead to incitement of an offence.

Elaborating on the point that "Prime Minister's Office has desired that comments of the Heads of the Security organizations involved may be obtained," the letter further said that:

---

[17] MoD letter dated March 7, 2005, accessed by author under RTI.
[18] Ibid.
[19] A.N. Tewari's letter accessed by the author using RTI.

In due course, DoPT may explore the possibility of an amendment to the Act to provide for selective exemption for Army, Navy, Air Force and Coast Guard in relation to activities undertaken in the course of warfare, defence of the nation's borders and anti-terrorism and anti-militancy operations could be considered. No exemption for these organizations may be granted when and if any of its forces are engaged in internal law and order and peace keeping operations.

So, the defense forces are still covered under RTI, but not the CBI, which was granted exemption later.

In case of the CBI, things were different. The file[20] regarding its inclusion into second schedule of RTI shows that things were moved very fast with regard to CBI. This file reflects the whole story that how the case of CBI was decided. After the enactment of the RTI Act, the CBI had requested that it should be exempted from RTI but, the Committee of Secretaries in its meeting on November 23, 2007, rejected the request saying: "The case of CBI was not considered necessary in view of the provisions of Section 8(1) (h) and other provisions that can be invoked for non-disclosure of sensitive information."

The chronology of the file movement[21] regarding CBI which was broken later using RTI is very interesting:

On July 22, 2010, in its meeting, the CVC had recommended that: "CBI would move the DoPT with a view to getting the Special Unit of CBI (dealing with collection of intelligence) exempted from purview of the RTI Act."

CBI forwarded its request for exemption to DoPT in September 2010, and again on February 14, 2011, CBI Joint Director A.K. Pateria forwarded a request to DoPT saying that "Exemption under RTI Act may be granted to the CBI (except matters pertaining to Administration, Personnel, Accounts/Finance, Budget and Training)."

Solicitor General of India Gopal Subramaniam advised on the file on March 14, 2011, that:

---

[20] Complete file regarding the CBI was accessed by the author. Available on http://indianexpress.com/article/india/india-others/cbi-sought-part-rti-exemption-govt-gave-it-full/, accessed December 31, 2016.
[21] Ibid.

The CBI can be considered to be added in the second schedule to the RTI Act, 2005 with the qualification that after setting out the words CBI, certain words in parenthesis will be added i.e., 'except matters pertaining to administration, personnel, accounts/finance, budget and training'.

Subramanium further wrote in his 23 page note that, "I am, however, not convinced that all aspects of the organisation of the CBI must be given exemption." The DoPT's joint secretary Rajeev Kapoor backed the CBI's original proposal of keeping only its intelligence gathering Special Unit out of the RTI Act. Pateria again wrote a cleverly drafted letter to the DoPT on May 2, 2011, saying, "As all the branches/units of CBI are involved in intelligence collection work for registration and investigation/enquiry, exempting only the Special Unit from purview of RTI Act, would not fulfil the requirements of CBI for seeking exemption from purview of the Act." And in a meeting with DoPT, he requested full exemption to the CBI and suggested that:

Even though it had originally been decided at the meeting held in the office of CVC that Special Unit of CBI (pertaining to collection of intelligence) may be exempted from the purview of the RTI Act, such a partial exemption (only in respect of Special Unit of CBI) may not serve the purpose.

A note of DoPT dated March 31, 2011, said:

It may also be noted that PMO had also sent us a note sent by Hon'ble Minister of Law to Hon'ble Prime Minister wherein the Law Minister had indicated that it has been decided to include CBI in the second schedule of RTI Act to the extent of issues relating to certain aspects of CBI working which will be fully specified in the second schedule.

The CBI was worried that "Exemption will not be available once investigation of case ends in closure or the prosecution of the case is finally over."

A DoPT note of April 2011 signed by its Secretary Alka Sirohi said that "partial exemption may not serve the purpose...according to the CBI they are in favour of full exemption". This note also recorded the anxiety of the PMO to exempt the CBI from the RTI

Act. A note from S.K. Sarkar, then additional secretary of DoPT, pointed out: "Shri M.N. Prasad, Secretary to PM, called me twice today to convey that the Law Ministry is obtaining the advice of the AG (Attorney General of India) the basis of reference from DoPT on the above subject."

The AG opined that:

> The CBI does intelligence work which is directly related to the security agencies and that it is legally feasible to include CBI in the Second Schedule.... It would not be feasible to exclude matters relating to administration, personnel, accounts/finance, budget and training from purview of the exemption because it would make intelligence gathering difficult.

The AG had also not found it necessary to limit the exemption only to that part of the CBI which deals with intelligence because security of the state is intertwined with investigation.

Law Minister M. Veerappa Moily, who did not recommend the exemption of CBI in his second ARC report as the chairman of second ARC, forwarded the AG's advice to the PM on May 10, 2011, recommending CBI's inclusion in the second schedule of the RTI Act. This proposal of DoPT was approved by the Committee of Secretaries in its meeting on May 13, 2011.

Finally, PM Manmohan Singh, being minister-in-charge of DoPT, approved this proposal on June 7, 2011, and the amendments notification was tabled in the Lok Sabha on August 17, 2011, and in the Rajya Sabha the next day.

So, while the provisions of the RTI Act were able to safeguard every aspect of the CBI's functioning which needed to be kept confidential in the public interest, it was clear from file notings and correspondence among related authorities that the government was more eager than the CBI itself to exempt the agency from the RTI Act. This exemption was much against the intention of the Parliament, and militates against the primary objective of the act which, as stated in the objects and reasons, is to contain corruption. If the CBI was under RTI, it would have been easy to know how the cases like Bofors and others were registered, investigated, tried, and ultimately closed.

Interestingly, efforts to get details about the anticorruption cases against IAS, IPS, and IRS officers for the story were fructified with the help of then CBI Director Vijay Shankar. In an interview[22] to the author on January 9, 2008, he had stated:

> The CPIOs in CBI have been instructed to follow the provisions of RTI Act in making available the information to the applicant. The officers are advised not to withhold information unless it is specifically provided for in the Act from disclosure. As an organization, CBI believes in transparency and as such, the officers are given training from time to time to make them aware of RTI provisions.

On hearing about the CBI's exemption from RTI, former Chief Information Commissioner Wajahat Habibulla wrote[23] to PM Manmohan Singh on May 16, 2011, requesting that: "The CBI remains within the ambit of RTI Act. Public interest would, in my view, be best served by keeping these bodies transparent and accountable within limits of the law." Wajahat Habibulla, quoting from his experience, said:[24]

> He (then director CBI Vijay Shankar) was, with the background of his experience of nine years in the CBI, in constant touch with me as Chief Information Commissioner to help improve the accountability of CBI. And this has borne fruit. CBI has effectively modified its systems making for ready access to information when required.

The replies received while doing anticorruption story brought out some interesting facts. Of the 48 IAS, 17 IPS, and 98 IRS C&CES officers, cases against 15 IAS, 7 IPS, and 34 IRS officers were still under investigation. Others were closed due to a variety of reasons and some were under trial in various courts. Two IPS officers against whom cases were filed had expired. While the total number of IAS, IPS, IRS and C&CES officers who were facing trial was 33, 8, and 64, respectively, only 12 IAS, 4 IPS, and 20 IRS

---

[22] Part of this interview was published in *India Today*. Available on http://india-today.intoday.in/story/'We+get+about+14,000+complaints+every+year'/1/6295.html, accessed December 31, 2016.

[23] See http://www.dnaindia.com/india/report-cbi-under-rti-will-prevent-misuse-1557208, accessed December 31, 2016.

[24] Copy was later accessed by the author using RTI Act. Available on http://www.dnaindia.com/india/report-cbi-under-rti-will-prevent-misuse-1557208, accessed December 31, 2016.

C&CES officers were ever arrested. As for cases which were under investigation, while none of the 16 IAS officers and 7 IPS officers had been arrested, only 4 of the 34 IRS and C&CES officers were taken into custody, most of them were trapped while receiving alleged bribe money.

Even worse was the state of affairs in the MHA, the cadre controlling authority for IPS officers. When a list of 17 IPS officers against whom CBI had registered cases over the years was sent to MHA, the reply[25] simply stated: "Two officers expired and as such no action is called for. In respect of seven officers, investigations by CBI are under progress. Cases against eight officers are under trial before the respective CBI courts and are sub judice." Matters were no different at the CBEC. Out of 47 C&CES officers[26] accused with corruption, only two were dismissed from service while three others faced minor penalties; others were acquitted for want of evidence, and as for the rest, their cases were pending.

It was not difficult to get information about the accused IAS and IPS officers from DoPT and MHA respectively. After some initial hesitation, the CBEC provided all required details about C&CES officers. But it was not possible from CBDT which denied the requests again and again.

The CBDT repeatedly tried to hide information which other cadre controlling authorities on other services had already provided.[27] When CBDT was asked for details about officers against whom prosecution sanctions were issued or pending, here is what Rakesh Gupta, then Additional Director (Vigilance) had to say[28] on November 9, 2012: "Names of the officers cannot be disclosed to the applicant as this information is third party information pertaining to such officers and relates to personal information the disclosure of which has no relationship to any public activity or interest." The FAA and director (Vigilance) of CBDT, Sanjay Puri, endorsed the stand taken by his CPIO by saying,[29] "Giving out any information regarding any individual who is merely facing certain charges in a disciplinary proceedings, which have

---

[25] MHA's response to author on RTI.

[26] Response of DG Vigilance, CBEC dated February 19, 2008.

[27] DoPT (for IAS), MHA (for IPS), CBEC (for C&CES) have regularly provided such list to author on RTI.

[28] In response to RTI application filed by the author.

[29] In response to First Appeal under RTI Act filed by the author.

not yet been proved, would violate his privacy and should not be given unless there is an overriding public interest involved."

Sadly, with the inclusion of CBI in the second schedule of the RTI Act, such disclosures from the agency have stopped. Gradually, the mind-set of the officers responsible for providing information has also been changed.

In the initial years of implementation of the RTI Act, it was comparatively easy to get details of complaints against IAS officers because the DoPT was much open toward RTI applications. Officers who were appointed CPIOs during the early years were very cooperative, but sadly they stopped being so gradually. Now it has become very difficult to get details of corruption cases pending against IAS officers as well. The authorities are now taking the defense of a Supreme Court order[30] in the matter of Gireesh Ramchandra Pande vs CIC which states that:

> The performance of an employee/officer in an organisation is primarily a matter between the employee and the employer and normally those aspects are governed by the service rules which fall under the expression 'personal information', the disclosure of which has no relationship to any public activity or public interest.

Particularly, if the cases are against senior officers, it is almost impossible to get the desired information. When the details of corruption cases against secretary rank officers were sought—just the names of the officers against whom the complaints were pending, along with the number of complaints received against each officer—the reply[31] stated that on January 14, 2010, a group of secretaries was set up to look into complaints against Secretaries to the Government of India consisting of the Cabinet Secretary (Chairman), Secretary to the PM, Secretary Co-ordination in the Cabsec, Secretary DoPT, and Secretary CVC as members. It further stated that "more than 275 complaints have been received against the Secretaries to the Government of India in this Secretariat so far…. 12 complaints are pending

---

[30] See http://judis.nic.in/supremecourt/imgst.aspx?filename=39615, accessed January 3, 2017.

[31] Response of the Cabsec dated June 20, 2013, to author under RTI.

before the Group of Secretaries as on date."[32] No additional details were given.

In pursuance to this reply, a separate RTI application was filed seeking to know the total number of complaints received against the Secretaries to the Government of India; list of officers against whom complaints were closed; and also the list of officers against whom any action was recommended. The CPIO again did not provide the details. And even after First Appeal, what was provided was merely the total number of complaints: "283 complaints were received by the Group of Secretaries…out of which 263 were disposed off by the Group of Secretaries."[33] As for other details requested in the application, the response was much the same as before:

> As far as providing the names of officers against whom the complaints were received, date of receipt and disposal are concerned, it is held that such information would fall under the expression 'personal information' the disclosure of which has no relationship to any public activity or public interest.[34]

It was in August 2010 that Sports Minister M.S. Gill advised[35] MPs to file RTI to know the details of Commonwealth Games projects when the MPs were raising the issue of corruption in Commonwealth Games projects.

CBI's exclusion from RTI has come as a shock for the people who were using RTI to get details of corruption cases. While all the required exemption was already there in the RTI Act, the decision of Manmohan Singh government was against the preamble of the RTI Act which says that the purpose of the RTI Act is to contain corruption. It will help the government if it wants to remove corruption that CBI must be covered under RTI again.

---

[32] Ibid.
[33] Response of the Cabsec dated October 18, 2013, to author under RTI.
[34] The Cabsec's first appellate order dated October 10, 2013, on author's appeal.
[35] See http://indiatoday.intoday.in/story/how-the-privilege-of-common-man-under-rti-is-more-powerful-than-of-the-parliament-members/1/112783.html, accessed January 3, 2017.

6

Streams of Filth: Cleaning the Rivers Through RTI

The belief the Ganga river is 'holy' has not, however, prevented over-use, abuse and pollution of the river.... The natural assimilative capacity of the river is severely stressed.[1]

—Richard Helmer and Ivanildo Hespanhol

Table 6.1:
Highlights of RTIs filed to know the pollution levels in rivers

Information	River pollution
Authority	Ministry of Environment, Forest and Climate Change; Central Pollution Control Board; Central Water Commission; State Pollution Control Boards.
Problems	Reports were old and technical; some authorities sent their entire reports.
Applications and appeals	39, for first story. (Excluding those filed for the follow up and other related stories.)
Time taken	Over a year
Story	Streams of Filth: Money is flowing like water into prominent government projects on river conservation, but there is little effect on the nation's lifelines (*India Today*, December 30, 2009)
Impact	River pollution, particularly of Ganga and its tributaries, gradually came into focus and after all, new government created a separate department to tackle the problem
Follow up by me	More applications were filed to check the status. Other stories were also published.
Follow up by others	My story was unique to interpret data in readable manner, and many other media followed it later

Source: Author.

---

[1] Richard Helmer and Ivanildo Hespanhol, ed. *Water Pollution Control—A Guide to the Use of Water Quality Management Principles* (United Nations Environment Programme, 1997).

This story can be considered a 'masterpiece', admittedly from among the stories explored through the RTI law. Although there were several stories that gave immense satisfaction as a journalist—and some of them had a huge impact—this one was different, in many ways. It was also the most internationally acclaimed, receiving some prestigious awards, which naturally gave lot of exposure abroad and recognition at home.

The story was awarded the first prize in Developing Asia Journalism Awards 2010[2] by the Asian Development Bank Institute at Tokyo in November, 2010, out of 180 entries from 20 countries of Asia Pacific. The European Commission for Development under the European Union awarded it the Lorenzo Natalie Journalism Prize[3] (first prize) in the Asia Pacific category in December 2010 in Brussels, and UNESCO published it as part of the *Story-Based Inquiry: A Manual for Investigative Journalists-2009*.[4] It was one of the 20 investigative pieces across the worlds which were compiled as UNESCO's *The Global Investigative Journalism Casebook* edited by INSEAD Professor Mark Lee Hunter.[5]

In October 2011, I was invited to make a presentation on 'Data Flood in India after RTI' at the Global Investigative Journalism Conference (GIJC)[6] in Keiv, Ukraine. This led to one opportunity after the other as there were invitations to give a talk on 'Use of RTI for Investigative Journalism' at Brussels by Europe's famous FoI activist Briggite Alfter[7] in May 2012, and again in May 2014 at their Data Harvest Conferences (DHC).[8]

***

The idea for this story came to mind from an editorial written by Aroon Purie, Editor-in-Chief, *India Today*, in the 33rd anniversary

---

[2] See http://www.adb.org/sites/default/files/publication/157767/adbi-news-v5n1.pdf, accessed December 29, 2016.

[3] See http://ec.europa.eu/europeaid/lnp/lorenzo-natali-prize/winners_en, accessed December 29, 2016.

[4] See http://unesdoc.unesco.org/images/0021/002176/217636e.pdf, accessed February 15, 2017.

[5] See http://www.storybasedinquiry.com/mark-lee-hunter, accessed December 29, 2016.

[6] See http://gijn.org/2011/10/, accessed December 29, 2016.

[7] See http://www.icij.org/journalists/brigitte-alfter

[8] See http://www.journalismfund.eu/dataharvest-conferences, accessed December 29, 2016.

issue of the magazine, dated December 29, 2008. In the editorial, he had lamented the fact that despite many achievements on many fronts, India had yet to successfully clean its rivers:[9] "While the economy has revolutionised our lives, what has not changed is our politics and governance. That's the paradox.... Even after spending thousands of crores of rupees we are yet to clean the Yamuna and the Ganges..."

There were articles in the media on pollution of the Ganga, Yamuna, and other major rivers and the action taken to clean them, based on Supreme Court orders, and MoEF and CPCB reports, time and again. But this new idea was for a comprehensive coverage on Indian rivers under the NRCP as whole. The story idea was structured around the fact of how much money was spent on tackling pollution in prominent rivers covered under the NRCP, and exposed how the NRCP had failed in its efforts, despite huge expenditure. It goes without saying that this story would have been impossible to undertake, and brought to a conclusion without the RTI Act.

Rajiv Gandhi initiated the process of cleaning the Ganga[10] when he took office as Prime Minister in 1984, and in February 1985 the Central Ganga Authority (CGA) was formed with an initial budget of ₹3.5 billion to administer the cleaning of the Ganga.[11] On June 14, 1986, the Ganga Action Plan (GAP)[12] was launched, which, in the course of time, included into its ambit the other major tributaries of Ganga: Yamuna, Gomti, and Damodar.[13] The program was further broad-based in 1995 and renamed as the National River Conservation Plan,[14] covering 18 grossly polluted river stretches in 10 states, at a projected cost of ₹7.72 billion. Till the new NDA government was formed in May 2014, 41 rivers were covered under its scope that includes every prominent Indian river. The rivers covered under NRCP[15] were: Adyar, Beas, Beehar, Betwa,

[9] See http://indiatoday.intoday.in/story/From+the+editor-in-chief/1/23057.html, accessed December 29, 2016.

[10] National River Conservation Plan, MoEF, New Delhi.

[11] See http://www.ecofriends.org/main/eganga/images/Critical%20analysis%20of%20GAP.pdf, accessed December 29, 2016.

[12] Ibid.

[13] National River Conservation Plan, MoEF, New Delhi.

[14] Ibid.

[15] See http://www.moef.nic.in/sites/default/files/NRCD/More.html, accessed December 29, 2016.

Bhadra, Brahmani, Cauvery, Chambal, Cooum, Damodar, Diphu and Dhansiri, Ganga, Godavari, Gomti, Khan, Krishna, Kshipra, Mahanadi, Mahananda, Mandovi, Mandakini, Mindhola, Musi, Narmada, Pamba, Pennar, Panchganga, Ranichu, Ramganga, Sabarmati, Satluj, Subarnarekha, Thamirabarani, Tapi, Tunga, Tungabhadra, Vaigai, Wainganga, and Yamuna. Later, Ganga and 11 of its tributaries were separated as part of a newly created scheme of Namami Gange[16] under the Ministry of Water Resources, River Development and Ganga Rejuvenation.

When the research for the story began, NRCP included 37 rivers; and when the story was published, the number had reached 39. Before filing the RTI applications, it was researched to find out how many authorities were involved in this ambitious plan. Based on these findings, RTI applications were filed one after another to the CPCB, a dozen state pollution control boards (SPCBs), the CWC, MoEF, and to the many state government departments of environment and forests.

From CPCB, initially, a copy of the report on the first sample of water taken from each of the 37 rivers, and then water quality reports based on the latest samples taken from these rivers was asked for. After getting the two water quality reports, they were asked for details of the total money spent on different rivers till that time.

Many responses were sought, more queries arose, and an added number of applications were filed, and so, all documents did not come at one go. In all, it took 39 RTI applications and numerous phone calls and personal visits to the public authorities to convince them to part with the information.

Also, the data on the total length of polluted stretches of every river and the year of inclusion of each of those rivers into the NRCP was received. As per the information available in the public domain, the 37 rivers had a total length of 22,127 km,[17] of which, as per the information received, 2,518 km in total were known as polluted stretches.[18]

---

[16] Union Cabinet decision dated May 13, 2015, http://wrmin.nic.in/forms/list.aspx?lid=277, accessed December 29, 2016.
[17] Calculation based on length of all these rivers found on internet by author.
[18] Response of CPCB, New Delhi, dated February 13, 2009, to author on RTI.

While Adyar and Cooum rivers were described variously as "drainage-only waste water is flowing",[19] for Mahananda it was told that they have "inadequate data",[20] and for Pennar it was told that the "river flows during monsoon only".[21] The CPCB provided the length of polluted stretches of big rivers. These were:[22] Betwa (15 km), Bhadra (18 km), Brahmani (85 km), Cauvery (160 km), Chambal (50 km), Damodar (90 km), Dhansiri (10 km), Ganga (125 km), Godavari (235 km), Gomti (130 km), Khan (20 km), Kshipra (20 km), Mahanadi (25 km), Musi (45 km), Pamba (20 km), Ranichu (5 km), Sabarmati (65 km), Satluj (120 km), Subarnarekha (25 km), Tamiraparani (50 km), Tapi (60 km), Tunga (20 km), Tungabhadra (18 km), Vaigai (10 km), Wainganga (30 km), and Yamuna (500 km). For Mandovi and Pennar rivers, the CPCB said, "Water quality improved, not polluted now."[23]

I managed to get parts of this information informally from various sources. It was a cumbersome process since the CPCB, in their wisdom, had sent a huge data[24] of 282 rivers at 1,085 locations being monitored by it. There was a mismatch in the pollution level data as provided by the CPCB, the River Data Directorate of CWC, and the SPCBs. All doubts were subsequently removed with new RTI applications and with the help of experts.

Dates of inclusion of every river into the NRCP were also obtained, using a separate RTI application. This was the information received:[25] Adyar was included in September 2000; Beehar in July 2007; Betwa, Bhadra, Brahmani, Cauvery, and Chambal in July 1995; Cooum in September 2000; Damodar in December 1996; Dhipu and Dhansiri in August 2005; Ganga in June 1986 (as GAP); Godavari in July 1995; Gomti in December 1996; Khan, Kshipra, and Mahanadi in July 1995; Mandovi in May 2002; Musi in April 2003; Narmada in July 1995; Pamba in May 2003; Pennar in August 2002; Ranichu in March 2005; Sabarmati in July 1995;

---

[19] Ibid.
[20] Ibid.
[21] Ibid.
[22] Ibid.
[23] Ibid.
[24] Response dated February 5, 2009, by CPCB, New Delhi, on author's e-mail dated February 3, 2009.
[25] Response of MoEF, dated March 26, 2009, to author on RTI.

Satluj in July 1995; Subarnarekha in July 1995; Tamiraparani in January 2001; Tapti in July 1995; Tapi in November 2008; Tunga in July 1995; Tungabhadra in July 1995; Vaigai in January 2001; Wainganga in July 1995; and Yamuna in December 1996.

All available information was put together, going through it carefully and cross-checking everything with the help of sources in the Ministry of Water Resources, MoEF, and CPCB, since most of it was scientific data. To analyze the impact of pollution-control mechanisms on these rivers, the worst locations of first sample reports were taken and their pollution status was compared to the latest data of same location, keeping in mind that they were all collected during the same season. Same season data was necessary, since the quality of water changes with change in temperature and flow of the water. Since many parameters were technical in nature, the levels of biochemical oxygen demand (BOD)[26] and dissolved oxygen (DO)[27] were taken into account in order to make it comprehensible to readers.

These are standard procedures to measure the amount of organic pollution in a sample of water. BOD is the amount of dissolved oxygen needed by aerobic biological organisms in a body of water to break down organic material. DO is a measure of how successfully the water has been treated. Raw waste water has very little DO. Simply put, higher the BOD, higher the pollution in the water sample; higher the DO, lower the pollution.

Water having BOD at 2 mg per liter or less and DO at 6 mg per liter or more can be used as drinking water without conventional treatment but after disinfection.[28] If water has BOD at 3 mg per liter or less and DO at 4 mg per liter or more, it can be used as potable water after conventional treatment and disinfection.[29] Water containing BOD at 3 mg per liter or less and DO at 5 mg per liter or more is fit for outdoor bathing.[30] If water has BOD at 2 mg per liter or less and DO between 4–6 mg per liter, it can be used for fisheries etc.[31] When BOD levels are high, DO levels

---

[26] See http://www.cpcb.nic.in/Water_Quality_Criteria.php, accessed December 29, 2016.
[27] Ibid.
[28] Ibid.
[29] Ibid.
[30] Ibid.
[31] Ibid.

decrease because the oxygen that is available in the water is being consumed by the bacteria. Since less DO is available in the water, fish and other aquatic organisms may not survive. After being aware of these facts through CPCB scientists and other experts on the subject, it was easy to identify at which locations water was suitable for drinking and at which it was suitable for bathing or for fisheries. So these parameters were applied to the sampled locations for which data was available.

But there were many figures given by the CPCB and the CWC, which created confusion:[32] While the CPCB reply indicated the BOD as 48 for Sabarmati in Kheda, the CWC reply said it was 58 at the same location. In another instance, the CPCB suggested the BOD as 70 at Okhla in Delhi, whereas the CWC reply said it was 100. The BOD at the Kshipra river (the Maha Kumbh Mela is held on this river every 12 years in Ujjain) according to CPCB was 8, while the CWC said it was 4.98. Huge difference in the quality of the water collected from the same location by different authorities raises doubts about their reports. In the case of the most polluted spot of river Tapi, while the CPCB said the BOD was 21 at Ajnand village (Maharashtra), the CWC gave a figure of 48 at Burhanpur (Madhya Pradesh).

While the monitoring of Yamuna was initiated by the CPCB in 1977,[33] the monitoring of Ganga was begun in 1980.[34] The first sample was taken from Ganga in Allahabad on January 9, 1985, and from Yamuna in Allahabad on January 11, 1985.[35] At the time of response, the CPCB was monitoring the water quality of 282 rivers.[36] According to the CPCB's reply, one such analysis costs around ₹9,500.[37] At the time of response on the RTI application, the CPCB was monitoring Ganga waters at 39 locations,[38] out of which 25 locations were monitored on a monthly basis, 13 locations on quarterly, and one location on a yearly basis.[39] Apart

[32] CPCB's response, dated August 20, 2009, and CWC's response, dated September 30, 2009, to author on RTI.
[33] Response of CPCB, New Delhi, dated January 28, 2009, to author on RTI.
[34] Ibid.
[35] Ibid.
[36] Ibid.
[37] Response of UPPCB, Lucknow, dated April 24, 2009, to author.
[38] Response of CPCB, New Delhi, dated January 28, 2009, to author on RTI.
[39] CPCB's response, dated October 9, 2012, to author on RTI.

from CPCB's monitoring of rivers, the CWC has[40] 258 water quality laboratories where it was monitoring the water quality of 27 rivers, as per its response.[41]

From the available data, it was found that only two rivers (the Narmada and Mandovi) were deemed clean among the sample reports. By making the claim that these two rivers were "not polluted," the CPCB contradicted itself, as it gave a level of BOD of 11.4 mg/liter for the Narmada at Hoshangabad, and 4.7 mg/liter for Mandovi at Tonca, Goa, which were much higher than the permissible levels.

The worst locations[42] on these rivers were identified as Betwa at Nayapura, Khan at Indore, and Narmada at Hoshangabad (Madhya Pradesh); Bhadra at Bhadravati, Tunga at Shimoga, and Tungbhadra at Ullanur (Karnataka); Brahmani at Pandosh (Odisha); Cauveri at Erode and Tambirparani at Murappanadu (Tamil Nadu); Chambal at Kota, Damodar at Narainpur, and Mahanadi at Siliguri (West Bengal); Dhansiri at Golaghat (Assam); Ganga at Kanpur and Godavari near Tapovan (Nasik); Krishna at Mahuli, Tapi at Ajnand and Wainganga at Ashti (Maharashtra); Kshipra at Siddhavat (Ujjain, Madhya Pradesh); Mandovi at Tonca (Goa); Musi at Nangole (Rangareddy, Andhra Pradesh); Pamba at Thakazhy (Kerala); Pennar at Somasila (Andhra Pradesh); Ranichu at Singtam (Sikkim); Sabarmati at Vautha (Gujarat); Satluj at Ludhiana (Punjab); Subarnrekha at Ranchi (Jharkhand); and Yamuna at Okhla (Delhi).

The rise in river pollution levels was alarming. When the GAP-I was initiated in 1985, the BOD in the Ganga at Kanpur was 6.9 mg/liter[43] while the latest sample of CPCB marked it at 21.[44] In 1980, the BOD in the Yamuna at Okhla in Delhi was 10.6 mg/liter,[45] while its latest sample analysis[46] by CPCB showed it at 70.

Starting from down South in Chennai to Punjab, Jharkhand, and Gujarat, rivers in the North, East, and West had a sorry state to tell.

---

[40] Response of CPCB, New Delhi, dated January 28, 2009, to author on RTI.
[41] Dated August 19, 2009, to author on RTI.
[42] Based on BOD and DO figures in CPCB's response, dated August 20, 2009, and CWC's response, dated September 30, 2009, to author on RTI.
[43] UPPCB's response, dated February 17, 2009, to author on RTI.
[44] CPCB's response, dated August 20, 2009, to author on RTI.
[45] CPCB's response, dated January 28, 2009, to author on RTI.
[46] CPCB's response, dated August 20, 2009, to author on RTI.

The Adyar and Cooum rivers in Tamil Nadu were found to be notorious for their industrial pollution. Kerala's Pamba was included in the first phase of the NRCP in 2003–04 and was slated for cleanup by 2008–09. But the data reflected that most of the 11 NRCP projects were under construction[47] and work was yet to begin on the largest one till 2008–09. The state government moved to set up an authority to monitor the slothful work only as late as in August 2008.[48] Rivers such as Chambal in Rajasthan and Satluj in the Punjab had much the same story to tell, based on available data.[49]

All this effort ultimately resulted in a big, impact-making, award-winning story, but it took complete one year to send applications, reminders, and appeals; make personal visits; and process the data with the help of many experts before that.

Finally, the story was published in *India Today*.[50]

This is what Professor Mark Lee Hunter[51] wrote in the Casebook[52] which he edited for UNESCO:[53]

> While mainstream print and broadcast media in Europe and the USA, with some exceptions, have suffered a triple decline of audience, revenues and human capacity over the past decade, India's media have been on the rise in more ways than one. The world's biggest democracy is presently the scene of a stupefying competition for expanding, newly prosperous media audiences, in print as in broadcast. Simultaneously, the establishment of a strong 'Right to Information' law (RTI for short) has given reporters potent new tools, and those tools are being used. In the piece published here, Shyamlal Yadav delivers a classic investigative theme—a bright promise that became another betrayal in a long list. He does so, on the basis of the government's own data. Thus, when you finish this story, you cannot argue about whether India's river conservation policies have failed (as you could, say, after reading an editorial on the subject). If you are not a liar, you will only ask what can be done about it. Part of the impact in this story resides in superb,

---

[47] "Streams of Filth", *India Today*, December 30, 2009, pp. 116–20.
[48] Ibid.
[49] Ibid.
[50] Ibid.
[51] See http://www.storybasedinquiry.com/mark-lee-hunter, accessed December 29, 2016.
[52] See http://www.storybasedinquiry.com/global-casebook
[53] "Can This Planet Be Saved", in *Global Investigative Journalism Casebook* (Paris: UNESCO), 69.

colorful graphics that make complex data immediately clear for the viewer—which is why we reproduce the article in its original published form.

The Casebook is explained on the UNESCO website as:[54]

UNESCO has consistently supported initiatives to strengthen investigative journalism throughout the world, which is crucial for freedom of expression and freedom of information. The Casebook aims to enable and enhance the exchange of good practices and networking in investigative journalism worldwide. The Casebook contains more than 20 recent investigative stories from around the world, covering a wide variety of topical subjects such as freedom of information, good governance, social and legal issues, the environment, health and gender. Each article is accompanied by an explanation of how the authors conducted their research and wrote their pieces. Many of the authors belong to the Global Investigative Journalism Network, and their stories exemplify the cutting-edge techniques and high standards developed within this network. At a time when media landscapes are rapidly changing, journalism today needs to clearly show its added value for public interest. In this light, credible investigative stories, like the kind promoted in this book, are increasingly important for highlighting the continuing importance of professional journalistic work. This Casebook thus serves as a key knowledge resource, providing a valuable learning opportunity for journalists and media professionals, as well as for journalism trainers and educators. It will also be used by UNESCO field offices to conduct training courses in investigative reporting.

The European Commission for Development, in an introduction to the Lorenzo Natalie Prize winners, wrote:[55]

Shyamlal has worked as a journalist for 17 years, but first came to national attention after the Right to Information (RTI) act came into force in India in 2005. Shyamlal began using the act for journalistic purposes and published a number of influential articles using the information he gathered.

---

[54] See http://www.unesco.org/new/en/communication-and-information/resources/publications-and-communication-materials/publications/full-list/the-global-investigative-journalism-casebook/, accessed December 29, 2016.
[55] See http://ec.europa.eu/europeaid/lnp/lorenzo-natali-prize/winners_en?qt-lorenzo_natali_lnp_winners=2#qt-lorenzo_natali_lnp_winners, accessed December 29, 2016.

The Lorenzo Natalie organizers further wrote:[56]

> Using India's Right to Information (RTI) act, Shymlal Yadav looked at the state of programmes being implemented to control pollution in India's major rivers. A scheme was launched in mid-1980s called the National River Conservation Programme (NRCP), within which vast sums were spent on improving the quality of some 37 rivers. But data shows that it had no positive effect on the rivers due to poor implementation.

The Story of Ganga–Yamuna During Maha Kumbh

In 2013, just three months prior to the Maha Kumbh[57] at Prayag (Allahabad), an idea came to mind. I thought it would be interesting to reveal the pollution levels, during Maha Kumbh, at Sangam—the conglomerate of Ganga, Yamuna, and the mythical Saraswati at Allahabad. So, the focus was on procuring data on the two rivers, Ganga and Yamuna. This data was collated in an article published in *The Indian Express* on January 13, 2013, see Figure 6.1.

CPCB and the SPCBs of UP, Uttarakhand, West Bengal, Bihar, and Jharkhand were asked to provide the latest findings from their samples. Since the reports of first samples from most of the locations were already available on these rivers, what was needed was only new data. Because some SPCBs had not provided complete information, some data was taken from the affidavit filed by the CPCB before the Supreme Court in November 2012.[58] Keeping in mind the date of January 14, 2013, the first *Shahi Snan* (Holy Dip) at Maha Kumbh,[59] the story was planned to be published just before that, and, as it so happened, the story[60] was published in *The Indian Express* just a day ahead of the first Shahi Snan.

---

[56] Ibid.
[57] See http://kumbhmelaallahabad.gov.in/english/index.html, accessed December 29, 2016.
[58] Accessed copy from CPCB.
[59] See http://kumbhmelaallahabad.gov.in/english/index.htm, accessed December 29, 2016.
[60] "What was once a river…," *The Indian Express* (New Delhi, January 13, 2013).

Figure 6.1:

What was once a river...

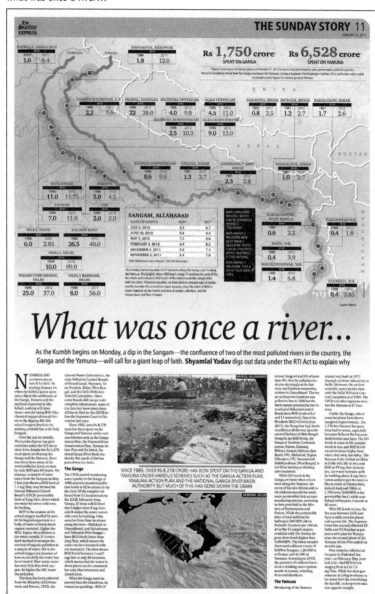

Source: The Indian Express (January 13, 2013).

The updated data from the latest responses of various departments revealed[61] that since 1985, over ₹82.78 billion had been spent on the Ganga and Yamuna under various schemes such as the GAP, the National River Conservation Plan, the Yamuna Action Plan, and the National Ganga River Basin Authority (NGRBA), but there was hardly any improvement in water quality.

The story of Ganga emerged from the data collected by the CPCB that, at the time of responding to queries, was monitoring pollution levels at 62 locations along the river. Of the samples collected from 51 locations along the 2,525-km-long Ganga, 22 showed a BOD level that was higher than 3 mg/liter, which makes the water unsuitable even for bathing.[62] At 26 locations, BOD levels were between 2 and 3 mg/liter, which means that the water in these places could be consumed, but only after treatment and disinfection. Only samples from three locations along the river— Rishikesh in Uttarakhand, and Nabadweep and Tribeni in West Bengal—had BOD levels lower than 2 mg/liter, which means the water was fit to be consumed without treatment.[63]

It was clear from the data that when Ganga starts its journey from the Himalayas, its waters are sparkling clean—BOD of zero at Gangotri and DO of more than 10—but the pollution levels rise alarmingly at the Raiwala and Hardwar monitoring stations in Uttarakhand. The water at even these two locations was pollution-free in 1986, but the latest reports provided by the Uttarakhand State Pollution Control Board had shown BOD levels of 6.4 and 12 respectively. Except for Rishikesh (BOD of 0.6 in June 2011), besides Gangotri, the Ganga had high levels of pollution all the way up to Diamond Harbour in West Bengal. Going by the parameters of BOD levels, the Ganga at Hardwar, Garhmukteswar, Narora, Kannauj, Bithoor, Kanpur, Dalmau (Rae Bareli, UP), Allahabad, Trighat (Ghazipur, UP), Varanasi, and Dakshineshwar (West Bengal) was not fit for drinking even after treatment, and not fit even for bathing. Yamuna was found to be worst between Delhi and Agra.

Interestingly, four samples collected at Sangam in Allahabad in February, May, June, and July 2012 had BOD levels ranging

---

[61] Ibid.
[62] Ibid.
[63] Ibid.

from 4.2 to 7.3 mg/liter.[64] This is the spot where many millions of people take a holy dip during the Kumbh Mela. This story was just to remind our faithful devotees of the holy dip at Sangam that if we do not change our attitude toward rivers, there will be a day when they will not find even dirty water to take a holy dip. It is shameful for us that we drink mineral water and offer this dirty water to our ancestors standing in holy rivers. We need to be most sensitive toward our rivers.

A New Beginning

Even before it came to power, the NDA, in its election campaign, had promised to take up the Ganga cleaning project on a priority basis. On assuming office in May 2014, the new government appointed Uma Bharti as minister of the newly created Ministry of Water Resources, River Development and Ganga Rejuvenation which has a mandate to clean the Ganga and its tributaries. The union cabinet approved the flagship "Namami Gange"[65] Programme with a budget outlay of ₹200 billion for 5 years, to clean and protect the Ganga river. It is a 100 percent centrally funded scheme.[66]

Earlier, when it was launched in 1985, the NRCP,[67] from which the present scheme has been segregated, had a 50:50 budget allocation between central and state governments. In 1997 it was converted to a 100 percent centrally funded scheme, but in 2001 it was re-converted to 70:30 between central and state governments (for new schemes) while 100 percent central funding continued for old projects.

By a notification dated July 31, 2014, the Ganga, along with its tributaries[68] Yamuna, Gomti, Damodar, Mahananda, Chambal, Beehar, Khan, Kshipra, Betwa, Ramganga, and Mandakini was

---

[64] Ibid.
[65] Union Cabinet decision on May 13, 2015.
[66] Ibid.
[67] Response dated December 10, 2008, from MoEF to author on RTI.
[68] See http://wrmin.nic.in/forms/list.aspx?lid=277, accessed December 29, 2016.

shifted to the newly created Ministry of Water Resources, River Development and Ganga Rejuvenation.

Prime Minister Narendra Modi has emphasized that the first goal of the project should be to stop all pollutants from entering the river, be it industrial effluents, domestic sewage, or religious offerings. But the top body to clean river Ganga, the NGRBA, seems to be struggling to take off. After being pulled up by the Supreme Court, the Central Government assured the court that the Ganga will be cleaned within a period of 18 years.[69] It is estimated to cost ₹510 billion.

We can only hope we don't see the billions flow down the 'drain' all over again. Usually the data accessed from the authorities would have not been considered newsy by many, but this effort has proved that data accessed can be made newsy and create and impact. RTI proved to be very helpful in all these efforts as it was not easy to approach all involved authorities to access such complicated data to make a readable story if the RTI Act was not there.

---

[69] See http://indianexpress.com/article/india/india-others/ganga-clean-up-to-take-18-years-says-centre/, accessed December 29, 2016.

7

Personnel in Personal Staff of MPs: All in Family

Moral and ethical concerns of the society weigh a great deal with those in public life as their behaviors is keenly watched by the people.... Members are expected to maintain high standards of morality, dignity, decency and values in public life.[1]

—Ethics Committee of the Rajya Sabha, headed by late S.B. Chavan, first report on December 8, 1998 (adopted by the Rajya Sabha on December 15, 1998)

Table 7.1:
Highlights of RTIs filed for information on Ministers' personal staff and MP's guests

Information	Ministers' and MPs' personal staff; MPs' guests
Authority	Lok Sabha and Rajya Sabha secretariats, Department of Personnel and Training (DoPT)
Problems	Both secretariats provided a list of personal staff, but finding out their relation with MPs was a tricky job. Likewise, both secretariats provided a list of MPs' guests but it was difficult to find out who were those guests
Applications and appeals	Three, for three stories (Excluding those filed for the follow-up and other related stories)
Time taken	Over four months
Stories	It's All in Family...*The Indian Express*, May 15, 2013; Despite DoPT ban...*The Indian Express*, July 29, 2013; MPs' guests, ex-MPs...*The Indian Express*, September 3, 2013
Impact	Rajya Sabha Ethics Committee passed a resolution to stop appointing relatives as PAs. Initially, guest accommodations were also in talk. New government under Narendra Modi asked ministers not to appoint persons who have served 10 years in personal staff.

(Continued)

---

[1] See http://rajyasabha.nic.in/rsnew/publication_electronic/ethics_committee.pdf, accessed December 27, 2016.

(Continued)

Follow-up by me	Several more applications were filed to know the follow-up action from Lok Sabha, Rajya Sabha, and also in DoPT.
Follow-up by others	All three stories were widely followed up by other media.

Source: Author.

Much of the performance of and the perception about any political leader depend on what type of persons are there in his/her personal staff. Once I did a story in *India Today* (Hindi) based on informal research about the personal staff of union ministers. The bottom line of the story was that there are a few dozen faces moving around in Delhi who were originally employed in different departments, but be it any regime and no matter which party is in power, these same individuals get employed with certain union ministers as their personal staff because they know how to manage all requirements of their bosses.

On July 22, 2008, a total of 11 MPs (10 from the Lok Sabha and 1 from the Rajya Sabha) were allegedly caught on camera by a private television channel while demanding money for asking questions in Parliament.[2] When this 'cash for query' scandal broke and some MPs were suspended as a result, I began seeking out facts about the personal staff of MPs. Getting deeper into the issue, these are some of the questions that came up and prompted me to find out who are the personal staff of MPs, where do they come from, who appoints them, do their appointments stand to scrutiny, what are their remunerations, and how long do their tenures last.

After trying for the information informally, the shelter was taken under the transparency law and, in the process, many interesting facts came out about the lives of ministers and MPs, and their staff.

On the other hand, years later, toward the beginning of 2013, using the RTI Act, the DoPT was asked for the copies of circulars pertaining to appointment of the personal staff of ministers with details of ceilings enforced and the relaxations granted to persons violating those ceilings. Information was provided by the DoPT which said a 10-year ceiling was imposed in March 2010

---

[2] This incident was widely covered in the media.

and that only the PMO had the authority to give relaxation to it. The DoPT also said that 87 requests for relaxation of those ceilings were approved since they were made applicable. According to the DoPT, despite having completed their prescribed tenure, 87 people continued to serve as personal staff of various ministers, after their appointments were cleared by the PMO.[3] This was published in *The Indian Express*.[4] In April 2013, the Appointment Committee of Cabinet (ACC) had apparently decided[5] to retain officials who had completed 10 years till the completion of the General Elections 2014, obviously due to requests from ministers so that they could continue their work unhampered. See Figure 7.1 for the story published in *The Indian Express*.

Figure 7.1:
Despite DoPT ban, ministers retain personal staff for over 10 years

Despite DoPT ban, ministers retain personal staff for over 10 years

SHYAMLAL YADAV
NEW DELHI, JULY 28

IN March 2010, the Department of Personnel and Training (DoPT) had directed that "a total ceiling of 10 years be prescribed beyond which an officer may not be permitted to be appointed in the personal staff of a minister, irrespective of level". But, despite having completed the prescribed tenure, at least 87 people continued to serve as personal staff of various ministers, after their appointments were cleared by the Prime Minister's Office (PMO) following requests from the ministries.

Among the ministers who sent such requests are Kamal Nath, Praful Patel, Sushil Kumar Shinde, K Rahman Khan, Jyotiraditya Scindia, Bharatsinh Solanki, K V Thomas, Mallikarjun Kharge, Salman Khurshid and Tusharbhai Chaudhary. The officials included six officers on special duty (U K Mitra, N K Gauri, V K Dhand, S V Pillai, S N Sharma and Giri Ketharaj) and three private secretaries (Z A Naqvi, D Vijayan and M Annadurai). Among the others are 29 additional private secretaries and 24 assistant private secretaries. Some of these officers are now no longer with the ministries.

In April this year, the Appointments Committee of the Cabinet also decided to retain officials who had completed 10 years as personal staff "till the completion of the next general elections".

According to information provided by the DoPT under the RTI Act, many requests were received from various ministries to allow some officials to continue as personal staff after the ceiling was imposed. Of these, 87 requests were approved. However, the DoPT circular directed that "no relaxation will be granted to these conditions".

Source: The Indian Express (July 29, 2013).

My initial efforts in this regard date back to 2005 when the story was published in *India Today* (Hindi) under the title "*Hasti Mitati Nahi Hamari*."[6] The story pertained to those working as personal

---

[3] Response of DoPT—dated June 24, 2013; February 20, 2013; and March 22, 2013 to author.

[4] "Despite DoPT ban, ministers retain personal staff for over 10 years," *The Indian Express* (New Delhi, July 29, 2013), http://archive.indianexpress.com/news/despite-dopt-ban-ministers-retain-personal-staff-for-over-10-years/1148057/, accessed December 27, 2016.

[5] DoPT informed vide letter, dated April 2, 2013, to author on RTI.

[6] "Hasti Mitati Nahi Hamari," by Shyamlal Yadav, *India Today* (Hindi), February 7, 2005.

staff to ministers and profiled many such persons employed in various departments who, once they joined the ministers' staff, had never returned to their parent services. Even if some had for a short period, they had managed to get readjusted with new ministers very soon. There are many such instances of people who have served over 20 ministers and boast unabashedly of their capabilities and dedication to their job.

Official Lives of MPs and Their Entourage

The Members of Parliament (Office Expense Allowance) Rules, 1988 (as amended up to December 13, 2010) says:[7]

> A member shall be entitled to receive office expense allowance under Section 8 of the Act at the rate of rupees forty five thousand per mensem, out of which- (a) Rupees fifteen thousand shall be for meeting expenses on stationery item and postage; and (b) the Lok Sabha or the Rajya Sabha Secretariat may pay up to rupees thirty thousand to the person(s) as may be engaged by a Member for obtaining Secretarial assistance and one such person shall be computer literate duly certified by the Member.

The rules are clear that MPs are not prohibited from appointing anyone from their family or close relatives for secretarial assistance. Therefore, if any MP appoints his/her relatives or family members, he/she is certainly not violating any rules. But let's not forget that India is a democracy where, on an average, a Lok Sabha MP is a representative of around 1.32 million voters.[8] During the 2009 general elections, there were 716.9 million voters registered[9] (though new figures are more than that, 2009 figures are used here because Lok Sabha MPs were elected in that 2009 general election). With 58.19 percent, that is, 417 million total votes polled, each constituency polled 767,000 votes on an average. If around

---

[7] See http://rajyasabha.nic.in/rsnew/msa_section/mpsalary.pdf, accessed December 27, 2016.
[8] Based on total voters registered during 2009 Lok Sabha elections.
[9] See http://eci.nic.in/eci_main/archiveofge2009/Stats/VOLI/05_StateWiseNumber OfElectors.pdf, accessed December 27, 2016.

30 percent votes polled were in favor of the winning candidate, it would imply that the said MP is voted by over 230,000 voters. Let us suppose that during their election campaign there were more than 200 who actively worked for those MPs and they must have been in their core group during election campaign. In cadre-based parties such as BJP and Communist parties, there is a chunk of dedicated workers who work for their party, without considering the party candidate. Sadly, though, after winning the elections, everybody among them is ignored and every post gets gradually captured by the MP's family members and relatives.

Appointing their relatives as their secretarial and personal assistants (PAs) reveals a lack of moral or ethical character. Since there is no limit to how many persons can be appointed as their assistants, many MPs were found to be appointing more than one.

So what happens to their reimbursements? Do they get divided? This thought would come to mind whenever one visits North Avenue and South Avenue, where many MPs live. One day, one of my sources told that while he works full time for his MP, he is given only half of his salary of ₹30,000. When he was asked what happens to the other half, he said that it is given to the MP's son who he has appointed as his other assistant, but who does not work. This astonishing fact impelled to further follow up on the matter.

On February 1, 2013, separate applications were filed to the secretariats of the Lok Sabha and the Rajya Sabha to get the list of persons appointed as secretarial assistants to MPs.

Both secretariats forwarded the list of such persons[10] after receiving the mandatory fee for photocopying. But the information was inadequate and not good enough for journalistic use. Therefore, a hunt started to get more information—a pursuit that was not possible through only RTI. After getting the directories of MPs of both Houses, I started calling them up personally, one-by-one. Picking each name given in the list of secretarial assistants provided by the secretariat, they were asked who he/she was. This was very tedious as almost all MPs were called, except 67 which were then union ministers. Majority of the MPs from the list of 543 from the Lok Sabha and 245 from the Rajya Sabha,

---

[10] Vide Rajya Sabha response dated March 15, 2013, and Lok Sabha response dated March 14, 2013.

(except vacancies and also union ministers) were called. By the end, after making calls to over 700 MPs, many did not cooperate, instead counter-questioned me about my credentials and the purpose of my query.

To get around this problem, I tried another ploy and started calling up their local landline numbers given in the directory. Fortunately, most of the MPs do not attend calls themselves and the persons who did so were naive enough to reveal the relationship of the secretarial assistants without querying too much. But some of the MPs who lived out of town created a problem. For instance, when I called the local landline number of Saifuddin Soz in Srinagar, he himself picked up the phone:[11] When I asked him for the name of his first secretarial assistant he said that he was his grandson. But when I enquired about the number two person in the list of his assistants, he countered, *"Aap kaun bol rahe hain* (Who is speaking)?" I introduced myself, but he again asked, "What will you do with this fact?" I replied, "I want to prepare a small profile of every MP." To which he replied: "How is my granddaughter concerned with my profile? Give me your number. I will be coming to Delhi day after so please meet me." I gave my number and said, "OK janab. Thanks." He had inadvertently given the answer in his confusion and confirmed that the second person was his granddaughter. There were some instances of threats and rude responses from MPs but I was only concerned with my story.

Finally, after collating the information, the story was published in *The Indian Express.*[12] This was the gist of the story:

At least 146 MPs—104 from the Lok Sabha and 42 from the Rajya Sabha—had appointed at least 191 relatives in their personal staff.... This army of family PAs includes 60 sons, 36 wives, 27 daughters, one father, seven brothers, seven daughters-in-law, four husbands and 10 cousins, among others.... Of the 146 MPs employing close relatives as PAs, 38 were from the BJP, 36 from Congress, 15 from BSP, 12 from Samajwadi Party, eight from DMK, seven from Biju Janata Dal, six from JD (U) and the rest from other parties.... Of these, 36 MPs had appointed more than one relative

---

[11] Author's own records.
[12] See http://archive.indianexpress.com/news/rs-ethics-panel-to-take-up-issue-of-mps-employing-relatives-as-pas/1116541/, accessed December 27, 2016.

as PA while at least four had appointed three family members as their personal staff.

There were instances where MPs had appointed a family member as one PA, paying them a large portion of the ₹30,000 monthly entitlement; and a nonfamily member as another PA (PA in the real sense) for the remaining, smaller amount.

It would be prudent to mention here that the Ethics Committee of the Rajya Sabha had presented its first report on December 8, 1998 (which was adopted by the Rajya Sabha on December 15, 1998), in which it was said, "Members are expected to maintain high standards of morality, dignity, decency and values in public life."[13] The first report of the Ethics Committee of the Lok Sabha, headed by former Prime Minister Chandra Shekhar, presented in November 2001, had also said, "Members should maintain high standards of morality, dignity, decency and values in public life."[14]

It was expected that issues raised in the story would get attention. Other media, including electronic and print, did follow-up stories. While the Ethics Committee of the Rajya Sabha reacted, the Lok Sabha Ethics Committee did nothing. When the story appeared on May 16, 2013, the Chairman of the Rajya Sabha Ethics Committee, Ram Gopal Yadav, stated[15] that he would take "suo motu cognizance" of the report and raise the issue before the Ethics Committee, and that his committee would take some decision. He went on to add:[16] "This practice is ethically incorrect.... The provision envisages employing people with secretarial skills, certainly not relatives. Employing relatives is wrong.... Parties should impose a code against this practice, and consider promoting party workers to these jobs." Ram Gopal Yadav, an MP from the SP, also declared[17] that he would seek his party leader Mulayam Singh Yadav's intervention to curb the practice among

---

[13] See http://rajyasabha.nic.in/rsnew/publication_electronic/ethics_committee.pdf, accessed December 27, 2016.
[14] See http://164.100.47.134/lsscommittee/Ethics/13_Ethics_1.pdf, accessed December 27, 2016.
[15] "RS ethics panel to take up issue of MPs employing relatives as PAs," *The Indian Express* (May 16, 2013), http://archive.indianexpress.com/news/rs-ethics-panel-to-take-up-issue-of-mps-employing-relatives-as-pas/1116541/, accessed December 27, 2016.
[16] Ibid.
[17] Ibid.

his party MPs. He stated all this after the story was published. In fact, repeated calls were made to contact Ram Gopal Yadav on his various landline and mobile numbers and sent SMSs to get his version, being the Ethics Committee chairman, before publishing the story, but he had not responded to any of them. After publication of the story he called Ravish Tewari of *The Indian Express* and expressed his reaction on the story.

Five months after the publication of the story, on October 17, 2013, the Ethics Committee of Rajya Sabha passed a unanimous resolution[18] that members should not appoint their relatives as PAs. The Lok Sabha, on the other hand, is yet to take cognizance of the matter.

To get an official response from both secretariats, an application was filed on September 23, 2013 to the Lok Sabha (enclosing a copy of the published story) asking, "Whether Hon'ble Speaker/Chairman of Ethics Committee have taken cognizance of the news report attached herewith? If yes, provide the details thereof." The Secretariat was also requested to provide a copy of the agenda items of the Ethics Committee meetings held since May 2013. Similar queries were also sent to the Rajya Sabha Secretariat regarding action taken by its chairman/chairman of Ethics Committee.

The Lok Sabha Secretariat responded:

No information is available about cognizance taken on the said news reports by Hon'ble Speaker or Chairman of the Ethics Committee. Moreover, the points raised by the applicant are hypothetical in nature and do not construe information under section 2(f) of the RTI Act. No agenda for the last meeting of the Ethics Committee is available since no meeting of the Committee has been held since May 2013.[19]

In contrast, the Rajya Sabha Secretariat responded[20] with a one-liner, "It may be stated that Chairman, Committee on Ethics has taken cognizance of the issue." On his part, Hamid Ansari, the vice-president of India and chairman of the Rajya Sabha, stated

---

[18] "'Members mustn't appoint kin as PAs'," *The Indian Express* (October 31, 2013), http://archive.indianexpress.com/news/members-mustnt-appoint-kin-as-pas/1189371/, accessed December 27, 2016.
[19] In response to RTI application filed by the author.
[20] In letter, dated October 24, 2013, to author on RTI.

that the ethics committees should take a view on the issue of MPs' relatives working as their personal assistants, and that ethical issues are to be decided by these committees with the Chair having no role. He was returning from Addis Ababa (Ethiopia) on an Air India One special aircraft from an official visit and I was accompanying him, when I broached the subject with him personally, and he had responded: "Tell me, is there any law against it? On ethical issues, there is an ethics committee in the Rajya Sabha. These issues are decided by that committee."

On November 12, 2013, in response to a reminder that was sent on October 5, 2013 asking for the deliberations of the Ethics Committee meetings held since May 2013, the Rajya Sabha Secretariat responded:[21]

> The information sought relates to the proceedings of the meetings of the Committee of Ethics. As per the Direction 55(1) of the Speaker, Lok Sabha, read with provisions laid down under subsection (1)(c) of section 8 of the RTI Act, only the information of the meetings of the Committee on Ethics which is included in the Report presented to the Council of States, could be divulged. It may be informed that in the recent past the Committee on Ethics has not presented any Report to the Council of States. Hence, the information sought by the applicant cannot be divulged.

Aware that many Rajya Sabha members were yet to remove their relatives as their assistants, another application was filed asking about the implementation of the Ethics Committee resolution. In a noncommittal reply, the Rajya Sabha responded:[22]

> It is informed that Committee on Ethics in its meeting held on October 17, 2013 inter-alia authorized Chairman of the Committee to convey a message, recommended by the Committee concerning ethical issues raised on alleged appointment of relatives by the Members of Parliament as their Personal Assistants to leaders of various political parties in Rajya Sabha. Leaders of Parties were informed, accordingly, by the Chairman of the Committee...No further action was proposed on this issue.

---

[21] Response dated November 18, 2013 to author on RTI.
[22] Response dated August 27, 2014 of Rajya Sabha to author on RTI.

In an interesting aside, the grapevine has it that when Prime Minister Narendra Modi read a news item that a BJP MP Priyanka Rawat had appointed her father Uttam Ram, as her representative in her constituency on May 26, 2014, he spoke to her, and on June 2, 2014 the MP withdrew her father's name and said, "My father or kin will not be appointed as my representative." This posture of the prime minister got headlines in several newspapers.

Soon after taking charge, the Narendra Modi government issued three successive circulars relating to appointments of personal staff of union ministers that left many ministers uncomfortable. Those who had imprudently identified officials and persons of their choice for their personal staff were told to hold back. Many officials who had already started working informally with ministers, with the assurance of imminent formal appointment orders, were sent back to their parent cadres. Many others were working with their favorite ministers, but getting salaries from other departments.

A June 19, 2014 communiqué issued by the DoPT said:[23] "Any officer/official/private person, who has worked earlier in the personal staff of a minister in any capacity for any duration, may not be appointed in the personal staff of ministers in the present government." However, following persistent pressure from several quarters, the DoPT issued a clarification on July 8, saying that the June 19 circular "shall apply only in respect of Private Secretaries who had worked in the personal staff of any minister for any duration in the last 10 years."[24]

Later, the government came out with a further clarification. In its order dated July 23, 2014, the DoPT, which functions directly under Prime Minister Narendra Modi, clarified that the June 19, 2014 circular would be applicable "in respect of Private Secretary, OSD, Additional Private Secretary, Assistant Private Secretary and First PA who have worked in the personal staff of any minister for any duration during the last 10 years."[25] The government reiterated that an instruction issued by the UPA government that barred a person who had been on the personal staff of any

---

[23] DoPT's circular No. 8/50/2013-CS-II(C) dated June 19, 2014.
[24] DoPT's circular No. 81/17/2014-EO(MM-I) dated July 8, 2014.
[25] DoPT circular No. 8/50/2013-CS.II(C) dated July 23, 2014.

minister for 10 years of his/her career from further employment in a similar capacity would continue.

But if Modi had given a message by calling Priyanka Rawat for barring her from appointing her father as her representative, his party MPs must have taken it as a message and should have taken it forward. But practically, it has not shown any impact on MPs as it was limited to Priyanka Rawat only. Clearly, the circulars[26] issued by the Lok Sabha and Rajya Sabha secretariats after the 2014 general elections in this regard did not mention any such restriction on relatives. Although the authority to decide these things for Lok Sabha and Rajya Sabha members is not the PM, but at least his party (BJP) MPs must have been advised to follow his line.

Story of Minimum Wages

The MP's 'relatives' story had many other aspects that were worth exploring. Around six months after the 2014 general elections, a list of assistants of members of the Lok Sabha was obtained along with their salaries as recommended by the MPs. Also, the copies of forms submitted by MPs recommending who they wanted as their assistants were obtained. After analysis of both sets of papers, it was found that at least 186 MPs pay their personal assistants wages that are less than the minimum mandated by law in Delhi. There were at least 321 underpaid assistants in the employ of these MPs of both Houses.[27]

The prevailing minimum wage in Delhi for skilled labor was ₹10,478 at that time. But the MPs have been paying their 321 assistants ₹10,000 or less per month; some of the MPs' assistants were getting as little as ₹4,000, ₹3000, or even ₹2,000. These MPs cut across all party lines, ranging from the Left and Socialists to the BJP and Congress. The list included 69 BJP MPs, 35 from the Congress, 10 from the All India Anna Dravida Munnetra Kazhagam (AIADMK), 8 from the Communist Party of India

---

[26] Lok Sabha Secretariat's response, dated June 6 and July 4, 2014, and Rajya Sabha Secretariat's response, dated June 2, 2014, to author under RTI.
[27] See http://indianexpress.com/article/india/india-others/but-several-mps-pay-their-pas-less-than-the-minimum-wages/, accessed December 27, 2016.

[Marxist] (CPI [M]), 7 from the Biju Janta Dal (BJD), 4 from the Janta Dal [United] (JD [U]), and 2 from the CPI, among others. Isn't it an irony, and a sad commentary on our political system, that MPs who are the custodians of people's rights and are supposed to fight against the violation of rights of others are themselves found to be violating the rights of their assistants?

MP's Guests

Chapter 4 of the *Handbook for Members of the Rajya Sabha* says:[28]

> Members are allotted accommodation for their guests on payment of rent in advance normally in the Western Court Hostel where messing is compulsory and other facilities are also available. Guest accommodation is also allotted in V.P. House, North and South Avenues and Meena Bagh under very exceptional circumstances. The House Committee is aware that a good number of guests do come to Members particularly during Parliament Session.... The Hostel accommodation, if allotted will be retained for a maximum period of one week, unless extension is obtained in writing from the Chairman, House Committee, Rajya Sabha or the officer of the House Committee. The extension would not be allowed beyond one week...(iii) Unless extension is granted by the Chairman, House Committee, Rajya Sabha, the allotment of accommodation, if made, will stand cancelled automatically and the recoveries on account of rent etc. will be made from the Member through his salary/T.A./D.A. bills in case the payment of rent etc. is not made at the Hostel Counter.

Similar is for Lok Sabha members as well.[29]

But these facilities do not go to the ordinary guests of MPs in many cases, it would appear. MPs have been found frequently getting these houses in the heart of Delhi allotted to former MPs or letting their guests stay for years. Of the 51 such houses occupied

---

[28] See http://rajyasabha.nic.in/rsnew/handbook/chapter-4.pdf, accessed December 27, 2016.
[29] See http://164.100.47.192/loksabha/writereaddata/Members/Downloads/guest accommodation.pdf, accessed December 27, 2016.

by guests of MPs of both Houses of Parliament, at the time of the response to RTI applications, 38 were with former MPs.[30] Of the 106 allotments made since 2007 on the recommendations of 96 MPs, 14 were allotted without even mentioning the name of the guests.[31] Housing committees of both Houses allot such guest houses, but the list of guests provided by the Lok Sabha and the Rajya Sabha secretariats indicated that the guests were not voters and ordinary citizens of the constituencies of the members but were former MPs who did not want to leave Lutyens' Bungalow Zone even after they had lost the elections years or decades earlier.[32]

Consider These Facts:[33]

- Bhim Singh of the Jammu & Kashmir National Panthers Party has been a guest of MPs from several parties. He was in V.P. House as a guest of S.S. Ahluwalia of BJP from June 1, 2007 to August 17, 2010. Another BJP MP, Bhagat Singh Koshyari, got Bhim Singh a house from August 17, 2010 to March 2, 2013. Singh was also a guest of NCP MP D.P. Tripathi for three months from October 26, 2012 when he had already been given another house as Koshyari's guest. At the time my story was published, he was a guest of independent MP Om Prakash Yadav in a flat in V.P. House.
- Congress treasurer Motilal Vora seems to have been a generous host. His guests included former MP Dwijendra Nath Sharma, who has been in V.P. House since September 14, 2012 and former MP K.C. Lenka, who was in V.P. House from May 1, 2005 to February 21, 2013. Lenka got this extended until August 19, 2013, on the recommendation of Dhiraj Prasad Sahu. Anuradha Vyas, was allotted a house on South Avenue from February 9, 2008 to March 31, 2013 and Vidya Dwivedi, got a house in Meena Bagh from April

---

[30] "MPs' guests, ex-MPs squat for years in their Lutyens houses," *The Indian Express* (September 3, 2013), http://archive.indianexpress.com/news/mps-guests-exmps-squat-for-years-in-their-lutyens-houses/1163708/, accessed December 27, 2016.
[31] Ibid.
[32] Ibid.
[33] Ibid.

8, 2009 to June 30, 2013. Vora also got five houses for his guests on North Avenue from January 2008 to March 2013 without mentioning the names of the guests.

- Congress MP Deepender Hooda from Rohtak had a guest accommodation for his grandmother, Har Devi, in South Avenue since September 22, 2009.
- When Ram Vilas Paswan was a Rajya Sabha member, he had accommodated his brother Ram Chandra Paswan, a former MP, as his guest on South Avenue from July 25, 2011.
- Ramesh Chennithala, a former MP and former Kerala PCC President, had a flat in V.P. House from December 2006 to October 2012 as a guest of P.J. Kurien. He also had a house on North Avenue since October 2009 as a guest of N.S.V. Chittan.
- Former minister of state in the DoPT, Suresh Pachauri, was the guest of his successor V. Narayanasami, living on South Avenue from August 10, 2010.

To give priority to former MPs, the Rajya Sabha Housing Committee in its meeting held on November 19, 2009 approved a guideline[34] which says, "In the allotment of guest accommodation, priority will be given to the applicants, where the guest happens to be an ex-MP." It further relaxes the earlier guideline and says,[35]

Initially the guest accommodation would be allowed for a maximum period of 3 months only. However, extension beyond this period may be granted by Chairman, House Committee on valid grounds, for a maximum period of 90 days. In any case, request for extension will be processed only if the rent has been paid up to date.

In response to the fresh RTI application, the Lok Sabha Secretariat said,[36] "The guest accommodations in respect of MPs of the 14th and 15th Lok Sabha have been cancelled consequent upon dissolution of the 15th Lok Sabha. No such guest accommodation is being extended during the 16th Lok Sabha." It also added that

---

[34] Provided to author vide letter dated February 10, 2014 on RTI.
[35] Ibid.
[36] Letter dated September 30, 2014 to author on RTI.

litigation in respect of all guest accommodations had been filed with the directorate of estates. In response to a subsequent RTI application, the Rajya Sabha Secretariat said[37] that it has asked the directorate of estates to 'initiate eviction proceedings' against the overstaying 'guests' of MPs.

The facts exposed in the stories of the personal staff of ministers and MPs and guest houses were very difficult, if not impossible, to be broken without the RTI Act. These are examples how journalists, with the help of transparency law, can track the lives of the elected representatives.

---

[37] Letter dated September 12, 2014 to author on RTI.

8

Light Every Corner: RTI Everywhere in the Government

Citizens should not only have the right to get copies of documents but also ask question and demand accountability from public authorities, because the right to ask questions is the very foundation of democracy and it will reinforce their faith in democracy.... If we limit RTI just to reply to questions, there will be no changes in governance. We have to analyse the RTI questions and ponder whether there is need to make changes in policy matters.[1]

—Narendra Modi, Prime Minister, on annual CIC conference on October 16, 2015

Breaking of Jan Dhan Story

It was a usual meeting with one of the senior officers of a public sector bank. I met him after one of my friends, a former journalist, told me that he has some story. During the meeting while he discussed the infighting going on in his bank and Department of Financial Services, I told him that I will discuss the same with my editors and will revert. He seemed so desperate for the said issue that he told me that he will give me another big story once I will do the story he was discussing. I asked him, "What is that?" In response, he gave me some tip off that billions of Jan Dhan accounts are being activated through ₹1 deposited by bank staffers.

Excited by the idea, I thought it would be a big story. Before discussing the same with my editors, I filed an RTI to all the public sector banks, including Bhartiya Mahila Banks, asking

---

[1] "Open up for trust, learn from RTI," *The Indian Express* (New Delhi, October 17, 2015); See the full speech: http://pib.nic.in/newsite/erelease.aspx, accessed December 27, 2016.

them for the total number of Jan Dhan account/total number of
Jan Dhan accounts opened by male/total number of Jan Dhan
accounts opened by female/total number of Jan Dhan accounts
that have zero balance/total number of Jan Dhan accounts where
total deposited amount is ₹1/total number of Jan Dhan accounts
where total deposited amount is ₹2–10/total number of Jan Dhan
accounts where total deposited amount is ₹11–20/total number of
Jan Dhan accounts where total deposited amount is ₹21–50/total
number of Jan Dhan accounts where total deposited amount is
₹51–100/total number of Jan Dhan accounts where total deposited
amount is more than ₹100. Few days later, I filed another round
of same applications with the banks asking about the same information with regard to regional rural banks working under them.
In addition, e-mail requests were sent to 10 major private sector
banks. While none of the private banks reverted to my e-mails,
responses from several other banks started arriving. A glimpse of
the story published can be seen in Figure 8.1.

The very first response was from Canara Bank, which was
encouraging as almost 10 percent of Jan Dhan accounts were
shown having total deposited amount of ₹1. When discussed with
the editors, they showed the same excitement and I was asked
to travel and meet the account holders of the accounts where ₹1
was deposited. The first visit I made was to Bareilly in UP where
I approached one of my friends, an officer, to arrange my visit in
some village. During my visit to Purnapur, a village around 20
kilometers from Bareilly city, I landed at the residence of village
Pradhan. On my request, the Pradhan arranged around 40 passbooks of Jan Dhan account holders, and very soon I found around
20 among them with no entries of any transaction. These all were
from Punjab and Sind Bank's nearby branch at Dhaurera Mafi,
nearly five kilometer from the village. On my request, Pradhan
sent two villagers with these 20 passbooks to the branch to get
them updated. When they returned, I found the entries of ₹1
deposited in seven accounts, and account holders told me that
they never deposited that amount. That was pretty exciting for
me, and I realized it will be easy to find out what I was looking for.

Interestingly, while sitting at Pradhan's home, I met the branch
manager of a nearby branch of Baroda Uttar Pradesh Gramin
Bank. It was a coincidence that I was there when he visited to persuade villagers about bank schemes. I was sitting by his side and,

Figure 8.1:
The one-rupee trick

AN EXPRESS INVESTIGATION

The One-Rupee Trick: How banks cut their zero-balance Jan Dhan accounts

Flagship scheme brings range of benefits to poor. There's a catch. Many officials are quietly depositing Re 1 from their pockets to erase zero-balance accounts — and dress up the data

SHYAMLAL YADAV &
JAY MAZOOMDAAR
NEW DELHI, SEPTEMBER 12

IN AUGUST 2014, a few weeks after the launch of Jan Dhan, the government's flagship scheme under which the unbanked get bank accounts, Kamlesh, a housewife at Purnapur village in Uttar Pradesh's Bareilly, opened an account at the Punjab and Sind Bank's local branch.

Wife of a farmer, the opening balance in her account was zero. This wasn't unusual — in fact, accounts like Kamlesh's, called zero-balance accounts, made up almost half of all the 17.90 crore Jan Dhan accounts a year later given that most of the holders were poor and had little by way of savings.

But on August 5 this year, when Kamlesh got her passbook updated, she was in for a surprise.

"Re 1 had been deposited in my account on September 29, 2015. I didn't deposit the money, I don't know where it came from. I will ask the bank about this," she said.

It's not just Kamlesh, and it's not just that branch in Bareilly, or even that bank.

Investigating information obtained from more than 30 nationalised and regional rural banks under the Right to Information (RTI) Act, *The Indian Express* went to more than 25 villages and cities spread across six states, checked individual passbooks and interviewed account holders.

To find that bank officials are quietly making one-rupee deposits, many from their own allowances, some from money kept aside for office maintenance.

Their ostensible goal: to reduce the branch's tally of zero-balance accounts.

CONTINUED ON PAGE 2

Passbooks with deposits of ₹1 at the office of a bank agent in Barh, Bihar. *Shyamlal Yadav*

THE INVESTIGATION

82 Banks
were approached under RTI Act, including regional rural banks

34 Banks
responded with data on Jan Dhan deposits

6 States
25 villages and 4 cities visited by Express

52
account holders were interviewed, most of them with ₹1 deposited without their knowledge

ZERO-BALANCE DOWN

August 28, 2014
LAUNCH OF PRIME MINISTER'S JAN DHAN YOJANA

17.90 cr

8.40 cr

August 26, 2015

24.10 cr

5.87 cr

August 31, 2016

■ Number of Jan Dhan Accounts
■ Number of 0 balance accounts

₹42094 cr
Total amount deposited in Jan Dhan accounts (Aug 31, 2016)

Source: The Indian Express (September 13, 2016).

without introducing myself, informally discussed with him the Jan Dhan scheme. Interestingly, he told me that there were hundreds of accounts where he had deposited ₹1. That was another confirmation. I visited another village, Fatehganj West, where one of my friends, who happens to be an officer, had arranged a meeting with some 30 farmers who were waiting for me with their Jan Dhan passbooks. There also I found a case, but really only one and that was from Punjab National Bank (PNB).

Next day, I visited three villages in Meerut with one my friends, an Associate Professor in CCS University Meerut. In two villages, I did not get any such account having ₹1 deposit, but in Machhra village I found many and returned after interviewing half a dozen account holders. Then, after a few days, I visited Etawah where efforts were not fruitful in three branches of separate banks. So, a little disappointed, I returned to Mathura the next day where I visited Naujhil town. I got a tip off from one of my friends in Delhi that Syndicate Bank's Naujhil branch has several such Jan Dhan accounts where ₹1 has been deposited. I visited two nearby villages with one of my local sources to collect passbooks of account holders having Jan Dhan account in Syndicate Bank, Naujhil branch. But, after coming back to the branch when the passbooks were updated, no such cases were found there as well. I encountered similar disappointments in Delhi's resettlement colonies Trilokpuri and Narela and some localities in Faridabad in Haryana. I had requested many of my friends to find out such accounts in Bilaspore and Raipur (Chhattisgarh), Chandigarh, Mumbai, Faridabad and Gurgaon (Haryana), Warangal (Telangana), Madurai (Tamil Nadu), Vadodara (Gujarat), Bhopal, Indore and Gwalior (MP), Lucknow and Allahabad (UP), Delhi and some other places but except few there were no good results. As per the information provided by some of them, they were aware that this is happening but were unable to find instances and details.

I travelled to Guwahati (Assam), Barh and Patna (Bihar), and Bhopal (MP), and details from Durg (Chhattisgarh) were arranged through one of my sources. In Guwahati, I visited a branch of Punjab & Sind Bank with one of my old friends and asked a bank official for the details of some Jan Dhan accounts where the balance is zero. Interestingly, he responded, "We have no zero balance accounts. We put ₹5 in all such accounts where the balance was zero." So, while I was satisfied with his answer, I asked the details of some of such accounts where the bank staff had deposited ₹5. He provided me the names and contact numbers of around 80 such account holders. I followed those addresses, located some of them, interviewed, and took their pictures with their passbooks. None of them were aware who deposited ₹5 in their accounts and how. In addition, while having tea from a tea vendor, Ajit Kumar Das, I asked whether he had a Jan Dhan account. When he said, yes, I asked him for his passbook which has no entries. I was sipping tea and requested him to go to the branch and get the passbook updated. He went there on his bicycle and returned very soon with the updated passbook which was reflecting credit of only ₹1 in his account, which was a value addition to my list.

From Guwahati I landed in Bihar and approached some senior officials of different banks in Patna. Interestingly, I met officers from four banks who confirmed that the story I was following was true, but they did not cooperate with the details of their own banks. They wanted the story to be broken out but keeping their banks out of it. So, I did not waste much time on them. Next day, I was heading toward Barh, where I had lined up some sources through some of my friends in Delhi. I stayed in a settlement of Musahar community in the outskirts of Patna. I entered in a government primary school where four teachers were sitting in a room and children were murmuring. Through the teachers, I called parents of some students with their Jan Dhan passbooks. Many of these passbooks reflected zero balance, and I sent them to nearby branch of Bank of India to get their passbooks updated but coincidently no passbook was found with such ₹1, ₹2 or ₹5 entries. I thanked the teachers and parents and moved towards Barh. In Barh, I found hundreds of passbooks lying at a PNB banking agent's kiosk. When asked if there are any passbooks where bank staff had put their own money, the agent responded that the passbooks lying there are only those types of passbooks. This agent helped me to call over to his kiosk some of the account holders who told me that they were not aware of the deposits made in their accounts. Through some of my friends in Delhi, I had lined up many contacts in other parts of Bihar as well, but I wanted to increase number of states. So, after getting bulk of such cases from Barh, I returned to Delhi.

I spent three days in Delhi's Trilokpuri, Bhalswa Dairy, and Narela areas with the help of some of my local friends. I checked over 300 passbooks in these areas and got them updated, if they were not updated, but none of them were helpful in my story. Many of my friends, who are bank officials in some banks, told me that it is a prevailing situation in their banks as well, but did not cooperate when I requested for the details of some accounts.

When I reached Bhopal, my friend, Sandeep Pathak, had already arranged two passbooks with deposit of ₹2 and had located account holders as well. But, from the city, I decided to go to some rural areas. I took help from another friend who connected me to a local official of MP Police who gave me some contacts in Raatibad, a village nearly 25 kilometer from Bhopal city. When I reached a newly settled area and inquired, I found several passbooks and many of them were reflecting a deposit of ₹1; even one of the passbooks had ₹0.10 entry. After interviewing half a dozen such account holders from this state, I returned to Delhi again. My colleague, Jay Mazoomdaar, visited Rajasthan and returned with details of many Jan Dhan accounts with total deposit of ₹1.

Along with all these travels, the information on my RTI applications filed with banks started coming one by one. Since most of them were online, I continued to compile all that information in one Excel file for further analysis. Numbers were telling the whole story; some of the examples are as follows:

- PNB said that out of their 13.6 million Jan Dhan accounts till the date of response on my RTI, 3.957 million accounts had total deposited amount just ₹1 each and further 722,000 accounts had total deposited amount of just ₹2–10.
- Bank of India had 13.4 million Jan Dhan Accounts out of which 449,000 accounts were having just ₹1 each and other 2.698 million accounts were having deposited amount of ₹2–10.
- Vijaya Bank had 1.414 million Jan Dhan accounts by that time, and while 183,000 had ₹1 deposit, other 136,000 accounts were with deposit of ₹2–10 only.
- State Bank of Bikaner and Jaipur had 3.646 million Jan Dhan accounts out of which over 80,000 accounts had ₹1 and other over 76,000 had ₹2–10 deposited amount.
- Dena Bank had 3.314 million Jan Dhan accounts by that time out of which 163,000 accounts had ₹1 and other over 92,000 accounts had ₹2–10 as deposited amount.
- In UCO Bank's around 7.461 million Jan Dhan accounts, over 1.106 million accounts had ₹1 and other 156,000 accounts had ₹2–10 as deposited amount.
- Bank of Baroda had 14 million Jan Dhan accounts by the time out of which 1.297 million accounts had ₹1 deposited amount and other 718,000 accounts had total deposited amount of ₹2–10.

- In Syndicate Bank's 4.058 million total Jan Dhan accounts, over 96,000 had ₹1 and other over 72,000 accounts had deposited amount of just ₹2–10.
- Allahabad Banks had a total of 5.094 million Jan Dhan accounts by that time out of which as many as 334,000 accounts had ₹1 deposited amount. Moreover, there were 796,000 lakh accounts where the deposited amount was ₹2–10.

I was excited with all this information coming one by one. However, some of the banks had chosen not to respond to my RTI application and some of them denied providing the information by saying that the information is confidential and not possible to give. The information coming from the regional rural banks was more exciting. Some of the information received is as follows:

- In Karnataka Vikas Grameena Bank, it has been found that out of total 1.333 million Jan Dhan accounts, 218,000 were such where total deposited amount was just ₹1 while in other over 12,000 accounts, the total deposited amount was between ₹2–10.
- In Baroda Uttar Pradesh Gramin Bank, the total number of Jan Dhan accounts was 1.485 million and 283,000 accounts were with the total deposited amount of just ₹1 and other over 63,000 were with ₹2–10.
- In Baroda Gujarat Gramin Bank, out of total 392,000 Jan Dhan accounts, over 51,000 accounts were with just ₹1 total deposit and other over 6,000 were with ₹2–10 deposited amount.
- In Baroda Rajasthan Kshetriya Gramin Bank, the total number of Jan Dhan accounts was 2.466 million out of which over 414,000 accounts were with deposited amount of ₹1 and other over 42,000 accounts with ₹2–10.
- In Saptagiri Grameena Bank's 121,000 total Jan Dhan accounts, 10,827 were with the deposit of ₹1 and other 1,336 were with the deposit of ₹2–10.
- In Jharkhand Gramin Bank's 403,000 total Jan Dhan accounts, deposit of just ₹1 was found in as many as 63,503 accounts and in other 64,303 accounts, total deposited amount was just ₹2–10.

- In Bihar Gramin Bank's 607,000 lakh Jan Dhan accounts, as many as 69,973 were with ₹1 deposit and other 85,754 were with deposited amount of just ₹2–10.
- The total Jan Dhan accounts in Gramin Bank of Aryavart were 1.339 million. While 159,000 accounts had ₹1 deposited amount, other 133,000 accounts had deposited amount of just ₹2–10.

The story was based on RTI data along with the groundwork published in *The Indian Express* dated September 13, 2016.[2] Same day several political parties in the opposition,[3] including Congress, Janta Dal (United), and CPI (M), attacked the government for the same. The next day, Union Finance Ministry issued a statement[4] that the matter is being looked into. Two days later, there was a meeting of chiefs of banks, and after that Finance Minister Arun Jaitley said[5] that four banks have been asked to inquire into the matter. Jaitley said that banks will submit their reports within 10 days, but the reports never came out. The story had the desired impact: When Prime Minister Narendra Modi announced demonetization of ₹500 and ₹1000 banknotes on November 8, 2016, from the very next day reports started coming out that Jan Dhan accounts were being used to park money by some, hence the deposits in Jan Dhan accounts started increasing.

After the publication of the story, a clarification was sought by the PMO from the Department of Financial Services (DFS). In response, a statement, based on the banks' clarifications, was prepared by the DFS on September 27, 2016 for the PMO.[6] The DFS

---

[2] See http://indianexpress.com/article/business/banking-and-finance/how-banks-cut-their-zero-balance-jan-dhan-accounts-one-rupee-trick-3028190/, accessed February 20, 2017.

[3] See http://indianexpress.com/article/india/india-news-india/jan-dhan-yojana-zero-balance-account-investigation-opposition-want-answers-inquiry-3029927/, accessed February 20, 2017.

[4] See http://indianexpress.com/article/business/banking-and-finance/one-rupee-deposits-zero-balance-account-jan-dhan-pm-modi-finding-facts-says-govt-3031771/, accessed February 20, 2017.

[5] See http://indianexpress.com/article/india/india-news-india/four-banks-looking-into-jandhan-account-deposits-arun-jaitley-3034210/, accessed February 20, 2017.

[6] See http://indianexpress.com/article/business/banking-and-finance/1-rupee-jan-dhan-trick-some-banks-admit-others-vow-tighter-vigil-zero-banalnce-

had once proposed to issue a press release on the clarifications received by the banks, but the idea was dropped later on.[7] A joint secretary of the DFS noted on the file on September 27, 2016:

> It is pertinent to mention here that in few of the cases of Bank of Baroda and Bank of India, deposit of ₹1 has been done which has been accepted by the banks concerned. Action needs to be taken as deemed fit in these cases so that in future such incidents are not repeated.[8]

The DFS statement to the PMO stated, "Bank of Baroda has informed that 2 per cent of PMJDY (Pradhan Mantri Jan Dhan Yojana) accounts have received ₹1 from P&L (Profit & Loss) Account. There are some cases in Bank of India where amount was transferred from BCs' (banking correspondents) account." Allahabad Bank said, "These accounts were opened in camp mode through various representatives like social bodies, village pradhan, NGOs, etc. Amount in these accounts were deposited by these representatives through the branch as these accounts were mobilised by them."[9] Bank of Baroda said,

> A sample verification of 3,799 Jan Dhan accounts covering 100 branches in Bihar, MP, Rajasthan, Chhattisgarh and UP were conducted. In two per cent of these accounts, cash was deposited by debiting P&L accounts. We sincerely regret the occurrence of this anomaly and shall ensure that suitable corrective action is taken.[10]

Bank of India said, "13.17 lakh accounts are funded by BC (banking correspondents) to keep the account active."[11] Bank of India also promised that it would "take all necessary steps to stop such practice in future."[12] Two account holders (one of Punjab National Bank and another of Bank of India) told that bank officials approached

---

modi-4468763/, accessed February 20, 2017.

[7] File notings accessed by the author from the DFS.

[8] Ibid.

[9] Under RTI Act, DFS provided the author copies of all these correspondence with PMO, DFS and various banks.

[10] Ibid.

[11] Ibid.

[12] Ibid.

them and were given a statement and asked to sign it.[13] They told the author that they signed the paper on which it was written that they themselves deposited the amount in their accounts.[14] Clearly, some banks tried to cover up the matter to save their skin.

The government did not take any action against any official for this trick adopted by them to reduce the number of zero balance accounts to impress their political bosses.

LIC: Whose Life is it Anyway?

Stories behind LIC's Historic Campaign

This story is an insight into the workings of India's public sector insurance company—Life Insurance Corporation (LIC)—with which almost every household in India is associated in some way or the other. They have an unquestioning faith in LIC, believing it to be a lifeline to an assured and comfortable future. This idea came to mind from an interaction with some insurance agents working for LIC who always persuade to take new policies but hardly persuade to revive and continue old policies which have lapsed because of unpaid premium. Granted, the primary job of an insurance agent is to sell insurance policies, but does the agent first enquire about his potential customers' old policies and offer advice on how to revive it if it has lapsed, before trying to hard sell a new policy to them?

To find out, a new hunt for a story was started under RTI with the LIC of India.

As a beginning, on October 18, 2007, an RTI application was filed[15] to LIC at their headquarters in Mumbai. Besides other queries, they were asked what time limit was provided to customers to revive their lapsed policies, and what were the total number of lapsed policies that were not revived during the last seven years

---

[13] Lallu Paswan of Barh (Bihar) and Rajesh Rao of Bhopal (MP) interviewed by the author.

[14] Ibid.

[15] By the author to LIC of India, Mumbai.

and had lapsed permanently from 2000–01 to 2006–07. Their response[16] arrived: "Policy holder can revive his policy within five years from the dates of first unpaid premium." They also provided the numbers of yearwise policies lapsed permanently during the given years. When the number of all such lapsed policies during the last seven requested years was totaled, it[17] came to 59,196,235. Predictably, to query regarding LIC's total earnings from policies that had lapsed permanently, they replied: "data is not available."[18]

Given that their data of 59.2 million lapsed policies were true, curiosity was where the colossal amount earned thereof might have gone? Even considering that a mere ₹2,000 had been paid against each such policy, the total earnings to LIC on this account would have been around ₹118.4 billion. I decided to pursue the matter.

To get more information, a first appeal was filed before LIC's managing director, A.K. Dasgupta. He responded[19] rather smugly: "The information required in point no. 4 even for any given policy is misleading without taking the cost to LIC in the competitive market. Therefore, it qualifies for exemption under section 8(1)(d)."

Since the first appellate had not helped to find out the requisite information, the next option was to approach the CIC with a second appeal, but being aware that the CIC was inundated with several such appeals and complaints which were taking months to be addressed, I believed, would kill the very idea of journalistic endeavor. Thinking of a more brazen option, a letter was written to the chairman of LIC requesting for disclosure of the required information. But this trick too backfired as a response from the executive director, Ms Thankom T. Mathew, on behalf of chairman, said:[20] "You may appeal to the CIC in case of any dissatisfaction with the order of the 1st Appellate Authority." Now there was no option but to resort to approach the CIC. Accordingly, the second appeal was filed before CIC.

---

[16] Letter No. CO/RTI/File No. 227, dated November 26, 2007, from LIC to author.
[17] Ibid.
[18] Ibid.
[19] Letter No. CO/RTI/file no. 227, dated January 6, 2008, from LIC to author.
[20] Letter No. RTI/CO/46A/K.S. dated February 27, 2008.

The concerned information commissioner at that time was A.N. Tiwari who was later retired as chief information commissioner. In response to the appeal, he decided[21] in favor of LIC on December 5, 2008 saying, "It is directed that there shall be no disclosure obligation for the requested information." In their submission,[22] the LIC had said, among other things, that: "In the first five years an insurance company incurs loss for death claims, lapses and surrenders. Therefore, there is huge loss due to lapsed policies to LIC."

The story was put on the website of *India Today*[23] on December 24, 2008, and in *India Today* (Hindi) magazine, dated January 7, 2009. The story was headlined: "5.91 Crore LIC Policies Discontinued in 7 Years." It was just a 300-word story and it had the desired impact. Within a month of its publication, an advertisement[24] surfaced in several leading newspapers about a new scheme for the revival of lapsed policies. The advertisement said, *"Has your policy lapsed? Then you are lucky to read this. LIC launches SPECIAL REVIVAL CAMPAIGN. From 19.01.2009 to 28.02.2009. Revival also allowed for policies lapsed for more than 5 years for the first time."*

This was clearly a reaction to the story. An officer in the customer relations management department of LIC confirmed this when he said: "We have launched this revival scheme for the first time as an experiment. After examining the responses of policy holders, we will decide what to do further with our rules."[25] The insurance company's managing director, A.K. Dasgupta, also confirmed that this indeed was the first such campaign in the history of LIC, when he said:[26]

Revival of policies lapsed over period of 5 years were allowed for the first time during Special Revival Campaign launched from

---

[21] See http://www.rti.india.gov.in/cic_decisions/AT-05122008–03.pdf, accessed December 27, 2016.

[22] Ibid.

[23] See http://indiatoday.intoday.in/story/5.91+crore+LIC+policies+discontinued+in+7+years/1/23493.html, accessed December 27, 2016.

[24] It was published in many daily newspapers on January 18, 2009 and after that as well.

[25] See http://indiatoday.intoday.in/story/LIC+launches+first+campaign+to+revive+policies+lapsed+for+over+5+years/1/25771.html, accessed December 27, 2016.

[26] On June 18, 2009 in response to RTI filed by author.

January 19, 2009 to February 28, 2009. In the earlier years, LIC had allowed revival of policies lapsed over 5 years as a routine revival, and not exclusively under the Special Revival Campaign.

Furthermore, he provided the data of beneficiaries:[27] "Total 14,221 policies which were lapsed over 5 years have been revived during this campaign."

It was a matter of satisfaction that such a large number of policy holders had benefitted due to this small effort.

Later, after joining *The Indian Express*, another application was filed for further details of such lapsed polices. A similar story was published in *The Indian Express* using LIC's latest data[28] that 44.2 million policies lapsed during the years 2005–06 to 2011–12. But LIC again refused to disclose the amount which was already deposited against those policies by the policy holders till the date of last premium paid.

Again, on March 1, 2012, another application was filed with LIC asking for yearwise information on "[h]ow much money deposited against the lapsed policies was forfeited by the LIC since 2005." They responded:[29]

The total amount deposited under a policy till the date of lapse, is not available as the same is never extracted for any of our routine purpose. The same cannot be calculated without going through the premium payment transactions under these policies. The number of premium payment transactions are nearly 500 million every year.

Interestingly, on each and every policy the LIC sends reminders for the payment schedule and the premium amount is also mentioned. In an earlier appeal which was decided by A.N. Tiwari, the request was to provide divisional office-wise information to which they took the plea that "[d]ivisions of LIC offices generate this information at the time of submission of D-return to the Central Office. However, total premium received against these lapsed policies, as requested by the appellant, has never been generated and so it is not available with us." In a new application of

---

[27] Ibid.
[28] See http://archive.indianexpress.com/news/lic-forfeits-money-lying-in-4.42-crore-lapsed-policies/915461/, accessed December 27, 2016.
[29] Response dated April 9, 2012 of LIC to author.

March 1, 2012, what was simply requested was the yearwise total amount deposited to LIC against the lapsed policies till the date of last premium paid. But again the ridiculous reply came that they do not maintain such data. It was unbelievable that LIC did not have a record of the total amount received till the date of last premium paid against lapsed policies for which premiums had not being paid since last five years.

Here again the first appeal was filed against the decision of the CPIO of LIC, Saroj Dikhale. As before, the first appellate, Susobhan Sarkar, upheld the CPIO's decision.[30] Once again, when the CIC was approached, the then Information Commissioner Deepak Sandhu, convinced with LIC's arguments, ruled[31] in favor of LIC. In her decision of August 22, 2013 she said:

> After hearing the averments of the respondents and on pursuing the facts on record Commission is satisfied that information as sought by the appellant is not maintained by the public authority and therefore cannot be furnished…. It is noted that the first appellate authority has provided year wise data of the number of policy which are in any lapsed condition for more than five years as on November 15, 2011.

While the LIC strongly put forth, before the CIC, arguable claims that it had suffered huge losses due to lapsed policies, the fact remains that it did not provide details of the money it had received as premium for those policies. This appears to be an obvious cover-up effort on the part of LIC to evade hard questions. A lot needs to be explored and the covert functioning of LIC needs to be exposed. And we can do it because LIC is a public sector entity and accountable toward RTI. The way insurance companies' agents pressurize for new policies with lucrative offers rather than focusing on the continuity of old ones, we wish those are also covered under transparency law. If it happens, such impact-making stories can be brought out from them and many hidden facts can be explored from the insurance business. Such exposes ultimately benefit the common man.

---

[30] CO/RTI/VN/9F/S Yadav dated May 18, 2012.
[31] See http://rti.india.gov.in/cic_decisions/CIC_DS_A_2012_002278_M_117586.pdf, accessed December 27, 2016.

Armed Aadmi

On a brief visit to New York in July 13–15, 2007 to cover the 8th World Hindi Conference which was inaugurated at the UN headquarters, I came across the famous pro-peace sculpture 'Knotted Gun' by Swedish artist Carl Fredrik Reuterswärd. The sculpture depicts a .45-caliber Colt Python revolver with its barrel knotted into a bullet-blocking twist. Sculpted in the late 1980s and offered to the UN by the government of Luxembourg in 1988, it was inspired by the assassination of John Lennon who was the sculptor's friend.

Coming from a state like Uttar Pradesh where the gun is a familiar and dreaded symbol of power and status, I found in the 'Knotted Gun' a powerful statement against violence. 'Knotted Gun' gave the idea for next story: Investigate and unearth facts relating to district-and statewise issuance of arms licenses to private persons living in India.

Admittedly, in rare cases and under certain circumstances, a private citizen might feel the need to possess a gun for his/her self-protection. But in a country where non-violence as propagated by the father of the nation Mahatma Gandhi is a creed we live by, is it not an anathema that using, possessing, and carrying a gun has become a custom in its many parts? These private guns, which are given in the name of self-defense, have often been used in offence and creating fear among the neighbors of the licensees. Figure 8.2 provides details about licenses issued in an article published in *The Indian Express* on February 7, 2014.

The fact is that the licensed arms are used not just for 'self-defense'. According to the National Crime Record Bureau (NCRB) data, during the six-year period 2008–13, at least 2,336 people were murdered across the country (574 in 2008, 371 in 2009, 340 in 2010, 404 in 2011, 323 in 2012, and 324 in 2013) using private licensed weapons. Incidents in which people may have died and the cases have been registered under section 304 of IPC (culpable homicide not amounting to murder) were not included in these figures. Though, admittedly, more persons than that were murdered using unlicensed weapons, the high number of murders committed using licensed arms was unsettling and reflected the

Figure 8.2:
Nearly 20 lakh private arms licensed in half of the country

Source: The Indian Express (February 7, 2014).

fact that they were being widely misused; people using them for 'offence' and not for 'self-defense[32]' or 'self-protection.'[33]

In today's new world order, India too is experiencing its own share of socioeconomic cataclysm, terrorism, and war. It is only natural, therefore, that states which have seen the terrorism menace and states with poor social indicators top the list of those with the highest gun-license demand by private persons.

---

[32] Most applicants claim the reason of seeking arms license.
[33] Ibid.

On return from New York, I got in touch with various sources in the MHA and state governments, but was disillusioned to learn that no countrywide data on firearms was available with them. For months thereafter, several attempts were made to find out how and from whom the information can be accessed, discussing the issue with friends in the police and administration across the country. These informal conversations did throw up a few interesting facts. In Uttar Pradesh, which is among the poorest states and arguably the most violence prone, many district magistrates confided[34] that they receive an unusually large numbers of recommendations from local politicians and senior officers for arms licenses. These recommendations, I was told, are many times the number of recommendations they receive for employment opportunities and facilities related to potable water, electricity, road, and other infrastructures which they desperately need. Here, MPs, MLAs, other political persons, senior officers, doctors, engineers, contractors, and businessmen, everybody wants a gun for themselves, their supporters, and near and dear ones.

Though quite a few of sources in central and state governments appreciated the idea and were eager to offer suggestions and opinion, I soon realized that it was all I could expect from them. It was apparent there was no informal way to get the information required, and for that reason the way was no other but the RTI Act.

Therefore, an RTI application was sent to the MHA on October 8, 2009, requesting for the number of arms licenses—of prohibited and nonprohibited bores separately—issued to private citizens in the country till the date of application: They were asked briefly: Does MHA have any estimate (through any source) of fire arms licenses issued to private persons in the country, statewise? Does the MHA have any estimate of illegal fire arms in the country? If yes, please provide the number statewise. But with this RTI, such a response was received that, later, over 700 RTI applications were needed to get the information which included almost all the district magistrates besides others, and, despite filing such a huge number of RTI and spending around four years, only the status of almost half of the country was clear. It was realized that fighting with the way too many thick-skinned district licensing authorities who were responding the queries, it will not be possible to get the nationwide figures easily.

---

[34] In an informal conversation with the author.

The MHA responded by initially stating that issuing arms licenses was a state subject and, therefore, the information can only be accessed from them. But, yes, they did give the total number of prohibited bores licenses issued to private persons, which was 2,191.[35] Prohibited bores licenses are issued by the Central Government and, therefore, they had the requisite information. As for nonprohibited bores licenses, the MHA was clueless. It was shocking that despite the rapid computerization in the country having taken place by that time, the government had not felt the need to prepare a single point database for the whole country regarding the matter.

In the next six months, three differently worded applications were filed for the same information, but the response[36] to each of them was the same: "Non-Prohibited Bore Licenses are issued by State Government/District Magistrate concerned and no data at present is available with MHA." In the middle of all this, on December 4, 2009, the MHA was gracious enough to inform:[37] "On 02.03.2009 a request was made to States/UT Administrations to indicate as to how many arms licenses have been issued by them. No specific time limit was prescribed. So far no information has been received from any state/UTs in this regard."

Later the MHA issued a circular[38] to state governments regarding arms licenses, which said: "It has been decided to maintain a database as may be specified and share the data with the Central Government which shall maintain a national database. National database including data on PB weapons may be maintained centrally by MHA."

Unfortunately, the circular did not have the desired effect as a majority of state governments ignored it. Since there was no required information, as a next step, similar RTI applications were filed to every states' director general of police (DGP) and commissioners of police (CP). Here again it was a failed effort, since a majority of them responded that licenses are issued by the district magistrates and, therefore, DGP offices do not have such data. Some DGP/CP offices transferred the application to the district authorities. A few of them responded, but

---

[35] MHA's response dated January 18, 2012 to author on RTI.
[36] Response of MHA dated June 28, 2010 on RTI.
[37] Response dated December 4, 2009 to author under RTI.
[38] Circular dated April 6, 2010, accessed by author using RTI.

most did not. Delhi Police were the only ones who provided the information.

Filing an application with each district is a lengthy and cumbersome procedure, so before doing so, fresh applications were filed to every states' principal secretary (Home). This time the Gujarat,[39] Haryana,[40] Nagaland,[41] Meghalaya,[42] Andaman-Nicobar,[43] Delhi,[44] and Tripura[45] governments provided the number of licenses issued in their states. The UP government responded:[46] "Licenses of Prohibited Bore are issued by Government of India and non-prohibited bore licenses are issued by District Magistrates. Therefore, no such information is maintained at State Government level." The rest of the states' Home departments also advised to approach the district magistrates since the licenses are issued by them.

Then, it was decided to try one more gambit before using the last option of approaching every district. Before every general election, the ECI asks state governments/district magistrates to surrender arms licenses. So it was asked from the ECI as to how many arms were surrendered before General Election 2009. The ECI replied:[47]

> To ensure free and fair election, the commission issues instruction from time to time on the matters such as ban on issue of license of arms, seizure of unlicensed arms and ammunitions, deposit of licensed arms, transportation of arms and ammunitions etc. No reply is sought from the CEOs thereon.

Then the applications were sent to the chief electoral officers (CEOs) of every state, some of whom forwarded it to every district. While the information was received in bits and pieces, it was

---

[39] Through letter, dated May 24, 2012, from Home Department, Gujarat, under RTI.
[40] Response dated July 4, 2012 from Home Department, Haryana, to author on RTI.
[41] Response dated July 12, 2012 from Home Department, Nagaland, to author on RTI.
[42] Response dated August 30, 2012 from Home Department, Meghalaya, to author on RTI.
[43] Response dated May 17 and May 14 from Andaman and Nicobar Administration to author on RTI.
[44] Response dated August 26, 2011 from Delhi Police to author on RTI.
[45] Letter dated July 12, 2012 from Home Department, Tripura, to author on RTI.
[46] Response dated October 10, 2011 from Home Department, UP, to author on RTI.
[47] Response of ECI, dated January 23, 2013, to author on RTI.

not sufficient. They told that only people of doubtful character are asked to surrender their weapons. This was of no help to me.

More than two years had passed since, and in November 2011 I left *India Today* and joined *The Indian Express,* but effort for the countrywide data of private arms licenses was continued.

Finally, succumbing to the circumstances, the final option was opted, which was to approach every district. In late 2012 and early 2013, around 600 of the total 644 districts at that time were approached through separate RTI applications. This gave me an insight into what the level of seriousness was toward RTI applications at the district level. Around one-third of the districts did not even respond to the application. Many of those districts which responded did not give information, avoiding it on one pretext or the other. The query was very simple: "Total number of arms licenses issued in your district as on December 31, 2012." The cut-off date differed with the date of filing of RTI application. If the application was filed in December 2012, the information as asked for was "as on November 2012."

From the long list of responses received, two things were apparent: First, it showed the mind-set of the public authority, and second, it reflected clearly that they had no intention to provide the number of licenses issued in their district till the given date. Some interesting, and often amusing, responses to very clearly worded application showed that the district authorities tried to ditch. This is evident from some of the responses mentioned below:

- "Arms licenses are issued for security of any person. It is related to internal security. Information has no public interest therefore it is not possible to provide this information."[48] —Collector, Alwar, Rajasthan.
- "Please mention the date of licenses issued for which the information is needed."[49] —Additional District Magistrate, Kasganj, UP.
- "Information sought by the applicant is related to third party. Such information can be sought only if the said third party

[48] Response dated February 25, 2013 from DM, Alwar, Rajasthan, to author on RTI.
[49] Response of DM, Kasganj, dated February 26, 2013, to author on RTI.

has authorised somebody to do this."[50] —Officer in-Charge of Arms, Etah, UP.

- "If you want to see the registers of licenses, you can do so. If you want to know the information about the license of any particular person, you can do so."[51] —PIO, Collector's Office, Mandsaur, MP.
- "In December 2012 this office has sanctioned 27 licenses for non-prohibited bores."[52] —Officer-in-Charge of Arms, Dehradun, Uttarakhand.
- "Corporate bodies and juristic persons cannot apply for information under the Act."[53] —Additional Deputy Commissioner, Chikballapur, Karnataka.
- "All licenses are maintained taluka wise. The total number of register is 72 and each are of 500 pages. According to the rules of RTI Act the amount will be ₹36,000 plus postage charges."[54] —Office of DM, Ahmednagar, Maharashtra.
- "On December 31, 2012 District Magistrate has issued licenses to 13 private persons."[55] —Officer-in-Charge of Arms, Allahabad.

Fortunately, around one-third of the districts provided complete information. Information of Delhi, Gujarat, Haryana, Nagaland, Meghalaya, Andaman-Nicobar, and Tripura was already available as their Home departments had provided it. When the information was processed, I realized that less than half of the country was covered. After filing more than 700 RTI applications and spending four years on an exercise which is primarily the government's job, data of just 324 districts was available, out of the 600 districts which were approached directly. The entire exercise brought home the point that getting information under RTI from district-level authorities is much more difficult than getting it from top government offices here in the national capital, or in state capitals.

---

[50] Response of DM, Etah, dated February 26, 2013, to author on RTI.
[51] Response dated March 19, 2013 from DM, Mandsaur MP, to author on RTI.
[52] Response dated March 16, 2013 from DM, Dehradun, to author on RTI.
[53] Response dated April 17, 2013 from DC, Chikballapur, to author on RTI.
[54] Response dated April 24, 2013 from DM, Ahmednagar, to author on RTI.
[55] Response dated May 20, 2013 from DM, Allahabad, to author on RTI.

From the data collected from different states pertaining to private arms licenses through various RTI applications, here are a few highlights and comparative figures based on the analysis of the information received:

- One in 62 households in these districts owns a licensed weapon (average of 324 districts, multiplied by the total number of districts, that is, 644 and then dividing that by the total number of households in the country as per Census 2011).
- Uttar Pradesh, which comprises 16.50 percent of the country's population, has issued nearly 30 percent of the country's arms licenses to private persons (average of UP districts data was spread in the entire state).
- If one were to take an average of the 324 districts that were spread across the country (total weapons in 324 districts, that is, total divided by 324), there would be 6,113 private arms licenses issued in each district.
- 21 of the top 50 private gun-holding districts, out of total 324, fall in UP, which include Lucknow, Varanasi, Moradabad, Ghaziabad, Muzaffarnagar, Meerut, Pratapgarh, Bareilly, Banda, and Azamgarh.
- 11 of these top 50, out of total 324, fall in Punjab, which include Patiala, Tarn Taran, Firozpur, Ludhiana, Hoshiarpur, Sangrur, Jullundur, and Muktsar Sahib.
- In the whole of Gujarat, there were merely 44,882 private arms licenses while UP's capital district Lucknow itself had issued 48,436 such weapons. Other statewise information was: Haryana had 144,543 private arms licenses, Meghalaya 12,291, Tripura 2,942, Sikkim 2,881, Andaman and Nicobar 2,931, Nagaland 57,123, and Delhi 63,329.

The Union Government has finally launched a project named National Database of Arms Licenses (NDAL) in 2012, under which, from March 31, 2016, it is mandatory for every licensing authority to put the details of every arms license issued. NDAL is part of Immigration, Visa and Foreigner's Registration & Tracking (IVFRT) under the national e-governance schemes. As a result, it is now possible to get the number of total arms licenses in the country.

Under the NDAL project, all licensing authorities are required to upload details of all existing arms licensees to generate a unique identification number (UIN). Arms Rules, 1962 have also been amended[56] to provide a cut-off date and after that the licenses without UIN to be considered invalid. An MHA communiqué[57] said that the data under NDAL "is proposed to be utilized for affecting appropriate policy changes in the implementation of the Arms Act, 1959 and Arms Rules, 1962 and other relevant matters."

The fact is that the process of arms licenses database was speeded up with the speed of this RTI exercise across the country, taking along the MHA, state governments, and district authorities. The story was published in *The Indian Express*.[58]

The Afzal Guru Files

Mohammad Afzal Guru was arrested, tried, convicted, and hanged to death for his role in the December 2001 terrorist attack on the Parliament of India. The Supreme Court confirmed his conviction and death sentence on August 4, 2005, following which his wife Tabassum Afzal filed a mercy petition with the President of India. His hanging kept being delayed and as a result he continued to be a hot news subject till the date he was hanged to death. His case became a serious political issue after the November 26, 2008 terror attack in Mumbai. In the 2009 general elections, the issue was repeatedly raked up, following which, the opposition parties, particularly the BJP, continued to pressurize and criticize the UPA government for delaying his execution. Finally, on February 3, 2013, the president rejected the mercy petition and Afzal Guru was secretly hanged in Delhi's Tihar Jail on February 9, 2013.

On the political front, there were allegations and counter allegations; the then home minister saying something, the

---

[56] Vide GSR No. 585(E) dated July 24, 2012: http://www.mha.nic.in/sites/upload_files/mha/files/ArmsRules1962–260813.pdf, accessed February 13, 2017.

[57] Letter dated February 3, 2015 from Home Secretary Anil Goswami to states.

[58] http://indianexpress.com/article/india/india-others/nearly-20-lakh-private-arms-licensed-in-half-the-country/, accessed December 27, 2016.

Government of Delhi saying something else, and the President's Secretariat putting in their bit. By filing several RTI applications, I had managed to gather a number of documents about the case from the MHA, the Department of Justice, and the Government of Delhi. When the MHA was requested to provide copies of its correspondence with the Government of Delhi, they provided the list of documents but did not provide the copies. Therefore, another application was filed with the Government of Delhi asking them for copies of the same correspondence. The PIO of the Government of Delhi was quite helpful as he provided the information[59] after I'd paid the cost of photocopying charges. After doing so, copies of all documents were provided and these were the startling facts gathered from the information accessed.

Afzal's wife Tabassum Afzal filed a mercy petition with the President of India in October 2006. The MHA forwarded it to the Government of Delhi the same day as the views of the government in whose territory the crime had taken place is taken before making any recommendation in mercy petitions pertaining to death sentences. In spite of the MHA writing many letters and reminders, the Government of Delhi kept the matter pending by not responding.

Interestingly, while the Government of Delhi sat on the file for nearly four years, the capital punishment awarded to the Pakistani terrorist Ajmal Amir Kasab in the Mumbai attacks case brought the issue into fresh focus. On May 17, 2010, then Delhi Chief Minister Sheila Dikshit made a statement that her government had not received any communication from the Central Government. "I have not received any letter (from Home Ministry). May be the Home Department (of the Government of Delhi) received it," she had said while talking to the media. Strangely enough, she herself was in charge of the Home Department!

After reading her statement, I scrutinized all documents available and then uploaded scanned copies of all correspondence between the MHA, the Government of India and her government on *India Today's* news portal. Documents showed that the MHA had sent 16 letters and reminders on the subject to the Government of Delhi, of which the Government of Delhi had provided copies

---

[59] Through letter dated December 24, 2009 and January 15, 2010, accessed by author under RTI.

of only nine. These documents were sufficient to counter the statement of the Delhi chief minister, and led to other media doing stories on the subject. As it happened, the very next day, on May 18, 2010, Sheila Dikshit sent the file to the lieutenant governor of Delhi who promptly returned it to the Government of Delhi the same day. So, finally the much awaited recommendation of the Government of Delhi reached the MHA, which later forwarded it to the President of India. The success of the RTI was that the chief minister of Delhi had to change her stand within 24 hours because there were all the documents from official channels, which were certainly difficult without RTI.

'Reserved' Toilets

While visiting and scouting around government offices, journalists come across interesting people, baffling behavior, and decadent practices, some of which kindle story ideas in their mind. I make use of most such ideas by filing RTI applications to unravel the truth and get to the bottom of the often mystifying problem. One such is the frequently seen boards outside the common toilets of many government offices which say "Reserved for Officers" or "Reserved for Senior Officers" or "Reserved for VIPs." On enquiring informally, officials told rather sheepishly that some of the toilets are kept reserved for officers/senior officers because it is difficult to keep all toilets neat and clean all the time. This could mean two things: Only senior officers could keep toilets clean or only they deserved clean toilets. The fact that many common toilets are reserved for officers/senior officers despite the fact that senior officers have attached toilets in their offices as well was perplexing. This practice reeked of a colonial mind-set, so it was decided to find it out.

In September 2013, separate applications were filed to the PMO, Cabsec, DoPT, MHA, MEA, MoEF, Ministry of Urban Development (MoUD), and the Central Public Works Department (CPWD) asking them for the number of toilets in their office premises and the number of toilets reserved for officers/senior officers among them. They were also asked for copies of instructions/circulars, if any, that authorize reserving toilets for senior officers. Blame it on a colonial hangover or the assumed superiority of bureaucrats in the corridors of power, some of these offices did actually have instructions in place that reserve some toilets exclusively for officers of a specified rank and above. This apparently allows senior functionaries to ease themselves in cleaner facilities and is in practice in most of the government offices.

While some departments were doing so informally, the PMO had issued a circular:[60]

> The Toilets attached to Room No. 54 (Conference Hall) and Room No. 153 (Conference Hall) are exclusively marked 'for officers only' and are meant to be used only by officers of the rank of Under Secretary and above and dignitaries visiting the PMO. However, it has been observed that staff not entitled to use these toilets is using the same, leaving the premises dirty. To avoid any embarrassing situation, all staff members are expected to refrain from using toilets that are exclusively marked 'For Officers Only', failing which administration will be constrained to take suitable action against staff defaulting on this count.

The PMO's reply to the RTI application also said that there are 13 toilets in the complex, of which two are reserved for senior officers.[61] A similar circular had also previously been issued three years back.[62]

The MHA in their reply stated that there are 25 toilets in North Block, 48 in NDCC-II building, and three in Lok Nayak Bhawan, out of which eight in North Block, three in NDCC-II building, and two in Lok Nayak Bhawan are reserved for senior officers. While it confessed that toilets are reserved for officers, it also said, "No such instruction/order is issued for reserving the toilets exclusively for officers/senior officers."[63] The MoEF replied that of the 24 toilets in Paryawaran Bhawan, the headquarters of MoEF, three were reserved for officers/senior officers, but clarified, "Copy of the instruction issued for reserving the toilets exclusively for officers/senior officers is not available."[64] The CPWD said, "No

[60] On August 23, 2013, copy accessed through RTI by author.
[61] PMO response, dated October 15, 2013, to author on RTI.
[62] On March 10, 2010, copy accessed through RTI by author.
[63] MHA response, dated November 20, 2013, to author on RTI.
[64] MoEF's response dated October 18, 2013.

such circular is available in this office."[65] The DoPT, when asked, replied, "DoPT has not issued any circular on the subject."[66]

After receiving responses from all the departments which were approached, an application was moved with the NHRC asking whether reserving some toilets for senior officers amounted to violation of human rights for the others. In response, the NHRC sent a copy of Protection of Human Rights Act, 1993 and said,[67] "The information sought, since requires interpretation of Law, it is not casting upon the public authority to interpret the Law and to furnish such non available information."

Granted that Indian society has unfair practices of differences and divisions, at least toilets in government offices must not follow such hierarchical practices that divide the staff in their rank. Since now government is on Swachh Bharat mission, one can hope that in the name of cleanliness this reservation will be ended.

Secret List of GoMs

The UPA government led by Dr Manmohan Singh started setting up the GoM and Empowered Group of Ministers (EGoM) within the cabinet, comprising key ministers to address specific important issues. Although, later, the list was available on the website of the Cabsec, initially it was not provided and it was only made possible through the directions issued by the CIC on RTI appeals.

It was on September 27, 2007 that I filed an RTI application before the PMO requesting for the names of GoMs, names of its chairmen and members, subjects they were assigned to handle, number of meetings held, and expected dates of submission of report with the actual dates of submission of report. The application was forwarded to the Cabsec by the PMO. Without disclosing any information, the Cabsec replied:[68]

From time to time the competent authority sets up a number of Groups of Ministers and these GoMs dispose of the business/

---

[65] CPWD response dated October 30, 2013.
[66] DoPT response dated October 8, 2013.
[67] NHRC response dated November 14, 2013.
[68] Cabsec's response, dated October 19, 2007, to author on RTI.

make recommendations on the specific issues referred to them. Consolidated data of this nature is not maintained in Cabinet Secretariat. However, issue of providing information of this nature is under consideration and as a matter of policy, a view will be taken with the approval of competent authority in due course.

Dissatisfied with their response, a first appeal was filed to the Cabsec on October 25, 2007. When the appeal was not replied to within the stipulated time, reminders were sent, such as "Whether the Cabinet Secretariat has set any time frame to reply to the applications under the RTI Act?" "If yes, please specify the time frame being followed by Cabinet Secretariat". "When can I expect an answer on my application?" When even these reminders were not responded to, a second appeal was filed before the CIC to direct the CPIO/FAA to provide the requisite information, look into the reason for delay, and fix responsibility. CIC was expected to pull the concerned authorities for not providing the information and not responding to the first appeal. But that did not happen.

On January 30, 2009, Habibullah was invited to address the Press Association of India at the Press Information Bureau (PIB) conference hall. I was among the audience. After his presentation, I stood up and raised[69] the issue before Habibullah: "You are saying journalists should use RTI for stories. In my case my stories are being killed due to pendency of complaints and appeals before the CIC." The order pertaining to the complaint had been uploaded the same day. Habibullah, deciding on the appeal, said:[70]

Because the 1st appellate authority has not addressed the questions of appellant, which are of direct concern to his public authority, the Commission has decided to remand this appeal to First Appellate Authority and Joint Secretary Shri Rajive Kumar, Cabinet Secretariat, Rashtrapati Bhawan, New Delhi to dispose of the appeal of Shri Shyamlal Yadav within 10 working days of receipt of this order.

---

[69] From author's own records.
[70] See http://www.rti.india.gov.in/cic_decisions/WB-30012009–02.pdf, accessed February 13, 2017.

After that, the appellate authority directed the CPIO to provide the list[71] of GoMs/EGoMs set up till that time. Later, during the tenure of UPA-II, the Cabsec was again asked for the list of GoMs/EGoMs and in response the Cabsec provided the copies of orders it had issued for Constitution and composition of all GoMs/EGoMs till that time. Then, along with more information collected through some informal research on the subject, the story was ready and it was published in July 2012, before Pranab Mukherjee was elected President of India. Majority of the GoMs/EGoMs were then headed by him. But by that time, the whole list of GoMs/EGoMs was available on the website of the Cabsec.

The story published in *The Indian Express*.[72] It is ironical that to know such obvious facts, a legal battle was needed under RTI. Such information would have been in public domain and there is no logic behind hiding such information, but it was RTI which forced to change the mind-set of authorities and ultimately brought this out.

Iftar Parties at Public Expense

On several occasions, while attending Iftar parties hosted by government functionaries my curiosity was to know whether they were being funded by the government exchequer. Although some of the government officers admitted during informal discussion that they had faced problems in their departments managing funds for such parties which were hosted by their political bosses, any definite or satisfactory answer did not come from them. Therefore, the next option was to take the RTI route.

When the DoE, Ministry of Finance was asked whether Iftar parties are allowed on public money, their response[73] was a curt "No." But responding to the queries, the PMO, MEA, Lok Sabha and Rajya Sabha secretariats, and the CPWD admitted that they

---

[71] Response of Cabsec, dated August 6, 2009, to author.
[72] "Every 6th working day, a new GoM, Pranab heads almost half," *The Indian Express* (New Delhi, May 22, 2012). Available at http://indianexpress.com/article/news-archive/web/express-exclusive-every-6th-working-day-a-new-gom-pranab-heads-almost-half/, accessed February 24, 2017.
[73] DoE's response dated August 26, 2011 to author under RTI.

had spent ₹17.5 million on 18 Iftar parties over the past 10 years, ending 2012.[74]

The Rajya Sabha Secretariat, which had spent ₹2.275 million on five Iftar parties since 2007–08, said:[75] "Yes, the secretariat bears expenses incurred in this regard." When it was asked, under which rule, it replied:[76] "There is no rule. It is as per the convention." It, however, added that[77] "expenditure is met on shared basis in the ratio of 2:1 between the Rajya Sabha Secretariat and the Ministry of External Affairs."

The Lok Sabha Secretariat said that spending public money on Iftar parties was allowed, and that it had spent ₹583,000 on two such parties in 2010 and 2011.[78] "Expenditure on Iftar parties is met from the hospitality grant of the Lok Sabha Secretariat," it added.[79]

The PMO's response to almost all RTI queries about Iftar parties, on the other hand, was most interesting:[80] "Information sought is not a part of records held by this office." The PMO had hosted six Iftar parties since 2004 at a cost of ₹10.3 million,[81] which, it said, was borne by the MEA and the CPWD.

The MEA, on its part, said it has spent about ₹4.148 million[82] since 2004 on 10 Iftar parties, including the ones hosted by the PMO. The MEA further stated on other related queries: "No specific information available."[83]

Although Railway Minister Lalu Prasad Yadav under UPA-I had hosted a few Iftar parties, the Railway Board evaded the issue, contending that: "The information asked for appears to be vague and not specific. Moreover, the data is not maintained and compilation of such information will disproportionately divert

---

[74] *The Indian Express* (New Delhi, August 6, 2012). Available at http://archive. indianexpress.com/news/mof-says-can-t-spend-public-money-on-iftar-but-govt- spent-rs-1.75-cr-in-10-yrs/984300/, accessed February 24, 2017.
[75] Response dated March 26, 2012 to author under RTI.
[76] Ibid.
[77] Ibid.
[78] Lok Sabha letter, dated December 26, 2011, under RTI to author.
[79] Ibid.
[80] PMO's letter, dated April 13, 2012, to author under RTI.
[81] PMO's letter, dated December 5, 2011, to author under RTI.
[82] Response of MEA, dated January 19, 2012, to author on RTI.
[83] Response of MEA, dated March 23, 2012, to author on RTI.

the resources of the public authority.... No catering arrangement for iftar party has been organized."[84]

But the impact of the story and the RTI exercise was felt later as there were almost no such parties on public expense after 2012. The Lok Sabha Secretariat informed[85] later that it had not spent any money on Iftar parties in 2012–13 and 2013–14. The Rajya Sabha Secretariat had also informed[86] that its last expense on an Iftar party was in 2011–12 which was for ₹82,900, and that it has not spent any money on Iftar parties since.

Telephone Interceptions

Under Section 5(2) of the Indian Telegraph Act, the Central and state governments can order interception/monitoring of tele-phonic conversations "on grounds of sovereignty and integrity of India, security of the State, relations with foreign states or public order or for preventing incitement to commission of an offence." Once cleared, the interceptions can be continued for two months and may be renewed twice. In any case, the interception cannot be in force for more than 180 days.

It was in 2010 that a chance was taken by sending an RTI application to obtain details of telephone interceptions since 2004, sanctioned by the Government of India on the request of various agencies such as the CBI, IB, ED, DRI, and NCB among others. The MHA refused to provide the yearwise and agency-wise information saying that "[r]ecords pertaining to such direc-tions for interception are destroyed every six months."[87] But when the applications were filed again with little revision of words, the MHA made the startling disclosure that "[o]n an average, between 7,500 and 9,000 orders for interception of telephones are issued by the Central Government per month" (Figure 8.3).[88]

---

[84] Railway Board's responses, dated December 9, 2011 and April 2, 2012, to author under RTI.

[85] Response of Lok Sabha, dated December 16, 2014, to author under RTI.

[86] Response of Rajya Sabha, dated November 27, 2014, to author under RTI.

[87] Response of MHA, dated December 13, 2010, to author under RTI.

[88] Responses of MHA, dated December 8, 2011 and December 19, 2011, to author under RTI.

Figure 8.3:
9,000 orders for phone interception in a month

9,000 orders for phone interception a month: Govt

SHYAMLAL YADAV
NEW DELHI, JANUARY 22

ON an average, the Union Home Ministry orders 250-300 telephone interceptions every day.

In response to an RTI application by *The Indian Express*, the Home Ministry has stated: "On an average, between 7,500 and 9,000 orders for interception of telephones are issued by the Central government per month." According to the Indian Telegraph Rules, the Union Home Secretary is the authority to grant approval for interception of telephones.

Under Section 5(2) of the Indian Telegraph Act, telephonic conversations can be intercepted/monitored inter alia on grounds of sovereignty and integrity of India, security of the State, relations with foreign states or public order or for preventing incitement to commission of an offence.

Once cleared, the interceptions can be continued for two months and may be renewed twice. In any case, the interception cannot be in force more than 180 days.

The Home Ministry, in its response to the RTI application, did not divulge details saying records pertaining to these interceptions are destroyed after six months, unless these are, or likely to be, required for functional re-

RIGHT TO **KNOW**

quirements. The agencies which get clearance for interception of telephones include law enforcement agencies functioning under the Central government.

Telephone interceptions are cleared as per Rule 419-A of the Indian Telegraph Rules. But these are not the only phones which are being intercepted. In fact, state governments have similar powers to intercept phones. In their case, requests for interception are cleared by the Secretary of Home Department.

The Centre and state governments are supposed to put these interceptions before a review committee headed by the Cabinet Secretary in case of the Centre, and by the Chief Secretary in case of the state.

Source: The Indian Express.

Rule 419-A of Indian Telegraph Rules 1951 says:

Directions for interception of any message or class of messages under sub-section (2) of Section 5 of the Indian Telegraph Act, 1885 [hereinafter referred to as the said (Act)] shall not be issued except by an order made by the Secretary to the Government of India in the Ministry of Home Affairs in the case of Government of India and by the Secretary to the State Government in-charge of the Home Department in the case of a State Government. In unavoidable circumstances, such order may be made by an officer, not below the rank of a Joint Secretary to the Government of India, who has been duly authorized by the Union Home Secretary or the State Home Secretary, as the case may be.

What was surprising was that if allowing that disposal of one request were to take two minutes for the competent authority, that is, the Home Secretary or a Joint Secretary authorized by him, all he must be doing the whole day would be disposing off such files. Indeed, he might need to put in extra hours because the requests that were rejected were not included in the MHA's figures. The revelations must have been embarrassing for the MHA, because, when a similar request was filed again after 3 years it was rejected saying that, "The desired information is exempted from disclosure."[89]

NAC Disbanded

After the UPA-I came to power at the Centre in May 2004, the NAC was constituted on June 4, 2004 headed by Sonia Gandhi to oversee the implementation of the NCMP and to monitor its progress. But Sonia Gandhi had to quit the NAC on March 23, 2006 over the Office of Profit Controversy, and Prime Minister Manmohan Singh accepted her resignation the same day. She also resigned as the MP from Rae Bareilly, though she was reelected later.

---

[89] Response of MHA, dated September 26, 2014, to author under RTI.

NAC was a government-funded body with Sonia Gandhi holding the rank of union cabinet minister. It was constituted to advise the coalition government on policy matters and soon acquired the tag of being a 'super-government'. But though Sonia Gandhi resigned, the NAC continued to function. An application was sent to NAC under the RTI Act on November 16, 2007 requesting the number of members as on date, meetings held after the resignation of Mrs Sonia Gandhi and the names of those who chaired these meetings, the list of members who attended those meetings, and the agenda of each meeting.

The NAC provided[90] the list of meetings, members who attended, and the agenda discussed, but regarding the query "Who chaired those meetings", they said[91] that "no member, NAC, chaired the meetings." When a first appeal was filed asking for clarification on this part of the information, the CPIO informed[92] that "Meetings were co-ordinated by NAC Secretariat."

Pursuant to this, a story was published in *India Today*.[93] But the RTI exercise had apparently already made an impact as the NAC was disbanded by the UPA government and no extension was given after March 31, 2008. (Though, it was reconstituted again on March 29, 2010 during UPA-II.) For nearly two years, the NAC occupied 2 Motilal Nehru Place, New Delhi bungalow, with its staff enjoying the perks and allowances, despite the fact that it was headless and many members did not attend the meetings. The RTI efforts evidently prompted the government not to extend its tenure beyond March 2008.

Scrutiny of Election Affidavits

When, following a Supreme Court directive of May 2, 2002, the ECI made it mandatory to file details of all candidates, criminal cases pending against them, and the assets and liabilities of their spouses and children before the returning officer, there was no

---

[90] NAC letter, dated November 29, 2007, to author.
[91] NAC letter, dated January 8, 2008, to author.
[92] NAC letter, dated March 12, 2008, to author.
[93] No attendance council, *India Today*, April 7, 2008.

system of scrutiny of those declarations. I filed a request to the CBDT on September 24, 2008 asking them whether there was any system in place to check the declarations made by electoral candidates while filing their nominations since 2004. Also, the copies of letters the CBDT might have written to its officials in this regard was sought. The CBDT replied on October 13, 2008 that "CBDT has not issued any circular after general elections 2004 to verify the affidavits filed by the contesting candidates." Based on this response, the story was published on the Internet edition of *India Today*.[94]

The ECI thereafter made the first request[95] before the 2010 Bihar assembly elections, and repeated it during all subsequent elections that were held, asking the taxmen to match the statements of assets and liabilities filed by all candidates with their income tax returns. But even after that, the CBDT failed to act. In June 2013, to find a solution, and following a meeting between CBDT and EC officials, it was decided to sort the affidavits of the candidates into categories and present the CBDT with the material in an easier-to-scrutinize format.[96]

A clutch of state elections has taken place since, but again the taxmen did not act. In fact, at the heart of the logjam was the disagreement over the volume of work to be undertaken: The CBDT wanted the EC to forward only selected affidavits to it, while the EC wanted the CBDT to download all affidavits for scrutiny. On October 23, 2013, the CBDT wrote to the EC that its guidelines (on scrutiny) "may need suitable modification particularly with respect to verification of affidavits of contesting candidates". The EC wrote back on January 3, 2014, stressing that the "verification of affidavits of contesting candidates may be done and reported to Commission within six months."[97]

A proper mechanism to scrutinize the affidavits of electoral candidates is still to be evolved, and the fight between the EC and

---

[94] See http://indiatoday.intoday.in/story/CBDT+has+no+system+to+check+candid ates'+affidavits/1/32650.html, accessed December 27, 2016.
[95] "Taxman sits on EC request for scrutiny of candidates' returns," *The Indian Express* (February 25, 2014), http://indianexpress.com/article/india/india-others/taxman-sits-on-ec-request-for-scrutiny-of-candidates-returns/, accessed December 27, 2016.
[96] Ibid.
[97] Ibid.

CBDT continues. As of now, it depends on the opponents of the candidates or the ordinary citizen to scrutinize the affidavits and bring in to the notice of EC authorities, if those are correct. But whatever the course of action taken and its future outcome, the sequence of events shows that things were speeded up after this was brought out using the RTI Act.

Missing Babus

Some of the officers of the Central Government are most concerned about the rotting system. These officers, when they come in contact with journalists, often give several interesting ideas. While moving around in the corridors of the DoPT, sometime in May 2012, I was told by one such officer that many IAS officers go abroad on assignments and extend their stay, spending many years there beyond their deputation or leave period. Some of these officers join UN agencies and other international organizations, only returning a little ahead of their retirement. Taking advantage of the complexities and disparity of rules between the Center and state governments, they manage to overcome every barrier and get their retirement benefits without any problem.

An RTI application was filed to gain access to the list of such IAS officers who were missing from their cadres without authorization.

The DoPT provided the list and all correspondences between the Center and concerned state governments. Rule 7(2) of All India Service (AIS) Leave Rules says:

> A member of the Service shall be deemed to have resigned from the service if he is absent without authorization for a period exceeding one year from the date of expiry of sanctioned leave or permission, or is absent from duty for a continuous period exceeding five years, or continues in foreign service beyond the period approved.

But the implementation of this rule was very difficult since the Center cannot take any action without the concerned states' consent.

The Center's helplessness was clear from the information provided by the DoPT, as at least one of those officers was on 'unauthorised absence' for 14 years. In most of the cases, the officers went abroad on study leave in the interest of service, but apparently decided to stay back in the interest of self-service. In other cases, they used postings in key ministries such as Ministry of Finance and Ministry of Commerce for coveted foreign assignments and did not return.

The RTI query[98] threw up some interesting cases. L.V. Nilesh, a Maharashtra-cadre officer, went on a two-year study leave in July 1999, but joined a California-based software firm in March 2000, under the name Nilesh Londhe. He was removed from service only in July 2012 after 11 years of unauthorized absence. Amit Kumar Jain (Sikkim-cadre officer, 1991 batch) has been absent without authorization since June 1, 2003. Anil Yadav (Madhya Pradesh-cadre officer, 1999 batch) has been missing since July 25, 2007. Alok Khare (Assam-Meghalaya, 1992) was granted study leave for two years on July 25, 2002, to pursue his PhD in the USA, and till December 31, 2008 he was on earned leave, then half-pay leave, and consequently on extraordinary leave (EOL). After January 2009, he was on unauthorized absence. Shishir Priyadarshi (Uttar Pradesh, 1980) was granted a one-year leave to join the World Trade Organization in July 1997 and rejoined the cadre after returning from the foreign deputation only on September 1, 2008. Subsequently, he again applied for leave, which has not been sanctioned. The DoPT sent over half a dozen reminders to the state government to initiate the deemed resignation process, but there was no response.

Sanjeev Ahluwalia (UP, 1980) was sent on a foreign deputation to Sudan as consultant of the World Bank on September 18, 2005, for one year. After September 18, 2006, the state government kept waiting for him to join back. In this case, again, the DoPT's reminders to the state government received no response.

---

[98] Responses of DoPT dated September 4, 2014; July 23, 2013; and August 1, 2012. *The Indian Express,* July 26, 2012; available at http://archive.indianexpress.com/news/the-missing-babus/979545/, accessed on February 24, 2017 and *The Indian Express,* September 10, 2012; available at http://archive.indianexpress.com/news/6-more-ias-officers–missing–govt-seeks-details-from-states/1000369/, accessed on February 24, 2017.

In the case of Saroj Kumar Jha (Orissa, 1990), it was only in 2009 that the DoPT realized that he had been absent from duty since June 5, 2002. While the DoPT requested the state government for details—sending the first request in November 2009—no decision was taken till June 2012. V. Ramakrishnan (Kerala, 1992) was granted study leave to go to the USA for two years with effect from June 16, 2000. On his return, he applied for EOL for another five years. The DoPT granted the same for three years, that is, till June 18, 2005. Seven years later, the DoPT had no information on his whereabouts. The DoPT also informed me that regarding IAS officers J. Radhakrishnan (Tamil Nadu, 1992), Namita Dutta (UT, 1991), Sanjay Agarwal (Maharashtra, 1996), Jyotsna Verma (Jharkhand, 1992), K.C. Mishra (Bihar, 1977), and Prashant (West Bengal, 1988) there was no intimation whether they had returned back from their foreign assignments.

Subsequently, two stories were published in *The Indian Express*.[99] After that, the DOPT sent urgent reminders to chief secretaries of all state governments asking them to provide details before September 30, 2012, about the missing officers. Since then, at least seven IAS officers were considered deemed to have resigned.[100] While the DoPT initiated action for deemed resignation against some of the missing officers, it was helpless in other cases as the state governments did not concede to the DoPT's advices. There have been many jottings on the files on the issue since, but the matter was never successfully addressed.

But, the DoPT issued a new instruction on November 3, 2015:

A Member of Service (MoS), if remains unauthorizedly absent after the sanctioned period of leave/study leave/tenure of Foreign Assignment there shall be a one month waiting period after the end of leave period/tenure of foreign assignment etc. After that the concerned State Government shall issue a show cause notice, thereby giving an opportunity to the MoS to explain his/her case. Thereafter,

---

[99] "The missing babus," *The Indian Express* (New Delhi, July 26, 2012), available at http://archive.indianexpress.com/news/the-missing-babus/979545/, accessed February 24, 2017; "6 more IAS officers 'missing, Govt seeks details from states," *The Indian Express* (New Delhi, September 10, 2012), available at http://archive.indianexpress.com/news/6-more-ias-officers–missing–govt-seeks-details-from-states/1000369/ accessed February 24, 2017.
[100] DoPT's response to author under RTI Act.

if the MoS does not return to duty, the State Government concerned shall initiate proceedings of deemed resignation and forward a complete proposal to the Central Government for effecting deemed resignation within next two months. If the State Government fails to comply with these instructions and does not adhere to the afore-said timeline, the Central Government shall initiate proceedings of deemed resignation on its own.

While this new instruction is intended for AISs such as the IAS, IPS, and IFoS, a similar list of missing officers exists in central services such as the C&CES, Indian Economic Service (IES), Indian Statistical Service (ISS), and in the medical field where some government doctors go abroad and do not return. The CBEC informed[101] that there are at least 14 officers whose whereabouts are not known since more than five years. But before the story was published, 11 of them were removed[102] as deemed to be resigned.

---

[101] In response to an RTI, on August 3, 2015 to author.
[102] "Absent for years, government sacks 11 IRS officers," *The Indian Express* (New Delhi, January 14, 2016). Available at http://indianexpress.com/article/india/india-news-india/absent-for-years-government-sacks-11-irs-officers/, accessed February 24, 2017.

9

NGOs Funded by Government: JSSs and KVKs

There is no public dissemination of this information. There is no public advertisement, for example, inviting offers from universities/colleges/ NGOs who might want to sponsor the KVKs. As a result, there is an inherent bias in favor of the existing state agriculture universities, with the exception of few well connected and really clued up NGOs.[1]

—Note of an Additional Secretary of the Ministry of Agriculture in the file of one Krishi Vigyan Kendra (KVK) in 2010

Table 9.1:
Highlights of RTI filed against NGOs getting funds from the government

Information	NGOs getting funds from the government
Authority	Ministry of HRD, and Ministry of Agriculture and Farmers' Welfare
Problems	Ministry of HRD provided the details of Jan Shikashan Sansthans (JSSs) and Ministry of Agriculture (ICAR on its behalf) provided details of Krishi Vigyan Kendras (KVKs), but to get more details, file inspection was carried out.
Applications and appeals	12, for two stories
Time taken	Over four months
Stories	Politicians' NGOs get 52 of 215 HRD resource centers.... *The Indian Express*, April 8, 2013; Seeds of political patronage… *The Indian Express*, May 16, 2013
Impact	Ministry of HRD stops sanctioning more JSS to NGOs, changes mechanism in new scheme; Ministry of Agriculture stops sanctioning more KVK to NGOs.
Follow-up by me	Several more applications were filed to know the follow-up action from both authorities along with ICAR and University Grants Commission for new scheme.

Source: Author.

---

[1] Note accessed by author from ICAR using RTI.

There are at least 3 million NGOs registered[2] under different pro-visions, and over 31,000 of them are registered[3] under FCRA to receive foreign contribution. One cannot run an NGO and get sufficient government funds without having connections in the government. While doing some stories[4] using online data in public domain with regard to grants received under FCRA, I was trying to get the details of funds received by NGOs from ministries, departments, and other government agencies. Several NGOs, those sanctioned and approved by different government ministries, receive substantial public grants from ministries and are being run directly (and at times indirectly) by politicians, bureaucrats, or their close relatives, with a complete lack of transparency in the way they function and in allotted government money.

It was started by scrutinizing those NGOs where links to government patronage could be conclusively established. Information was explored from social sector ministries such as Health and Family Welfare, Women and Child Development, HRD, and Social Justice and Empowerment among others, and the search was narrowed down to two types of NGOs, one funded by the Ministry of Agriculture and other by Ministry of Human Resource Development (MoHRD).

Jan Shikshan Sansthans

Jan Shikshan Sansthans (JSSs) are funded by the MoHRD, and have a mandate to provide vocational skills to nonliterates and neo-literates as well as school dropouts. The list of JSSs in the country was available on the website of the MoHRD. After studying their system of sanctioning and their pattern of fund release, it was found that the MoHRD gives[5] ₹2.5–3.5 million or more per

---

[2] See http://indianexpress.com/article/india/india-others/india-has-31-lakh-ngos-twice-the-number-of-schools-almost-twice-number-of-policemen/, accessed December 28, 2016.

[3] See https://fcraonline.nic.in/fc8_statewise.aspx, accessed December 28, 2016.

[4] See http://archive.indianexpress.com/news/the-ngos-that-will-come-under-the-lokpal-s-ambit/894896/, accessed December 28, 2016.

[5] See http://mhrd.gov.in/jss, accessed December 28, 2016.

year to each JSS for recurring expenses, ₹1.0–1.5 million per year for nonrecurring expenses, and a one-time building grant of ₹2 million. Printouts of the list of the 215 JSSs existing in the country in early 2012 was taken for further research.

The information available on relevant websites was insufficient, and listed contact numbers were mostly inaccessible, so two separate RTI applications were filed in June 2012 to the MoHRD asking for a list of employees and the policy being followed by the JSSs regarding recruitments. Another application was filed soon after, requesting for details of funds they had received in the last five years, with copies of utilization certificates submitted for those funds. The MoHRD provided[6] the details of funds released to various JSS in two years and forwarded[7] the other application to all the JSSs in the country, and detailed information about the employees, funds, and their utilization certificates was received. But this was not sufficient to put together a comprehensive story. The names of people behind these JSSs are still needed. Moreover, the information to another application filed in May 2012 to the MoHRD, for copies of complaints received against the JSSs was yet to be provided.

Therefore, in August 2012, a request was filed to the MoHRD to allow inspection of relevant files pertaining to sanctioning and funding of the various JSSs. For the next two months,[8] after getting the requisite permission, I visited the Shashtri Bhawan office of MoHRD to inspect each and every file relating to their sanctioning over the years. The real purpose behind this move was to locate the names of people behind the JSSs. From the many recommendation letters and correspondences which were part of the files, it was easy to identify who they were. The reason it took two months was that I was unable to visit their office daily on account of other commitments, and also because the files were spread across many sections of the ministry. Besides, the inspection depended greatly on adjusting to a mutually convenient time.

JSSs are normally run by societies. During the tenure of Dr Murli Manohar Joshi as HRD Minister, many of the JSSs were

---

[6] Vide letter dated January 23, 2012 to author on RTI.
[7] Copy was endorsed to author as well.
[8] On dates mutually convenient to officials and to me.

sanctioned to societies[9] under the control of BJP leaders or their relatives as given in the article in Figure 9.1. After his departure from the ministry, his successor Arjun Singh did likewise when he sanctioned many such JSSs to Congressmen of his choice.[10] Visibly, there was no transparency in these sanctioning and the ministers had brought in their own men in an arbitrary manner.[11] There was virtual mismanagement in the sanctioning and funding of these societies.

Websites of many JSSs and of the societies behind them were also accessed. Interestingly, there was no mention of those societies whose proposals had been rejected in the selection process. As for the files inspected, these pertained to existing JSSs. Each JSS had two files; one related to their society and the other to their release of funds. It was becoming increasingly clear that it was important to find out the names of societies whose proposals had been rejected. Concerned officers of the MoHRD were also asked but they said that they do not have such information. This denial was needed 'on record,' so after completing the inspection of records and analyzing all available information, a fresh RTI application was filed to the MoHRD, on January 31, 2013, asking them what procedures were followed for getting proposals sanctioned for JSSs, their selection process, the criteria for selection and, most important, they were asked for copies of proposals that were rejected in the districts where the particular JSS had been cleared by the ministry. MoHRD categorically confessed:[12] "Only those proposals and their feasibility study reports are kept by this Department for record whom the Jan Shikshan Sansthan was sanctioned." Now it was on record that the MoHRD did not have the files of rejected cases. This again was clear that there was a complete lack of transparency in the selection process.

Now the story was ready. In essence, the key points were: The government favored organizations that had links to politicians. Almost a quarter of the JSSs approved by the MoHRD since 2000 have been found to belong to leaders of key political parties or

---

[9] See http://indianexpress.com/article/news-archive/web/political-resource-development/, accessed December 28, 2016.
[10] Ibid.
[11] Ibid.
[12] Vide letter no. 2–8/2013-NLM-3 in response to author's RTI dated January 31, 2013.

Figure 9.1:
Political resource development

POLITICAL RESOURCE DEVELOPMENT

There are 271 Jan Shikshan Sansthans or JSSs in the country to help boost education programmes in the districts and 215 of them came up after 2000. At least 52 of these bodies were given to NGOs linked to politicians, mostly in the BJP and Congress, indicating that a significant chunk of the programme was converted into political largesse by both parties when they were in power. The following is the list of these NGOs:

17 JSSs linked to BJP leaders

LOCATION: BOKARO, JHARKHAND
NGO: Randhir Verma Memorial Society (RVMS).
Political link: RVMS was founded in the memory of the late husband of Rita Verma, who is patron of the NGO and was MoS, HRD, until end-2003.
Date of sanction: February 4, 2004.

LOCATION: ETAWAH, UP
NGO: Munna Smriti Sansthan.
Political link: Sarita Bhadauria.
Date of sanction: October 2006

LOCATION: AMETHI, UP
NGO: Atal Gramodyog Sewa Samiti.
Political link: Wife of former BJP MLA Yamuna Prasad Mishra.
Date of sanction: March 2003.

LOCATION: MIRZAPUR, UP
NGO: People's Association for Development.
Political link: former Allahabad BJP president Sunil Jain.
Date of sanction: January 2004.

LOCATION: FARRUKHABAD, UP
NGO: Shri Ram Vivekanand Shiksha Samiti.
Political link: Sunil Dwivedi, earlier with BSP.
Date of sanction: February 2002.

LOCATION: AMBEDKAR NAGAR, UP
NGO: Thakur Gurudati Singh Smriti Sewa Sanstha.
Political link: Shakti Singh, known to be close to BJP
Date of sanction: March 2000.

LOCATION: JAUNPUR, UP
NGO: Pratap Gramin Utthan Samiti.
Political link: Former state minister Brajesh Sharma.
Date of sanction: March 2000.

LOCATION: BAHRAICH, UP
NGO: Gramodaya Sansthan.
Political link: Faizabad BJP leader Aditya Narain Mishra.
Date of sanction: March 2003.

LOCATION: GAUTAM BUDH NAGAR, UP
NGO: Ujjain-based Vasudhaiva Kutumbakam Sansthan.
Political link: Veerendra Kawadia, brother of Ashok Kawadia, who was aide of former HRD minister M M Joshi.
Date of sanction: February 2004.

LOCATION: GWALIOR, MP
NGO: Gwalior Udyamita Vikas Prashikshan Kendra.
Political link: Shobha Mishra.
Date of sanction: January 2003.

LOCATION: GOA
NGO: Vidyaprobodhini.
Political link: Prabhakar Bhate, known to be close to BJP.
Date of sanction: May 2001.

LOCATION: SHIMOGA, KARNATAKA
NGO: Vivekananda Vidya Samsthe.
Political link: former chief minister B S Yeddyurappa who has since quit BJP
Date of sanction: April 2000.

LOCATION: BAGALKOT, KARNATAKA
NGO: BVVS Sangha.
Political link: Bagalkot MLA Veeranna C Charantimath.

Date of sanction: June 2004.

LOCATION: WASHIM, MAHARASHTRA
NGO: Mahila Utkarsh Pratisthan.
Political link: MP Bhavna Gavli, who wrote to former HRD minister Joshi with recommendation letters from 27 prominent BJP leaders.
Date of sanction: January 2003.

LOCATION: RAIGAD, MAHARASHTRA
NGO: Yuvak Pratisthan.
Political link: former MP Kirit Somaiya and his wife Medha.
Date of sanction: February 2004.

LOCATION: MAU, UP
NGO: Shiksha Prasarini Samiti.
Political link: Ghazipur BJP leader Parasnath Rai.
Date of sanction: March 2004.

LOCATION: SULTANPUR, UP
NGO: Vidyadhan Sansthan.
Political link: Anil Tewari, who was a BJP minister in the state.
Date of sanction: March 2000.

30 JSSs linked to Congress leaders:

LOCATION: SHAHJAHANPUR, UP
NGO: Srijan JP Foundation.
Political link: Trustees include MoS HRD Jitin Prasada, Union minister Rajiv Shukla and Haryana minister Kiran Choudhry.
Date of sanction: February 2006.

LOCATION: RAE BARELI, UP
NGO: Rajeev Manav Sewa Samiti.
Political link: Local leader Suresh Pratap Singh.
Date of sanction: February 2006.

LOCATION: FATEHPUR, UP
NGO: Shri Vighneshwar Paryavaran Sansthan.
Political link: Yamuna Prasad Pande, who contested 1993 assembly polls from Handia.
Date of sanction: May 2005.

LOCATION: KAUSHAMBI, UP
NGO: Shri Vighneshwar Paryavaran Sansthan.
Political link: Yamuna Prasad Pande, who contested 1993 assembly polls from Handia.
Date of sanction: October 2006.

LOCATION: SONBHADRA, UP
NGO: Pandit Kamlapati Smarak Samiti.
Political link: Society in memory of late Congress leader Kamlapati Tripathi.
Date of sanction: October 2006.

LOCATION: MATHURA, UP
NGO: Rajendra Behari Mathur Chetna Sansthan.
Political link: UP Assembly leader Pradeep Mathur.
Date of sanction: 2008-09.

LOCATION: SIDHARTHNAGAR, UP
NGO: Surya Bux Pal Charitable Trust.
Political link: Wife of Congress MP Jagdambika Pal.
Date of sanction: February 2006.

LOCATION: AURANGABAD, BIHAR
NGO: Chanakya Vihar Sewa Sansthan.
Political link: Thakur Sanjay Kumar Singh Chauhan.
Date of sanction: October 2006.

LOCATION: DEVAS, MP
NGO: Sankalp Sewa Samiti.
Political link: Pankaj Sanghvi.
Date of sanction: October 2006.

LOCATION: ALIRAJPUR, MP
NGO: Mahashakti Seva Kendra.
Political link: Also headed by Indira Iyengar.
Date of sanction: 2009.

LOCATION: BHOPAL, MP
NGO: Manav Sansadhan Vikas Samiti.
Political link: former state minister Mukesh Naik.
Date of sanction: March 2000.

LOCATION: GUNA, MP
NGO: Azad Nirdhan Bal Kalyan Samiti.
Political link: Sachin Kumar.
Date of sanction: August 2000.

LOCATION: SIDHI, MP
NGO: Savyasachi Center for Urban and Rural Development.
Political link: Rajendra Singh Bhadauria.
Date of sanction: January 2005.

LOCATION: HOSHANGABAD, MP
NGO: Jawaharlal Youth Welfare and Social Resource Center.
Political link: Mahendra Singh Chauhan.
Date of sanction: January 2005.

LOCATION: CHHATARPUR, MP
NGO: Bundeli Vikas Samiti.
Political link: Twice MLA Shankar Singh Bundela.
Date of sanction: February 2006.

LOCATION: AZAMGARH, UP
Organisation: Shivji Inter College.
Political link: Former MP Santosh Kumar Singh.
Date of sanction: October 2006.

LOCATION: BAREILLY, UP
NGO: Ansari Krishi & Gramin Vikas Sewa Samiti.
Political link: M M Ansari, son of a former Congress MLC.
Date of sanction: May 2007.

LOCATION: LUCKNOW, UP
NGO: All India Minorities Welfare Action Group.
Political link: Syed Ahmad Zameel.
Date of sanction: October 2007.

LOCATION: BILASPUR, CHHATTISGARH
NGO: Abhiyan.
Political link: Bilaspur Mayor Vani Rao.
Date of sanction: October 2007.

LOCATION: SAGAR, MP
NGO: Gyanveer Sewa Samiti.
Political link: MLA Govind Singh Rajput.
Date of sanction: April 2006.

LOCATION: WEST GODAVARI, ANDHRA PRADESH
NGO: Kavuru Foundation.
Political link: MP K Sambasshiva Rao.
Date of sanction: October 2007.

LOCATION: SABARKANTHA, GUJARAT
NGO: Gram Vikas Mandal.
Political link: State Congress secretary Gopal Singh N Rathod.
Date of sanction: October 2007.

LOCATION: SAMASTIPUR, BIHAR
NGO: Prayas.

Political link: Former IPS officer Amod Kanth who contested 2008 Delhi Assembly polls on Congress ticket.
Date of sanction: 2009.

LOCATION: JHABUA, MP
NGO: Mahashakti Seva Kendra.
Political link: Headed by former member of state minorities commission Indira Iyengar, considered close to then HRD minister, late Arjun Singh.
Date of sanction: October 2006.

LOCATION: DELHI
NGO: Prayas.
Political link: Former IPS officer Amod Kanth.
Date of sanction: 2000.

LOCATION: CHANDAULI, UP
NGO: Asha Education Society.
Political link: Congress leader Avdhesh Singh, earlier with BSP.
Date of sanction: October 2007.

LOCATION: KOTTAYAM, KERALA
NGO: Bharat Sevak Samaj.
Political link: State Congress committee member B S Balchandran.
Date of sanction: October 2000.

LOCATION: SITAPUR, UP
NGO: Momin Ansar Welfare Association, Pilibhit.
Political link: State Congress leader Anusuya Sharma.
Date of sanction: February 2006.

LOCATION: KANPUR DEHAT, UP
NGO: All India Minorities Welfare Society.
Political link: Zafar Ali Naqvi, Lok Sabha MP from Kheri Lakhimpur.
Date of sanction: 2008-09.

LOCATION: BHADOHI, UP
NGO: Badrinarain Dhanraji Devi Gramotthan & Shikshan Sansthan (Allahabad).
Political link: Chairman Keshav Deo Tripathi was a prominent Congress leader who later joined the Tewari Congress.
Date of sanction: 2005.

5 JSSs linked to leaders of other parties:

LOCATION: GORAKHPUR, UP
NGO: Gramin & Samajik Vikas Sewa Sansthan.
Political link: BSP MLA from Sahjanva, Brijesh Singh alias Rajendra.
Date of sanction: February 2006.

LOCATION: EAST MIDNAPORE, WB
NGO: Haldia Service Society.
Political link: Former CPM MLA Tomalika Panda Seth.
Date of sanction: October 2007.

LOCATION: JORHAT, ASSAM
NGO: Former AGP MLA Arun Kumar Sarma.
Political link: Former AGP MLA Arun Kumar Sarma.
Date of sanction: February 2004.

LOCATION: SINDHUDURG, MAHARASHTRA
NGO: Manav Sadan Vikas Sanstha.
Political link: Former Union minister Suresh Prabhu of Shiv Sena.
Date of sanction: March 2000.

LOCATION: RAIPUR, CHHATTISGARH
NGO: IRCEN.
Political link: Former Rajya Sabha MP from Meghalaya, Thomas A Sangma of National People's Party.
Date of sanction: March 2000.

Source: The Indian Express (April, 8, 2013).

their relatives and friends. At least 52 of the 215 JSSs were controlled by politicians or their near and dear ones—including 30 with Congress links, 17 with BJP links, and the rest 5 with links to other parties.[13]

Interestingly, when Kapil Sibal got the portfolio of MoHRD in UPA-II, he could not sanction a single JSS, as his predecessor Arjun Singh had exhausted the entire quota of 73 JSS that were supposed to be allotted during the 11th Five Year Plan.[14] To be on the safe side, in the story, in the list of 52, only those JSS were included where there was no doubt about their connections. Also, those JSSs were excluded which were not directly connected with the powerful.

Documents available regarding selection of NGOs clearly showed how some of them sought to impress the ministry about their standing. For instance, the first page of the proposal for a JSS in Jhabua district of Madhya Pradesh, submitted by Mahashakti Seva Kendra, was a letter from Congress President Sonia Gandhi acknowledging and accepting a gift sent to her by the NGO.[15] It also had an acknowledgment letter written by BJP leader Najma Heptullah in response to New Year greetings from the NGO.[16] The NGO was found to be headed by Indira Iyengar, a Congress leader. Her NGO was selected to run a JSS. Her NGO was later allotted another JSS in Alirajpur, also in Madhya Pradesh.

The files also showed that JSS applications by several BJP leaders or their relatives were approved in the first quarter of 2004, just before General Elections 2004[17] were held that summer.[18] Similarly, many Congress leaders or their relatives got JSSs approved during 2008–09 in the last quarter of the UPA-I government Lok Sabha elections 2009 were announced on March 2, 2009 when Arjun Singh was the HRD minister.[19]

The story was published in *The Indian Express*.[20] Now new JSSs are not being sanctioned and the MoHRD has taken cautious steps

---

[13] See http://indianexpress.com/article/news-archive/web/political-resource-development/, accessed December 28, 2016.
[14] Ibid.
[15] Author found it during inspection of files.
[16] Ibid.
[17] Lok Sabha elections 2004 were announced on February 29, 2004.
[18] Ibid.
[19] Ibid.
[20] "Politicians' NGOs Get 52 of 215 HRD Resource Centres," *The Indian Express* (April 8, 2013), pp. 1, 2.

while finalizing its similar schemes. The new NDA government has launched a scheme of skill development, and UGC is sanctioning Kaushal Vikas Kendras[21] for various universities and institutions. UGC is not giving funds to NGOs/societies directly[22] but to these universities and institutions which are collaborating with 'industry partners' at the local level.

Krishi Vigyan Kendras

In the early 1970s, the Ministry of Agriculture, through the Indian Council for Agriculture Research (ICAR), began setting up KVKs or farm science centers to educate farmers to increase agricultural production in order to improve their socio-economic condition.[23] One of the mandates of KVKs was to work as resource and knowledge centers of agricultural technology to support the initiatives of public, private, and voluntary sectors for improving the agricultural economy of their district.[24] Many NGOs who met the required criteria were allowed to start their own KVKs. A list of such NGOs was availed along with the details of funds they received in previous five years from ICAR since the ICAR provides funds to run the KVKs.[25] Over the years, a small but significant portion of KVKs have ended up as channels of political favor, having been allotted to politicians across the spectrum or to their friends and relatives.[26]

Through the year 2012, the details relating to the running of KVKs were gathered informally as well. Like in the case with the JSS story, the ICAR website was surfed to access the list of KVKs run by NGOs. There were 99 KVKs, from among a total of 630 KVKs, which were being run by NGOs. More information was

---

[21] See http://www.ugc.ac.in/pdfnews/4880344_Amended-KAUSHAL.pdf, accessed December 28, 2016.

[22] UGC responded dated September 10, 2015 on author's RTI application.

[23] http://www.icar.org.in/en/krishi-vigyan-kendra.htm accessed December 28, 2016.

[24] Ibid.

[25] Vide Letter dated August 1, 2012 from ICAR by author under RTI.

[26] See http://archive.indianexpress.com/news/seeds-of-political-patronage/1116240/, accessed December 28, 2016.

needed, so the first RTI application was filed to the Ministry of Agriculture on May 15, 2012 to get the list of KVKs from them, and also for details of funds released to them in the last five years. Once this information was received, another request was filed to inspect the files related to all 630 KVKs. In three weeks in December 2012, files related to all the 630 KVKs were inspected. Files of the 99 KVKs which were being run by NGOs were separated. While going through these files minutely, it was found that in many cases arbitrary decisions had been taken.[27] Over 650 pages were identified from the files of the 99 KVKs and photocopies were arranged. Those copies were received in mid-January 2013 with the help of which the story[28] (Figure 9.2) was processed.

Some files had their own encouraging stories to tell. For instance, Rajiv Mehrishi, then the additional secretary in the Ministry of Agriculture, observed during a selection process in 2010:

> There is no public dissemination of this information. There is no public advertisement, for example, inviting offers from universities/colleges/ NGOs who might want to sponsor the KVKs. As a result, there is an inherent bias in favor of the existing state agriculture universities, with the exception of few well connected and really clued up NGOs.[29]

On the same file, K.V. Thomas, Minister of State in the Ministry of Agriculture, Food and Public Distribution, after seeing the guidelines, noted: "I don't find the guidelines are very comprehensive at all. Lot of ambiguities remains."[30]

From the information gathered, it was clear that, of the 99 KVKs run by NGOs, at least 39[31] were closely linked to politicians or their relatives, if not directly controlled by them, and three KVKs were run by NGOs belonging to former IAS officers. The prominent names included Agriculture Minister Sharad Pawar, then Bihar Governor D.Y. Patil, former President Pratibha Patil's son Rajendra Shekhawat, former Haryana Chief Minister Om Prakash Chautala's son Abhay Chautala, UP Congress MP Sanjay Singh,

---

[27] Ibid.
[28] Ibid.
[29] Copy of notes received by the author using RTI.
[30] Ibid.
[31] See http://archive.indianexpress.com/news/seeds-of-political-patronage/1116 240/, accessed December 28, 2016.

Figure 9.2:
Seeds of political patronage

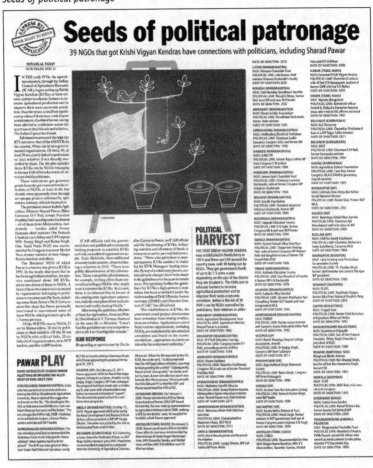

Source: *The Indian Express* (May 16, 2013).

and former Lok Sabha MP from Congress Ratna Singh. One Tamil Nadu NGO had been recommended by Congress treasurer Motilal Vora, former Minister of State Gingee Ramachandran, and others. Of the 99 KVKs run by NGOs, 25 were found to be in Maharashtra, with 18 of them run by politicians or their relatives. Of the total 39 KVK run by NGOs with political links, 20 were linked to Congress leaders, six to NCP, and five to BJP, among others.

The files also revealed some interesting decisions made by Sharad Pawar who was the one who had decided or influenced allotment of KVKs since 2004. Like, in the case of Aurangabad (Maharashtra), where a site selection panel had recommended sanctioning the KVK to Marathwada Agriculture University. But Pawar rejected the suggestion and wrote[32] on the file, "We should give this KVK to Mahatma Gandhi Mission. I am confident their performance will be better." The Mahatma Gandhi Mission got the KVK in July 2009. This Mahatma Gandhi Mission and the KVK belong to Kamal Kishore Kadam, a former Maharashtra minister and NCP leader. In the case of Ahmednagar, the site selection panel had recommended Mahatma Phule Krishi Vidyapeeth. But Pawar noted[33] on the file that "other options need to be explored." The KVK was later allotted to the Marutrao Ghule Patil Shikshan Sansthan, run by NCP MLA Chandrashekhar Marutrao Ghule, with Pawar approving the proposal on August 29, 2011. Again, in Akola (Maharashtra), on May 13, 2010, Pawar approved a KVK to be run by the Rural Development and Research Foundation whose president was BJP MP Sanjay Dhotre.[34] The name was picked by the site selection panel from a list of nine contenders.

Similar was the case in UP's Sitapur where on February 23, 2011, Pawar approved[35] a KVK for Ranvir Rananjay Degree College Association, Amethi, run by Sanjay Singh, then Congress MP from Sultanpur. The proposal had been made just a few days before, on February 8, 2011, and came with a handwritten note from a bureaucrat marked[36] "urgent." The site selection panel picked this over three other proposals by different societies.

Likewise, in Belgaum (Karnataka), the KLE University, whose chancellor, Prabhakar B. Kore was a BJP MP from Rajya Sabha, got a KVK. It had been recommended in response to a proposal from the University of Agricultural Sciences, Dharwad. When the file was sent to the DG, ICAR, he wrote[37] that, "as discussed with Hon'ble AM (agriculture minister), case may be kept pending for

---

[32] Copy of notes received by the author using RTI.
[33] Ibid.
[34] Ibid.
[35] Ibid.
[36] Ibid.
[37] Ibid.

a while." Subsequently, Pawar wrote[38] "put up early" on a letter written by Kore. A new site selection panel was formed after the issue was "discussed with Hon'ble AM and PS to Hon'ble AM"[39] and Pawar sanctioned the KVK to KLE University, rejecting the claim of the University of Agriculture Sciences, Dharwad.

Pawar again sanctioned a KVK in Sitamarhi (Bihar) on February 1, 2006, this time to the Samta Sewa Kendra of former JD (U) MP Nawal Kishore Rai. Rai had been making representations to agriculture ministers since 1996, seeking a KVK for the district. Later, he sought it for his NGO and Pawar approved it forthwith. In Ariyalur (Tamil Nadu), on January 3, 2008, Pawar sanctioned a KVK to the NGO CREED after its case was recommended by then Minister of State Gingee Ramachandran, MPs Vasanthy Stanley and Motilal Vora, and former MPs R.D. Athithan and S.K. Kharventahan.[40]

These many overrulings would have been difficult to access from government records had there not been the RTI Act in place. Here, it is interesting to note that all this was happening at a time when curtailing the discretionary quota of ministers were being discussed everywhere, and DoPT was gathering data of discretionary quota of ministers and issuing several guidelines and circulars in that regard.[41]

After computing research and inspection of files, it was tried to get the concerned authorities to commit their mismanagement on record. On February 11, 2013, an e-mail was sent to Sharad Pawar for his comments. This is what he was requested to clarify: "Only well connected institutions, including NGOs belonging to politicians, apply for and are granted approval for KVKs for which neither applications are solicited nor advertisements issued; there are no clear guidelines for issuing KVKs; and no efforts to bring transparency in these approvals."

---

[38] Ibid.

[39] Ibid.

[40] Author inspected the documents and got copy of all these notes.

[41] UPA government constituted a GoM on January 6, 2011 to consider and advise on "relinquishing discretionary powers enjoyed by Ministers at the centre," and DoPT was gathering information from different ministries in this regard: http://ccis.nic.in/WriteReadData/CircularPortal/D2/D02ser/372_14_2012-AVD-III-16042012.pdf, accessed December 28, 2016.

Later, an under secretary in ICAR responded[42] on his behalf:

> For establishment of KVKs the concerned Zonal Project Directorates have now-a-days been issuing notifications in websites... For updating further the guidelines for KVKs a high-powered Committee has been constituted.... The functioning of KVKs including sanction and allotment of funds is totally transparent and as per well laid procedures.

After the NDA government came to power in May 2014, the Ministry of Agriculture began a review of the functioning of all 639 KVKs. At a meeting held over August 19–20, 2014 at the ICAR in Delhi, Minister of State for Agriculture and Farmer's Welfare (ministry renamed by the new government) Sanjeev Balyan warned KVKs to improve their functioning or face consequences.[43] Later, in December 2014, the Minister of Agriculture and Farmer's Welfare Radha Mohan Singh constituted a committee[44] headed by former Agriculture Secretary J.N.L. Srivastava which submitted its report in February 2015 and recommended[45] that KVKs must follow the norms, though it was not a thorough enquiry as the committee visited only four KVKs near Delhi, that is, Gurgaon, Muzaffarnagar, Karnal, and Ambala, and prepared its report. Presently, there are on an average one KVK in each district, and these are not effective because they are not properly managed. Later, Minister of Agriculture and Farmers Welfare Radha Mohan Singh said that, "The first thing our government did was to ensure that KVKs were not given to NGOs."[46]

---

[42] ICAR's response dated March 18, 2013 to author.

[43] See http://indianexpress.com/article/india/india-others/agriculture-ministry-cracks-down-on-mismanagement-in-kvks/, accessed December 28, 2016.

[44] See http://indianexpress.com/article/india/india-others/panel-to-inquire-into-functioning-of-kvks/, accessed December 28, 2016.

[45] Report accessed by the author on March, 2015 using RTI: http://indianexpress.com/article/india/india-others/follow-norms-says-krishi-kendra-review-panel/, accessed December 28, 2016.

[46] "Who is a farmer leader? Rahul just speaks about them, but BJP has most farmer MPs: Union Agriculture Minister Radha Mohan Singh," *The Indian Express* (New Delhi, January 17, 2016). Available at: http://indianexpress.com/article/india/india-news-india/idea-exchange-whos-a-farmer-leader-rahul-just-speaks-about-them-but-bjp-has-most-farmer-mps-whos-a-farmer-leader-rahul-just-speaks-about-them-but-bjp-has-most-farmer-mps-union-agriculture-m/, accessed January 16, 2017.

NGO Activities Only on Paper

Almost every government department, particularly those working in the social sectors, have their own schemes to involve NGOs
in their activities to take the development to the end users. Amid
the controversy of the NGO Zakir Hussain Memorial Trust, run
by former Minister of External Affairs Salman Khursheed and his
wife Louise Khursheed,[47] I was invited to make a presentation on
RTI at a conference organized by the Dr Ambedkar Foundation
(DAF), in collaboration with the Indian Institute of Public
Administration (IIPA), at Delhi. During the presentation, I noticed
the poor attendance of NGOs. Since the conference was for the
NGOs working for the weaker sections, I would have expected
them to be interested in the subject and to attend in larger numbers. When asked, the organizers informed that they had diffi-
culty in locating and identifying such NGOs. So, after returning
from the conference, different RTI applications were filed before
the DAF and the IIPA. Both of them provided the information
without any hesitation; copies of complete file noting from both
offices were received. The DAF, under the Ministry of Social
Justice and Empowerment, had found that most NGOs working
for scheduled castes and weaker sections of society, and receiving
funds from the government, remain inactive, except on the birth
and death anniversaries of Dr Babasaheb Ambedkar.

Preparing a list of just two dozen participants for a five-day
workshop on capacity-building of such NGOs took the DAF two
years. Being that as it were, DAF also found that most of these
NGOs are run by people from nonweaker sections. A note by the
DAF based on an informal study of about 100 NGOs working for
weaker sections in Delhi and the NCR, said:

> Most of the active NGOs working for SC/weaker sections are
> run by non-SC/weaker sections; most of these are 'one man
> shows' and some are found active only on April 14 (birth anni-
> versary of Dr Ambedkar) and December 6 (death anniversary of

---

[47] On October 10, 2012, Aaj Tak channel broke the story that Khursheed and his
wife ran a trust for the disabled and forged officials' signatures to get grants the
beneficiaries never received.

Dr Ambedkar); Most of these are lying dormant as the decision to set up the same was more impulsive rather than professional; They have very limited information about the initiatives taken by the government for development of weaker sections.[48]

Interestingly, the decision to hold the workshop was taken at a governing body meeting of the DAF on July 24, 2009. It was postponed again and again, and took place finally in June 2012 due to the paucity of getting proper nominees. After prolonged attempts to shortlist NGOs, the DAF sent out invitations to 22 Delhi-based NGOs receiving funds from the government for empowerment of weaker sections in February 2011. But after many months of effort, "only three NGOs confirmed their participation and four letters were returned undelivered."[49] The DAF wrote to the National Commission for Safai Karamcharis and the National Safai Karamcharis Finance and Development Corporation for names of more such NGOs, but were told they "do not have list/addresses of NGOs working for SCs." Following many more reminders and postponement of schedule, only 21 participants belonging to 10 NGOs finally attended the workshop.[50]

Notwithstanding, and on the assumption that "NGOs are playing a very vital role in development/awareness programs not only on their own but also as an extended arm of the government and quasi government organisations", the DAF had decided to hold more such workshops for NGOs working in other states. However, in Maharashtra, of the 50 NGOs that were sent invitations in early November, the DAF note said that only two indicated their willingness to participate. A sorry state of affairs, indeed![51]

Granted, some of the NGOs are playing a crucial role in taking governance up to the grassroots level, but it is equally true that bungling of government funds by NGOs is more than in the government sector. Sadly, since NGOs are beyond the RTI ambit, it becomes difficult to catch them under the RTI Act directly. But

---

[48] Note accessed by the author using RTI from the DAF and IIPA.

[49] Ibid.

[50] Ibid.

[51] 'NGOs getting government funds...' *The Indian Express*, New Delhi, January 8, 2013. Available at: http://archive.indianexpress.com/news/ngos-getting-govt-funds-for-sc-welfare-are-inactive-study/1055982/, accessed February 16, 2017.

there are ways to get around this problem. Where they are funded by government agencies, or even when they get funds from international bodies, NGOs are supposed to follow certain guidelines. There are ways to scrutinize them; since government agencies are where NGOs get their funds or seek approvals. All it takes is to put RTI applications to the relevant government agencies to get information. With the help of the RTI, there is no doubt that more and more such mismanagement can be exposed in order to improve the transparency and accountability among the NGOs.

10

Passing the Buck: Misuse of RTI by Public Authorities

It had long since come to our attention that the Public Information Officers (PIO) under the guise of one of the exceptions given under Section 8 of RTI Act, have evaded the general public from getting their hands on the rightful information that they are entitled to.[1]

—Supreme Court, on December 16, 2015 in RBI vs Jayantilal N. Mistry and others

In the last 10 years that I have been using RTI for journalistic work, I have dealt extensively with the whole gamut of government machinery—from the president's secretariat, PMO, Cabsec, chief ministers' offices of states, central and state ministries, public sector undertakings, investigation agencies, and police organizations, down to the district collectors and district superintendents of police of the remotest districts of each state—trying to garner information from them on a wide range of issues of national importance. But despite the RTI Act, getting crucial information from the government is a tough, tedious, and often frustrating engagement where, it would appear; anti-transparency is a statement of belief and hiding the information and passing the buck the favorite diversionary activity. Having overcome their initial fear, several government departments try to make every effort to undermine the RTI Act, since the very beginning.

The fact is that whether the seeker of the information will get it or not and what will happen to the RTI application, it all depends on the mindset of the person sitting on the other side of the table, that is, the PIO. An application with queries can return with complete information from one office, and from another office a similar application with similar queries may come back with claims of

---

[1] See http://judis.nic.in/supremecourt/imgst.aspx?filename=43192, accessed December 29, 2016.

exemptions for denial of information. It can be forwarded to hundreds of offices just to confuse the seeker and defeat the purpose of information. There are many such experiences while dealing with government offices and officials on RTI which are necessary to share in order to understand this observation.

For instance, section 6(3) of the RTI Act says:[2]

> Where an application is made to a public authority requesting for an information—which is held by another public authority; or the subject matter of which is more closely connected with the functions of another public authority—the public authority, to which such application is made, shall transfer the application or such part of it as may be appropriate to that other public authority and inform the applicant immediately about such transfer: Provided that the transfer of an application pursuant to this sub-section shall be made as soon as practicable but in no case later than five days from the date of receipt of the application.

Further, section 7(9) says:[3] "An information shall ordinarily be provided in the form in which it is sought unless it would disproportionately divert the resources of the public authority or would be detrimental to the safety or preservation of the record in question." There are many rulings of information commissions and one from Madras High Court that section 7(9) cannot be used for denial of any information.

But, both these sections have been variously misinterpreted and exploited by several public authorities. Section 6(3) has been most commonly misused for denying information and indulging in their favorite diversion tactics of passing the buck. On many applications, I have got disconcerting, and often alarming, responses from ministries and departments such as the CPWD, Department of Revenue, CBDT, MHA, Department of Posts, Ministry of Water Resources, ECI, and state DGPs, among others. These are lessons for those who always criticize transparency law for so-called 'misuse' by users and claim that valuable time of public authorities is being wasted. There are examples that several of their colleagues are themselves misusing the law

---

[2] See http://www.righttoinformation.gov.in/webactrti.htm, accessed December 29, 2016.

[3] Ibid.

and wasting the time, energy, and resources by unmindful use of section 6(3), forwarding the application to hundreds of officers without making an effort to know who is the custodian of the requisite information.

ECI's 2000 Envelopes

The first such big shock I experienced, and definitely the most baffling, was while dealing with the ECI. On an application filed with the ECI, I must have received in total an overwhelming 2000 envelops but hardly any information—all they said was either, "The requisite information may be treated as NIL!" or "Your application is being forwarded to" other CPIO. My applications were first forwarded by the ECI to CEOs of all states and then onwards to district election officers (DEOs), that is, district magistrates by CEOs. In most cases, even the DEOs managed to adroitly pass the buck by forwarding my queries to returning officers of every assembly constituency to respond directly.

In fact, during the ongoing controversy related to Bangladeshi migrants, requests were filed to the CEO of Delhi, MHA, the Delhi-based Foreigner Regional Registration Office (FRRO), and the ECI for information about Bangladeshi migrants. Applications[4] were filed to all these authorities with changed words. The application filed before the ECI was in these words:

> Whether the ECI has so far received any request from the Ministry of Home Affairs, Government of India to identify and delete the names of suspected Bangladeshis from the voter's list? If yes, when did the ECI receive this request? Provide copies of such requests giving details of action taken by the ECI in this regard. In how many states has the ECI directed verification of names of voters in the voters' list by door-to-door surveys? How many names of suspected voters have been deleted till 30th April 2008 from the voters' list during this campaign? Provide this information state wise. Whether the ECI has any estimated number of voters who are suspected to be Bangladeshis? If yes, please provide this information.

---

[4] Filed on May 21, 2008 by the author, with little changed words, to all these authorities.

The MHA forwarded the application to the ECI, emphasizing that the ECI was concerned with that issue. The ECI's CPIO J.K. Rao responded that[5] "[n]o request from the MHA to identify and delete the names of suspected Bangladeshis from the voter's list has been received in the Commission in recent years." He further said,[6] "Recently, the door-to-door verification has been carried out in Uttar Pradesh, Madhya Pradesh, Gujarat, Karnataka and NCT of Delhi. It is presumed that 'suspected voters' mentioned in this item (application) is intended to refer to 'electors whose citizenship is suspected'." And he forwarded the application to CEOs of all these states and also said that "Commission does not have any estimated number of voters who are suspected to be Bangladeshis."

The CEO of Delhi responded:[7]

A monthly meeting of the Monitoring Authority to review the progress of deportation of illegal Bangladeshi nationals in Delhi is being held under the chairmanship of Joint Secretary (Foreigners), MHA, Government of India. In this meeting, an officer of the Election Department, Govt of NCT Delhi is also invited, as FRRO, Delhi sends a list on a monthly basis of the persons detected from NCT of Delhi. This list is sorted out Assembly Constituency wise and further sent to the concerned ERO with the direction to take immediate necessary action for deletion of names from the Electoral Rolls after following the due process as laid down in the election law.

J.K. Rao, the CPIO of ECI further clarified:

There was Special Revision of Electoral Rolls of intensive nature/ house-to-house verification with reference to January 1, 2008 as the qualifying date…. During the exercise, all the EROs were directed to include the names of only Indian nationals and to take special care for dealing with foreign nationals.

Interestingly, the application was also put to CEOs of some states, and they had forwarded the application to DEO, and many DEOs

---

[5] Vide letter dated June 18, 2008 to author under RTI.
[6] Ibid.
[7] Through response dated June 10, 2008 to author.

forwarded it to the officials in charge of the electoral rolls revision in every assembly constituency. I was unperturbed by the influx of envelopes on my table as I realized that every letter forwarded by one officer to another was being marked to me. At the end, there were thousands of envelops but there was almost no information.

States and districts, supposedly harboring large numbers of suspected Bangladeshis, either did not respond or they forwarded the application to the sub-division level so the response was not consolidated. One day I visited the ECI office and met Deputy Election Commissioner R. Balakrishnan and told him about the bundles of worthless envelopes received. According to him, the problem of Bangladeshi migrants was mainly in Assam; to which I countered that I had not got responses from many districts and subdivisions of Assam. He was asked what he thought I should do. He immediately called up the CEO of Assam who informed him that in Assam there were around 150,000 names of "D Category" voters identified during the revision of electoral rolls. So, obviously the CEO of Assam had the information but his PIO had unnecessarily, or with the intention of stalling, forwarded the application to the ground level.

Much the same happened when another RTI application was filed to ECI on January 12, 2010 to get details of cash seized during General Elections 2009, and action taken in the matter. But the application was forwarded[8] to CEOs of all states and they in turn forwarded it to the district level interpreting section 6(3) of the RTI Act. But later, the ECI improved the system as when similar query was asked for General Elections 2014, the ECI provided countrywide data[9] from Delhi itself.

The CBDT

There are other departments which have very often used section 6(3) of the RTI Act without applying sensitivity. On a single application with three queries that was filed before the

---

[8] Vide letter dated March 16, 2010 from ECI.
[9] Of cash seized, through letter dated March 3, 2014.

CBDT under the Department of Revenue, Ministry of Finance, over 500 envelops were received for each query. The first was for details of outstanding taxes against societies/NGOs, the second, for copies of Income Tax returns filed by political parties, and the third, for details of exemptions received by political parties. The application was directed to the CBDT, but they forwarded it to almost every income tax office in the country, one after another, though that information concerned only a few offices.

The CBDT has always had a predictable approach toward RTI applications. In an interesting case, an application was filed to several departments which are cadre-controlling authorities for various services under the Central Government, such as the DoPT (for IAS), MHA (for IPS), Ministry of Health and Family Welfare (for doctors of several Central Government run hospitals), CBDT (for IRS), CBEC (for C&CES), Ministry of Statistics and Programme Implementation (for ISS), and DEA (for IES). They were simply asked for the list of officers who are missing from their duty without authorization. Responses were received[10] from all of them except the CBDT. Even its brother organization CBEC provided the list of such officers of C&CES. In predictable style, the CBDT forwarded the application to all chief commissioners under it in the country to respond directly. They, in turn, thoughtlessly following CBDT's example, forwarded the application to their various subordinate officials. As a result, over four hundred envelops were received, most of them stating that they didn't deal with the concerned issue. The information must certainly be available with the division looking after personnel matters in the CBDT, but their approach to the application showed that they certainly did not want to give out the information. They treated similarly the application filed to get the copies of letters written from ECI to CBDT and vice versa with regard to scrutiny of affidavits filed by electoral candidates. The application was forwarded to the entire country, to all income tax offices, one after another. In such cases, envelops were received but the information came from only half a dozen offices. In my experience, the CBDT is among the worst departments with regard to RTI.

---

[10] Except CBDT, all other departments provided the list of such officers to author under RTI.

IITs and IIMs

There were many cases where I was informed that I cannot be provided the requisite information since being in a media organization I can't be treated as a citizen of India. Isn't it strange that based on the mere mention of my designation and office address for correspondence, I was told that being a representative of a media organization I cannot be considered a citizen of India? Shockingly, many such replies came from the hallowed centers of educational excellence such as IITs and IIMs. For instance, when an application was filed to all seven existing IITs in May 26, 2011, IIT Madras, while denying the information, responded[11] in this bizarre and insulting manner: "Only citizens shall have right to information. Corporation, firm or association of persons and trusts etc, are not treated as citizens under the Constitution. They are not entitled to file application for information before the PIO."

The case with IIM Ahmedabad was quite similar. Their CPIO denied information on my two requests saying: "Please note that as per section 3 of the RTI Act 'All citizens shall have the right to information.' You are applying in a capacity of Senior Editor of India Today, which is not citizen of India."[12] One of the queries was to know the funds received by each IIM from various sources in the last five years; the other to know the total number of PhD degrees awarded in the last five years.

To all such denials by IITs and IIMs, I filed first appeals in these strong words:

> In the said application I have sought certain information by cate-
> gorically mentioning my name and whereby I have also written my
> designation and the name of institution where I work but the infor-
> mation so sought was purely on personal basis and the language
> and contents of the said application are crystal clear. The desig-
> nation and institution where I work cannot be construed as that
> the institution is seeking information from the concerned organ-
> isation and any such conclusion is absolutely erroneous, perverse,
> illegal, meaningless and unconstitutional. The information sought
> by me is purely by me as an individual who is very much a citizen

---

[11] Letter dated June 6, 2011 from IIT Madras to author under RTI.
[12] IIM Ahmedabad's letter, dated June 3, 2011, to author under RTI.

of this country and below the name of the information seeker i.e. me, I have mentioned my designation and the name of institution where I work as my personal introduction and identification which doesn't mean at all that the institution has sought the information from the concerned body. It is also to make clear that if information has to be sought by anybody, they will file it in their letter head and also supported by a resolution authorising any authorised representative of the body to file the same with due documentation. Any institution cannot file the application under RTI in such a simple manner as there are formalities to be completed in any institution as the decision taken there is not individual but collective. It is also necessary to say that had the concerned authority was having any doubt regarding my citizenship, they would have sought clarification to that effect but denying the information on the ground of the same is absolutely illegal, unwarranted and against the purpose of transparency under RTI Act.

I would also like to submit that the purpose of the Act is to harmonize the conflicting interests while preserving the paramount of the democratic ideals and furnishing information to citizens who desire to have it. I am the citizen of this country and I am born in the territory of India and my parents have also born in the territory of India and there cannot be any doubt on that.

Presumably, if the argument given by PIO rejecting my application is believed to be right, even then, in the case of R.K. Morarka vs Central Bank of India, Appeal no. 908/CPB/2007, dated 17.9.2007, the Central Information Commission clarified that the commission consistently has taken a view that directors of the companies, partners of firms, and office bearers of association of persons could also seek information on behalf of the companies, firms and associations respectively. Therefore, the CPIO should not reject the application on the sole ground that a company is not a citizen even otherwise. Therefore directors, partners and office bearers as above can seek information under the RTI Act.

This perhaps did the trick, for I got the information in due course of time.

The appellate at IIT Madras responded:, "I have given direction to the concerned operating personnel to give the available information so as to reach you within 45 days."[13] Later the information was provided.

---

[13] First appellate order, dated July 14, 2011, to author on under RTI.

Although I was not surprised with their denial the first time, what was shocking was that when an application was filed a year later, the concerned institutions treated that in the same manner, appearing to have forgotten the experience of the previous year. Similar denials were received from both IIT Madras and IIT Kharagpur. IIT Kharagpur's CPIO took the denial route despite the fact that earlier, in June 2011, he had replied to my queries a year back when I was with *India Today* after the first appeal was filed. This time around he again said[14] that the RTI Act

[c]onfers the right to information on all 'citizens' and not on all 'persons.' The 'citizenship' can only be a natural born person and it does not even by implication include a legal or juristic person. Hence, you, being a person of The Indian Express, New Delhi, are not entitled to seek any information under the RTI Act. (See letter in Figure 10.1)

But when the first appeal was filed he again provided the information. IIT Madras, which had earlier provided the information after the first appeal was filed again a year later, responded on another RTI that, "[c]orporation, firm or association of persons and trusts etc are not treated as citizens under the Constitution. They are not entitled to file application for information before the Public Information Officer."[15]

IIM Ahmedabad's CPIO denied information, later almost repeating what he had said in his earlier response. He said: "You are applying in a capacity of Senior Assistant Editor of The Indian Express, which is not citizen of India."[16]

It is truly amazing that officials dealing with the RTI Act in such centers of excellence did not remember, or did not have on record, what had happened to their earlier illogical responses. Also, the fact that they were unaware of the CIC order on a similar topic was deplorable, in spite of having reminded them of it in first appeals earlier. And, despite their views being turned down on the first appeals earlier, they did the same again!

Another response from an IIT was very interesting. In fact, an RTI was filed in the MoHRD about the list of students who were

---

[14] IIT Kharagpur's response, dated June 19, 2012, to author.
[15] Response dated June 21, 2012 from IIT Madras to author.
[16] Response of IIM Ahmedabad, dated June 21, 2013, to author.

Figure 10.1:
Reply to RTI application from IIT Kharagpur

भारतीय प्रौद्योगिकी संस्थान
खड़गपुर-721302, भारत

INDIAN INSTITUTE OF TECHNOLOGY
KHARAGPUR - 721302, INDIA

डॉ. अनाथबंधु पात्र
उप कुलसचिव एवं जन सूचना अधिकारी
Dr. Anathbandhu Patra
Deputy Registrar and Public Information Officer

SPEED POST

I.D. No.: IIT/RTI/060612
Dated 19 June, 2012

To
Shri Shyamlal Yadav
Senior Assistant Editor
The Indian Express, 9 & 10,
Bahadur Shah Zafar Marg,
New Delhi- 110 002

Sir,

Please refer to your application dated 12/06/12 (received on 18/06/2012).

This is to inform you that the RTI Act, 2005 confers the right to information on all "citizens" and not on all "persons". The "citizenship" can only be a natural born person and it does not even by implication include a legal or a juristic person. Hence, you, being a person of The Indian Express, New Delhi are not entitled to seek any information under the RTI Act, 2005.

Source: Author.

dropped during study in last five years from various IITs. The MoHRD forwarded the list to all IITs and they provided the information, except for IIT Kanpur. This was the first such denial case on my RTI where a public authority had denied the information because of the fact that the application was forwarded by another public authority. IIT Kanpur did not provide the information and told[17] the MoHRD to "inform the applicant" that the "information is not available with public authority (i.e. MoHRD)."

A Simple Request Turned Down Repeatedly

There was an attempt by the PMO and the Cabsec not to provide the list of persons who had been conferred the rank of union

---

[17] Copy of the letter dated March 30, 2015 was endorsed to the author as well.

cabinet ministers and union ministers of state. The first application on the issue was filed on July 30, 2009 to the CPIO at the Cabsec asking for the list of persons availing the rank of cabinet minister and ministers of state outside the Union Council of Ministers. The CPIO of the Cabsec forwarded the request to the MHA based on the fact that the MHA is the custodian of such information. The MHA, on its part, responded[18] saying, "To confer the status of Union Cabinet Minister on a person, are processed by the individual administrative Ministry/Department for approval of the Prime Minister directly. A centralized list is not maintained by this Ministry." After getting this reply from the MHA, an application was sent to the PMO and Cabsec asking them "Whether the Prime Minister approves the files to confer anybody the rank of Union Ministers/Minister of State; if yes, to please provide the required information of the persons conferred the rank of Cabinet Minister/Minister of State since May 2004." The PMO's response on this new application was just that: "Yes, on proposals which require the approval of the Prime Minister as established procedures." On this also, the response from the MHA via the Cabsec said that they do not have a compiled list.

Between 2009 and 2010, at least four efforts were made using RTI applications to the PMO and the Cabsec for a list of such persons, but they failed to get a proper answer. PMO was specially asked to provide the list of persons to whom the prime minister had granted the rank of cabinet minister or Minister of State since 2004 and each time the PMO forwarded the request to the Cabsec, and the Cabsec forwarded it to the MHA. The Cabsec, while forwarding the applications to the MHA, maintained the same line: "Cabinet Secretariat is not the appropriate public authority to respond to your application. However, your application is being transferred to the Ministry of Home Affairs with the business allocated to that Ministry." And the MHA forwarded the list of persons holding the rank of cabinet minister and the Minister of State in the MHA thrice, but said that they did not have the information about such persons in other ministries and departments.

Since it is the prime minister who approves all such files pertaining to whom these ranks are given, I reminded the PMO that

---

[18] MHA's responses, dated August 19, 2009 and September 28, 2010, on author's RTI.

they must have the information on how many such proposals the prime minister has approved. But they again denied the information reiterating their earlier stand.

This time, just to take a chance, an application was filed to the President's Secretariat for a list of persons invited during the last oath ceremony of newly inducted union ministers, hoping that all persons I was after must have also been invited to the ceremony. I thought that once the list is received it would not take long to dig out the required names of persons enjoying the rank of cabinet ministers and Minister of State outside the Union Council of Ministers. But, it came as no surprise that the CPIO of the President's Secretariat denied the information. When a first appeal was filed, it too met the same fate.

But now I tried another ploy. An application was filed to the PMO asking whether persons availing the rank of union cabinet minister and Minister of State are supposed to declare their assets and liabilities to the PMO, just as members of the Union Council do. If yes, to please provide the list of such persons who have declared such details, along with the list of defaulters. With the availability of such a list, the answer to the queries would be complete, I had thought. But once again there was disappointment as the PMO responded[19] that the code of conduct for members of Union Council is not applicable on such persons who hold the ranks of cabinet ministers and Minister of State outside the Union Council.

Finally, after denials on three applications on the same issue, the MHA provided[20] a list of 11 persons availing the rank of cabinet minister and 27 others availing the rank of union minister of state who were not members of the Union Council of Ministers. It was shocking that an answer that should have been forthcoming on only one application took more than two years of repeated efforts.

Foreign Visits of Sonia Gandhi and Rahul Gandhi

Some of the most curious foreign trips undertaken during 10 years of the UPA regime were of Sonia Gandhi and Rahul Gandhi.

---

[19] Letter dated June 23, 2011 to author.
[20] Vide letter dated October 15, 2010 to author on RTI.

Although it is not mandatory for MPs to declare details about their personal foreign trips, most MPs make it a point to inform the Lok Sabha and Rajya Sabha secretariats.[21] But Sonia Gandhi and Rahul Gandhi have never intimated the Lok Sabha about their personal foreign trips.

When the MEA was requested for a list of persons who are exempted from political clearance and asked if there is any such exemption to the Special Protection Group/National Security Guards (SPG/NSG) protectees, MEA wrote back,[22] "We are requesting the CPIO of the Ministry of Home Affairs, New Delhi, to directly provide you with the list of public functionaries protected by SPG/NSG or any other security outfit who are exempted from taking political clearance from going abroad, if any." But on the request to provide details of foreign trips made by Sonia Gandhi and Rahul Gandhi since June 2004, the MEA said:[23]

As the Lok Sabha/Rajya Sabha Secretariat approaches the Ministry of External Affairs for issue of political clearances for visits of Hon'ble Members of Parliament, we are endorsing a copy of this reply to the CPIO, Lok Sabha Secretariat with a request to directly provide the information available in this regard.

The Lok Sabha Secretariat had already reverted on another application filed before it:

As per the convention, the Members of Lok Sabha inform the Hon'ble Speaker, Lok Sabha about their foreign visits (private and/or official). However, there is no rule available in the Rules of Procedure or Direction by the Lok Sabha or any other document in the Lok Sabha Secretariat, whereby it has been made mandatory for the Members to give prior/subsequent information about their foreign visits to the Hon'ble Speaker, Lok Sabha.[24]

Now, again the Lok Sabha Secretariat responded,[25] "Smt Sonia Gandhi, MP and Shri Rahul Gandhi, MP have not been part of any

---

[21] Response dated January 27, 2012 to author under RTI.
[22] Response of MEA, dated May 23, 2012, to author under RTI.
[23] Ibid.
[24] Response dated January 27, 2012 to author under RTI.
[25] Response of Lok Sabha Secretariat, dated June 19, 2012, to author under RTI.

Indian Parliamentary Delegation going abroad under bilateral exchange during the year 2004–12. Therefore, political clearance for them was never sought from MEA."

The MHA, in response to the application forwarded by the MEA, said:[26]

> The matter of exemption from taking political clearance from going abroad is related to MEA, who have already replied to you. However, a copy of your RTI application is being forwarded to CPIO, Cabinet Secretariat and NSG for providing information, if any to you directly.

Interestingly, the Cabsec replied,[27]

> It is not clear as to why your application has been transferred to the Secretariat as the matter relating to political clearance for visits abroad is solely the prerogative of the MEA. There have been no instructions issued by this secretariat in this regard. Accordingly the application is being remarked back to the MEA.

As for the NAC—which was chaired by Sonia Gandhi with the rank of cabinet minister—it said,[28] "As regard the foreign visits of the Chairperson/Members, NAC since the inception of the council (visits made on NAC account), it is mentioned that the then chairperson travelled to Bangkok in July, 2004 on which total expenditure of ₹2,22,939 (approx) was incurred."

Later the NAC clarified, "As per the Cabinet Secretariat order dated May 31, 2004, all the expenditure incurred in the functioning of National Advisory Council would be met by the Central Government through the PMO and the PMO is custodian of all information."

But when a fresh RTI application was filed in the PMO after Narendra Modi took charge as Prime Minister, the PMO said:

> Information regarding the foreign trips undertaken by Ms Sonia Gandhi and Mr Rahul Gandhi does not form part of records held by this office. However, as per PMO records, Ms Sonia Gandhi,

---

[26] Response of MHA dated June 20, 2012 to author under RTI.
[27] Cabsec's response, dated June 22, 2012, to author under RTI.
[28] Response of NAC dated November 29, 2007 to author on RTI.

in her capacity as chairperson, NAC, undertook an official foreign visit to Bangkok, Thailand, during 14–17 July 2004 to attend the International AIDS Conference.[29]

So, during the 10 years of UPA rule, information of none of the foreign trips, except that of Sonia Gandhi's Bangkok trip, was available to the PMO, MHA, MEA, or NAC as per their responses. After struggling to get information from several departments which are custodians of the information related to foreign travels of public figures, I realized that the information about foreign trips made by both the MPs of Congress's first family is nowhere.

While several public authorities constantly complain about the so-called misuse of RTI by applicants, they never reflect on the approach of their own officers toward RTI. Such officers are the ones who are misusing the manpower, money and time of public authorities. In doing so, they are definitely harassing the RTI applicants, and what is more important, it is unethical and goes against the very spirit of the RTI Act.

---

[29] Response dated August 26, 2014 to author under RTI.

11

How a Journalist Can Use RTI and See the Change

Frequent the checks and more piercing and deeper the investigation, the better is the monitoring of the system.[1]

—View of the workshop organized by the Press Council of India on RTI on August 10–11, 1996

What I have observed in the last 10 years of the implementation of RTI Act is that while its users have tried to learn how to use it, public authorities have already learnt how to deny the information, claiming exemptions using various circulars of the DoPT and respective departments of state governments, orders of the central and SICs, and of the Supreme Court and various High Courts. Moreover, they quite often give out confusing information, or information worded in such a way that it cannot be understood. While there is no standard for filing an application, and the outcome of the application can greatly depend on a number of factors, not least on the person occupying the chair of PIO, here are some guidelines which journalists may follow while using RTI for their stories. These are based on my experiences of filing many thousand RTI applications across government offices in the country.

1. **Conceptualize the idea:** More than the techniques of using RTI, what is important is to first conceptualize the idea. It is important to ensure, as far as possible, that one does not use RTI for information which is already available in the public domain. This can be achieved only if one is well informed and up to date. First, carefully go through all available means of information to get ideas. Information may be accessed through annual reports, budget speeches,

---

[1] Future of Print Media, Press Council of India, New Delhi, 132.

government documents and publications, websites of various departments, Parliament and assembly questions, and interactions with sources in the relevant departments. Very often, RTI users file applications for information pertaining to minor, irrelevant topics. So before starting any RTI exercise, get an idea of its possible impact based on a broader public interest.

2. **Begin by getting available information without RTI:** Once the idea is conceptualized, it is important to first explore whether the information can be obtained without using RTI. The best thing about using the Internet is that we can explore all accessible information available in the public domain. Once one has accessed all available information, only then one should draft the RTI application to get information which is not available in the public domain. Before filing an RTI application, reading the RTI Act is important to help one understand how to proceed with an idea under RTI.

3. **Don't question, just ask for information:** The RTI Act gives us the right to information and we can ask for any information which is available in any format. Just concentrate on getting that information. Read the definition of the information given in Section 2(f) of the RTI Act.[2] One may now also use Prime Minister Narendra Modi's comments on RTI which he made in the annual RTI convention on October 16, 2015 at Vigyan Bhawan in Delhi. He said, "Citizens should not only have the right to get copies of documents but also ask question and demand accountability from public authorities, because the right to ask questions is the very foundation of democracy and it will reinforce their faith in democracy."[3]

4. **Be simple and clear in format and be aware of the loopholes:** While drafting the application asking for information, keep the format simple and easy to comprehend. It is always better that a journalist seeking information does not disclose the idea and just asks for that part of information he/she wants from the concerned public authority. In some states and departments, they have designed their

---

[2] See Note 29 of Chapter 1.

[3] "Open up for trust, learn from RTI," *The Indian Express* (New Delhi, October 17, 2015). Available at: http://indianexpress.com/article/india/india-news-india/open-up-for-trust-says-narendra-modi-learn-from-rti/, accessed February 20, 2017.

own formats and they reject the queries if it is not filed in their format, therefore, before filing the request, one must check with the particular departments whether it has any format. Also, be aware that the officer to whom the queries are addressed has a load of excuses to pass the buck. Like, under section 7(9) which says, "An information shall ordinarily be provided in the form in which it is sought unless it would disproportionately divert the resources of the public authority or would be detrimental to the safety or preservation of the record in question." But while the public authorities are often taking shelter of Section 7(9) of the RTI Act, the CIC has decided in several cases that information can't be denied under this section. Notable is Decision No. CIC/OP/A/2009/000204-AD dated January 12, 2010: "The Commission holds that Section 7(9) of the Act does not allow denial of information but denial of providing the same in the form in which it has been sought in the event this leads to disproportionate diversion of resources of the Public." And the decision in Appeal No. CIC/OK/A/2008/01256 dated January 9, 2009 stated:

> The denial of information on the basis of Section 11 and Section 7(9) of the Act was without any basis in law. Denial of information can only be under Section 8(1) or Section 9. Section 11 sets out a procedure for giving the opportunity to a third party to give his objections and Section 7(9) can be invoked only to state that information in the format demanded by the appellant is not possible. However the PIO would have to offer the information in an alternate format when invoking Section 7(9).

Moreover, the judgment of Madras High Court dated January 7, 2010 in W.P.No. 20372 of 2009 and M.P.No. 1 of 2009 is more clear.

> 4. The Commission, after notice to the petitioner Archives and also to the Central Survey Office, held that Archives cannot refuse to furnish any information unless it is covered by Sections 8 and 9 of the Right to Information Act.... 13. The other objections that they are maintaining a large number of documents in respect of 45 departments and they are short

of human resources cannot be raised to whittle down the citizens' right to seek information. It is for them to write to the Government to provide for additional staff depending upon the volume of requests that may be forthcoming pursuant to the RTI Act. It is purely an internal matter between the petitioner archives and the State Government. The right to information having been guaranteed by the law of Parliament, the administrative difficulties in providing information cannot be raised. Such pleas will defeat the very right of citizens to have access to information.

One must also need to understand the implications of why Supreme Court Justices R.V. Raveendran and A.K. Patnaik's observation made in their order dated August 9, 2011 is being widely quoted by public authorities these days while denying information. The order states: "The nation does not want a scenario where 75% of the staff of public authorities spends 75% of their time in collecting and furnishing information to applicants instead of discharging their regular duties." We must remind the PIOs that the same Supreme Court in its same order dated August 9, 2011 has also said that, "The right to information is a cherished right. Information and right to information are intended to be formidable tools in the hands of responsible citizens to fight corruption and to bring in transparency and accountability." We can also remind the PIOs of another observation dated December 3, 2007 of Delhi High Court Justice S. Ravindra Bhat, who said in an order that

> Access to information, under Section 3 of the Act, is the rule and exemptions under Section 8, the exception. Section 8 being a restriction on this fundamental right, must therefore is to be strictly construed. It should not be interpreted in manner as to shadow the very right itself.

At the same time, one must take into account a DoPT circular which says

> Only such information can be supplied under the Act which already exists and is held by the public authority or

held under the control of the public authority. The Public Information Officer is not supposed to create information; or to interpret information; or to solve the problems raised by the applicants; or to furnish replies to hypothetical questions.

The lesson to be learnt from all this is that in order to avoid the denials, be simple, be aware, and be focused.

5. **Know the exemptions before you exercise the right:** We must carefully go through and understand Section 8(1) of the RTI Act before exercise our right to information. It says:

> Notwithstanding anything contained in this Act, there shall be no obligation to give any citizen, (a) information, disclosure of which would prejudicially affect the sovereignty and integrity of India, the security, strategic, scientific or economic interests of the State, relation with foreign State or lead to incitement of an offence; (b) information which has been expressly forbidden to be published by any court of law or tribunal or the disclosure of which may constitute contempt of court; (c) information, the disclosure of which would cause a breach of privilege of Parliament or the State Legislature; (d) information including commercial confidence, trade secrets or intellectual property, the disclosure of which would harm the competitive position of a third party, unless the competent authority is satisfied that larger public interest warrants the disclosure of such information; (e) information available to a person in his fiduciary relationship, unless the competent authority is satisfied that the larger public interest warrants the disclosure of such information; (f) information received in confidence from foreign Government; (g) information, the disclosure of which would endanger the life or physical safety of any person or identify the source of information or assistance given in confidence for law enforcement or security purposes; (h) information which would impede the process of investigation or apprehension or prosecution of offenders; (i) cabinet papers including records of deliberations of the Council of Ministers, Secretaries and other officers: Provided that the decisions of Council of Ministers, the reasons thereof, and the material on the basis of which the decisions were taken shall be made public after the decision has been taken, and the matter is complete, or over, Provided further that those matters which come under the exemptions specified in this

section shall not be disclosed; (j) information which relates to personal information the disclosure of which has no relationship to any public activity or interest, or which would cause unwarranted invasion of the privacy of the individual unless the Central Public Information Officer or the State Public Information Officer or the appellate authority, as the case may be, is satisfied that the larger public interest justifies the disclosure of such information: Provided that the information which cannot be denied to the Parliament or a State Legislature shall not be denied to any person.

In this regard, one Supreme Court observation is much helpful to information seekers. On December 16, 2015 in the matter of Reserve Bank of India vs Jayantilal N. Mistry and others Supreme Court Justices M.Y. Eqbal and C. Nagappan have said that:

> It had long since come to our attention that the Public Information Officers (PIO) under the guise of one of the exceptions given under Section 8 of RTI Act, have evaded the general public from getting their hands on the rightful information that they are entitled to.

6. **Try all concerned public authorities for same information:** If the same information is available with multiple authorities, more than one authority can be approached. It often happens that one authority denies the information, while another provides the same without any ifs and buts. For example, in 2009, when I requested the MHA to provide copies of its correspondence with the Delhi Government on the Afzal Guru case (given in Chapter 8), copies were not provided. But Delhi Government's PIO was quite helpful as he sent me the information after I'd paid the cost of photocopying charges, etc.

7. **Get familiar with PIOs:** We must try to meet and discuss things with the relevant PIOs before sending an RTI application. There are several PIOs in the government who are ready to share the information. Normally, the PIOs belong to junior cadres like the Central Secretariat Services (CSS) and have a tendency of being at odds with their senior officers like those from the IAS. Since crucial decision-making

in government starts at the joint secretary level, the PIOs of junior rank such as section officers, under secretaries, and deputy secretaries do not have much at stake if any embarrassing information is released under the RTI. The officers themselves often give ideas for exciting stories once they are familiar with the applicant and if they are sure that the information will be used in public interest. We must utilize this conflict among government officials to explore and collect crucial information.

8. **Moving targets:** We should not give the impression to particular government departments or public information officers that we use RTI only pertaining to them. We must work with an approach of *"Na kahoo se dosti, na kahoo se bair* (No friendship with anybody, no enmity with anybody)." So, we should always keep visiting new departments, governments (like state governments), and ministries and be in constant touch with them for our ideas, because the truth is that stories are everywhere.

9. **No need to reveal identity of a journalist:** If we think some particular authority may not respond favorably if it knows you are a journalist, avoid giving identity. Sometimes, some public authorities, afraid that the information they are providing will be published in the media and will create an impact, hesitate in giving out information. Right to information is meant for every citizen of India so we do not need to disclose who or what we are. Several public authorities respond to queries without asking about the applicants, so it is up to you whether you feel the need to disclose your identity or not and to file your application giving your office address or home address.

10. **Be prepared for any response:** Some PIOs may initially confuse the applicant by turning down the applications on one pretext or the other. They try to borrow time and delay our information. Even when we file a request on behalf of our news organization, the PIO may turn it down, as happened to me in the case of IIT Kharagpur and IIM Ahmedabad. They turned down my applications saying that the RTI Act "Confers the right to information on all 'citizens' and not on all 'persons'. The 'citizenship' can only be a natural born person and it does not even by implication include a legal

or juristic person." In such a situation, take recourse to the CIC order dated September 17, 2007 which said that "directors of companies, partners of firms, and office bearers of association of persons could also seek information on behalf of the companies, firms and associations respectively."

11. **Remember, a NO doesn't always mean NO:** When officers dealing with RTI respond in a negative way or do not provide the information, it does not necessarily mean that they don't want to provide the information. Sometimes, an informal, personal meeting with them does the trick, while a first appeal against the order creates extra pressure on them to provide the necessary information. We should keep in mind that PIOs work under several seniors and the fact is that they respond on behalf of their departments. Sometimes he/she is personally inclined to provide the information, but their seniors pressurize them not to. Quite often, when we meet them personally, they will tell how to deal with the hurdles and show the way to get the information. There are many instances in my experience where the information was denied formally, but the same officers provided the same information later, informally.

12. **Don't waste time, file online or by post:** In some states such as Maharashtra and Odisha and with the Central Government, one can file an RTI online and submit hard copies to any public authority or send it through postal services. One does not need to go everywhere to submit the applications; the best way to save time is to do so online or send them through post offices. It does not cost much and saves valuable time. The easiest means of processing the fee is an Indian postal order which can be bought from any post office. Also, in the name of Central Government departments, the Postal Department has started issuing e-postal orders which can be printed through India Posts' website after making an online payment.

13. **Be patient, be persistent:** During the tedious and boring process of taking the RTI route, one will often feel frustrated. But one must not lose patience because the type of story one can get using RTI is usually not possible through other means of investigative reporting. So, once the story is finalized, published, and creates an impact, one will

feel vindicated and elated. Sometimes such stories will be among the award-winning entries. So keep persisting with efforts. I myself have filed many thousand applications, and a majority of them were mere wastage of time, but I do not bother for I have always concentrated on the positive outcome of the efforts. Even without RTI, when a journalist explores some story, often it needs much time and wasteful efforts, so what if that happens under RTI as well? So, a journalist must be prepared always for such efforts in search of a good story.

14. **Do extra work on information:** The information we access through RTI is hardly useful or adequate for stories in the form in which it is supplied. It depends entirely on us what information we finally manage to unearth after repeated efforts and, more importantly, on how best we utilize them in formulating our idea and writing the story. Very often, we will need to prepare multiple drafts to give maturity to the idea and need to work several weeks or months to convert all the accessed information into a hard-hitting story. Although several RTI activists and NGOs supply and give access to information to journalists, only a few of them have an impact, since it is not processed and analyzed in a proper and effective journalistic manner.

15. **Have sensitivity toward RTI officials:** While using RTI, journalists must always be sensitive toward the person sitting across the table. One must be sensitive to the fact that he/she is not given any extra remuneration for supplying information and in case of any blunder he/she may have to face the consequences. Also, we should remember that these officials are employed on public money and they have to deal with RTI applications along with their other official duties. While the government has enacted the RTI law, it does not fill the vacant posts in the departments, so the officers are loaded with work. So, as far as possible, we should avoid filing multiple requests in the same department for the same information. And, we should not seek information which is already available in the public domain. I realize through my experience that most of the officials who deal with RTI provide the information without any hassle if they are convinced that the applicant has only the public interest in mind. Therefore,

we should try to win their trust and make them realize that we are just doing our job with the purpose of bringing about reforms in the system, nothing else.

16. **Take help from information commissioners:** Since most of the information commissioners are retired bureaucrats, they understand the functioning of the government system and they know well what information is kept with which department. Although some commissioners may be protecting particular persons, they largely would like to be seen as pro-transparency and supportive of openness. We should take benefit of their experience and utilize it to get ideas and in understanding how, when, and where to move RTI. As far as I am concerned, I avoid taking my cases into CIC because it takes much time. What I prefer is to meet the officials and file again another RTI with changed words in the hope of access to information. But this must not be a principal for all users. One must take its appeals to CIC/SICs if information is denied by PIO/FAA.

17. **Inspection of documents:** As per section 2(j) of the RTI Act:

> Right to information includes the right to: inspection of work, documents, records; taking notes, extracts or certified copies of documents or records; taking certified samples of material; obtaining information in the form of diskettes, floppies, tapes, video cassettes or in any other electronic mode or through printouts where such information is stored in a computer or in any other device.

This provision of inspection of documents must be utilized by journalists as, with its help, one can easily penetrate any government office in order to develop contacts for further stories besides getting the particular information on hand.

18. **Stories from the ground:** Real stories of grassroots-level development are with the district administrations, several other government agencies at the district level, panchayats, and offices at the ground level. So far, many stories have not come, though there have been several efforts by some vernacular media; but in the absence of proper ideation and training, all the process seems to be held up now. Media at the grassroots level, like in most cases at the Center and states as well, depends on the information accessed by

NGOs and activists. For proper ideation and effective use of RTI in public interest, vernacular and regional media persons working at the grassroots level must be trained for that. Media men working outside Delhi should take interest in that regard. Getting information from the Central Government is easy, but it is very difficult to get correct and timely information from district administration and grassroots level offices of government.

19. **State-level stories:** The same situation is at the state level. While many big success stories have come from the Central Government on broad public interest issues, in the states the case is not like that. Although some journalists in the states have been using RTI, the need is to appoint a reporter in news organizations as a full-time user of RTI who coordinates with other colleagues on possible RTI-based stories and facilitates exploring those ideas. In the absence of proactive use of RTI by media in public interest, the RTI is losing its shine in many states, and in some states such as UP, Chhattisgarh, Bihar, and Odisha it depends on the luck of a user whether the request is responded to and the information would be supplied or not and also the number of months the response may take. Some state governments have become more and more resistant toward RTI year after year, and one thing they never bother about is the time limit of replying to an RTI request.

20. **Follow up, follow up:** It is the beauty of the RTI Act that one can keep the public authorities always on watch on any issue. Once the story is filed, we must not forget the issue. What I do in many cases is file an RTI application just after publishing the story to know the impact of the story. It makes our work impact-making and significant. So, after publishing any story which is of public interest, one may file an RTI application to know the follow-up. Once a story is published, one may not do the follow-up story, but RTI itself makes an impact if we ask for the information regarding what was done by the concerned authorities after the publication of the story.

Index

About the Author

Shyamlal Yadav is one of the pioneers of the effective use of RTI for investigative reporting and asking questions of the powers that be. His work on India's polluted rivers, *Streams of Filth* (India Today, December 30, 2009) was selected by UNESCO as one of the 20 best investigative reports across the globe. A member of the investigative bureau of *The Indian Express*, his reports like foreign travel of ministers and bureaucrats, MPs appointing their relatives as their personal assistants, bank staff putting their own money to reduce the total number of zero balance Jan Dhan accounts have had an impact and influence. He is the only two-time winner of the prestigious Ramnath Goenka Award for Excellence in Journalism in Investigative Reporting category. Shyamlal has been awarded with the Lorenzo Natalie Journalism Prize by the European Commission for Development, Brussels; Developing Asia Journalism Award by the ADB Institute, Tokyo; National RTI Award by NDTV-PCRF; Statesman Rural Reporting Award; and Ganesh Shankar Vidyarthi Award for Excellence in Journalism among others. He has addressed several conferences on RTI and Media at a range of platforms including Columbia University, New York at Rio de Janeiro; European Investigative Journalism Conferences at Brussels; Global Investigative Journalism Conference at Kiev; Asian Investigative Journalism Conference, Kathmandu. Having earlier worked at *Jansatta, Amar Ujala,* and *India Today* Shyamlal is presently Senior Editor at *The Indian Express*.